Shakespeare's Great Stage of Fools

Also by Robert H. Bell

Jocoserious Joyce: The Fate of Folly in Ulysses (1991)

Critical Essays on Kingsley Amis (1998)

A Reader's Companion to Infinite Jest by William C. Dowling and Robert H. Bell (2005)

Shakespeare's Great Stage of Fools

Robert H. Bell

First published in 2011 by
PALGRAVE MACMILLAN®
in the United States—a division of St. Martin's Press LLC,
175 Fifth Avenue, New York, NY 10010.

Where this book is distributed in the UK, Europe and the rest of the world,
this is by Palgrave Macmillan, a division of Macmillan Publishers Limited,
registered in England, company number 785998, of Houndmills,
Basingstoke, Hampshire RG21 6XS.

Palgrave Macmillan is the global academic imprint of the above companies
and has companies and representatives throughout the world.

Palgrave® and Macmillan® are registered trademarks in the United States,
the United Kingdom, Europe and other countries.

ISBN: 978-0-230-11511-8

Library of Congress Cataloging-in-Publication Data

Bell, Robert H. (Robert Huntley), 1946–
    Shakespeare's great stage of fools / Robert Huntley Bell.
        p. cm.
    ISBN 978-0-230-11511-8 (hardback)
        1. Shakespeare, William, 1564–1616—Characters—Fools.
    2. Shakespeare, William, 1564–1616—Characters—Clowns.
    3. Fools and jesters in literature. 4. Clowns in literature. I. Title.
PR2992.F6B45 2011
822.3'3—dc22   2011006317

A catalogue record of the book is available from the British Library.

Design by Newgen Imaging Systems (P) Ltd., Chennai, India.

First edition: September 2011

D 10 9 8 7 6 5 4 3 2

Printed in the United States of America.

Once more for Ilona.
This time I mean it, really. No fooling.

Contents

Acknowledgments

Though I have been joyfully teaching Shakespeare at Williams College since 1972, recently and for the first time I team-taught Shakespeare with my colleague and partner Ilona Bell. Together over many years, we have discussed thousands of lines, debated feminist critiques and the textuality of history, attended scores of productions, and watched hundreds of films. If life without Shakespeare would be sadly impoverished, life without Ilona is truly unthinkable.

I first taught Shakespeare in Reuben Brower's Humanities 6 course at Harvard. At one weekly staff meeting, Ben stressed how wonderfully undergraduates *absorbed* Shakespeare. "As a boy working on the farm," he mused, "I couldn't get those speeches out of my head." Brower dedicated his last book, *Hero and Saint: Shakespeare and the Graeco-Roman Heroic Tradition*, to a former colleague he dubbed "teacher of teachers." Ben Brower was my teacher of teachers whose words I can't get out of my head. Another boon from Humanities 6 was the beginning of a lifelong friendship with Philip Weinstein of Swarthmore College. I deeply appreciate his rigorous critique of my manuscript.

Among the friends and colleagues with whom I've talked about Shakespeare, literary criticism, and teaching are Chris Pye, Stacy Cochran, Jean-Bernard Bucky, William C. Dowling, Suzanne Graver, David L. Smith, Stephen Fix, Rob Baker-White, Michael Ferber, Christopher Bolton, John Kleiner, and John Limon. I am grateful for institutional support to Tom Kohut, Bill Wagner, Bill Lenhart, and Peter Murphy.

To many research assistants I am beholden: Mariah Robbins, Molly Joplin, Caroline Henry, Zoe Jenkin, Kaitlin Bell-Barnett, and Amanda Bell. Special thanks to Samantha Barbaro.

Sections of this book have appeared as articles. Part of the introduction was published in *Southwest Review*. Particular thanks to Willard Spiegelman for editorial acumen and much else. The discussion of Falstaff appeared in an earlier form in *Humor: International Journal of Humor Research* ("The Anatomy of Folly in Shakespeare's 'Henriad,'" *Humor: International Journal of Humor Research* 12, no. 2 (2001): 181–201; www.reference-global.com). Several paragraphs about Thersites were part of my article, "Homer's Humor," published by *Humanitas*. I am grateful for permission to reprint.

And I applied my mind to know wisdom and to know madness and folly.
I perceived that this also is but a striving after wind. For in much wisdom
is much vexation and he who increases knowledge increases sorrow.

—Eccles. 1:17–18

I like to fool—oh, you know, you like to be mischievous. ... What do I
want to communicate but what a *hell* of a good time I had writing it? The
whole thing is performance and prowess and feats of association.

—Robert Frost

But someone will say, so what? What is all this leading up to? Listen,
then, to how I will develop the argument.

—Erasmus, *Praise of Folly*

CHAPTER 1

In Quest of Folly

What is folly? "Foolery...shines every where"[1] in Shakespeare's plays. It encompasses infatuation, homicide, jokes, or holiness; follies can be sublime or ridiculous, tragic or trivial.[2] Folly's basic meaning is lack of reason, wisdom, or understanding—hence error, misperception, confusion. Derived from the French *folie*, it suggests madness. Homer's "Ruinous Folly" is the goddess Até, who distracts and blinds mortals.[3] To the Hebrew prophets, folly denotes evil or sin—either plain ignorance or willful defiance of God: "The fool hath said in his heart, there is no God" (Ps. 14:1).[4] It is a subject to which Jeremiah, Isaiah, Ecclesiastes, and the prophets return repeatedly: "As a dog returneth to his vomit, so a fool returneth to his folly" (Prov. 26:11). To fool someone can also mean to trick or deceive. In either sense, to be fooled might be amusing or confusing, painful or disastrous. Finally, the conception of folly as what fools say and do gives the more abstract notion of folly a local habitation and a name. Very often *fool* comes attached to another epithet: "moral fool," "vain fool" (*Lr* 4.2.58, 4.2.62), "a bitter fool and a sweet one" (*Lr* 1.4.138), godless fool, wise fool, holy fool, Christian fool. Elizabethans often distinguished between a natural fool, meaning a simpleton or lunatic, and an artificial fool, who "professionally counterfeits folly for the entertainment of others"[5] and is conscious of the role he plays.

Fool and *folly* have multiple valences, attaching indiscriminately and making "strange bedfellows" (*Tmp.* 2.2.40). The folly/fool cluster evokes a plurality of meaning. All these myriad, contradictory, and nebulous meanings—or to use Shakespeare's phrase, all this "superfluous folly" (*AWW* 1.1.105)—are extravagantly displayed in Erasmus's *Praise of Folly*, written in 1511 and immediately translated and widely read throughout Europe.[6]

It's possible that the "words, words, words" (2.2.192) Hamlet reads are Erasmus's encyclopedia of foibles and chapbook of fooling. *Praise of Folly* is a stirring dramatic monologue, for "Folly Herself Speaks" (9). *Moria*, as Erasmus calls Folly, is an engaging performer, exuberantly entertaining and deftly instructive: "For just as nothing is more trivial than to treat serious matters in a trivial way, so too nothing is more delightful than to treat trifles in such a way that you do not seem to be trifling at all. . . . But unless I am completely deceived by '*Selflove*,' my praise of Folly is not altogether foolish" (4). Moria is never foolish enough to define her subject or herself: no one "should expect me . . . to explain my subject matter—myself—by a definition, much less to divide it into parts" (12). Because the terms *fool, fooling*, and *folly* undergo so many metamorphoses, they can be maddeningly slippery. Mercurial Moria could drive anyone bonkers!

Initially, Moria's charming ebullience and freedom from constraint provoke congenial laughter: "The human race is propagated by the part which is so foolish and funny that it cannot even be mentioned without a snicker" (18). Moria boasts that "no glorious deed was ever performed except at my instigation" (35). Her works pleasure and benefit mankind. To wisely overlook things makes possible both intimate relations and "soothing self-delusions" (64). Yet wily Moria suddenly becomes an angry scourge of abominations. Protean and elusive, she can be perplexing and exasperating. Her hocos-pocos—now you see it, now you don't—alternately flaunts and obscures specious reasoning.[7] Of course, Moria *would* be a sophist.[8] She wants "everything suddenly reversed" (43). Playfully celebrating harmless peccadilloes or pillorying serious transgressions, now tongue-in-cheek, now derisive, she is the bane of logic. Moria resembles the Cretan declaring that all Cretans are liars.

The festive host Moria exhorting "illustrious initiates of Folly" (138) to applaud and drink ultimately transforms into a veritable prophet. Recalling that Christ became "somehow foolish in order to relieve the folly of mortals" (130), Moria sanctifies folly: "What is foolish to the world, God has chosen" (Erasmus 128; 1 Cor. 1:27), for "the wisdom of this world is foolishness with God" (1 Cor. 3:19). Like Paul, she urges us to be "fools for Christ's sake" (4:10) because "the Christian religion taken all together has a certain affinity with some sort of folly and has little or nothing to do with wisdom" (132).[9] Moria affirms "Folly's part, which shall not be taken from her by the transformation of life, but shall be perfected" (137). Citing Paul, her conclusion is compelling, gorgeous, and altogether earnest: "So much beyond the body are the things of the spirit; things unseen, beyond what can be seen. This indeed, is what the prophet promises" (137).

Moria's "glorious laudation of folly" poses problems that inspire my own quest of folly: its connections with grace and redemption; its Pauline inversion of wisdom and error; its shifting ironies and incongruous tones; its range of meanings from iniquity to blessedness; its protean transmutations of the foolish narrator whose self-justification is compelling and self-consuming; its mélange of brilliant insights and sophistry, nonsense and visionary lucidity, culminating in Paul's faith in things unseen: "Eye has not seen, nor ear heard, nor has the heart of man conceived what things God has prepared for those who love him" (Erasmus 137; 1 Cor. 2:9). Truly, folly works in mysterious ways. When Shakespeare's Bottom (a simple weaver and bumptious community theater actor) awakes, befuddled and amazed, he echoes Moria's revelation: Bottom's "most rare vision" (*MND* 4.1.204–5) bears witness to a seriocomic "transformation of life" (Erasmus 137). Not even Bottom could miss Moria's cue as it appears in Chaloner's 1559 rendition: "Was neuer mans eie sawe, nor eare heard, nor thot of hert yet compassed, what, and how great felicitee god hath prepared unto such as dooe loue him."[10]

As Feste proclaims, "Foolery...shines every where" (*TN* 3.1.38–39). *Shakespeare's Great Stage of Fools* dissects four kinds of folly. Chapter 2, "This Great Stage of Fools," traces the development of the clowns and fools, jesters, and foolosophers who populate the plays from *Comedy of Errors* through *The Tempest*. This chapter begins by construing fooling narrowly as the activity of so-called artificial fools, those self-identified or self-evident jesters such as Feste or Touchstone. These proper fools, as it were, are licensed performers with conventional techniques of foolery. Shakespeare's clowns expand into significant commentators and problematic figures whose discourse both complicates and illuminates. Chapter 3 explores the "Henriad," in which folly is represented by intimate antagonists, the foolosopher king Falstaff and the madcap Prince of Wales. Falstaff, Shakespeare's greatest apostle of folly, and Hal, apostate from folly—both complexly divided—embody and stage a dialectical drama.

"Fools for Love," chapter 4, examines the competition between fooling and feeling in *Much Ado About Nothing*, *As You Like It*, and *Twelfth Night*. In the first two, which epitomize Shakespeare's great romantic comedies, foolery between hero and heroine is relatively beneficent and follies are felicitously reparable. However, these comedies do not license and authorize folly. Though fooling permits self-affirmation and relatedness, it also impedes self-awareness and love. How, in a world of duplicities and "counterfeiting" where fooling is interrogated, does Shakespeare's audience determine the validity of particular attitudes and feelings? Not necessarily simple or harmless misapprehension, fooling also entails complex deception and dubious trickery. In these three plays, some feelings really do matter and mean something. Warily licensed and seemingly celebrated in *Much Ado* and *As You*

Like It, folly in *Twelfth Night* takes the form of madness and maintains its troubling persistence amid the requisite happy ending.

The play of contraries that shapes the "Henriad" continues into the next chapter, "Folly is Anatomiz'd," which focuses on Shakespeare's obnoxious and persuasive scourges: Mercutio, Jaques, Malvolio, and Thersites. Appalled, disgusted, or outraged, they embody the power of folly even as they repudiate and denigrate it. Chapter 6, "There the Antic Sits," considers Romeo, Richard II, Hamlet, Lear, and Othello, who play the fool both deliberately and willy-nilly. In its tragic incarnations, forms of folly variously inspire, confound, entrap, and undo Shakespeare's heroes in motley. *Fool* is Goneril's term of abuse for her good husband, and "poor fool" is Lear's term of endearment for his murdered Cordelia. Contagious and insinuating, folly links "mighty opposites" (*Ham.* 5.2.62) who, as the Prince of Denmark observes, are a "little more than kin" (1.2.64). The stubborn intractability of folly and the disturbing tendencies of foolery give *The Tempest* its peculiar and haunting resonance. Prospero painfully discovers that the cursed "folly of this island" (*Tmp.* 3.2.4) is pervasive and deep-rooted within—where the antic abides.

Shakespeare's Great Stage of Fools explores the uses, meanings, virtue, and value of foolery as represented and advocated by clowns, fools, and jesters—virulently critiqued by self-proclaimed anatomists of folly, regarded and practiced by comic and romantic protagonists, perceived and enacted by tragic heroes. Fools are indeed everywhere we look, except in the mirror. Whether it is possible to study folly without becoming a fool remains "a question to be ask'd" (*1H4* 2.4.410). Teaching Shakespeare for the first time, I was asked why a fool carries a "glass." I was confidently explaining the symbolic implications of an hourglass when my student objected: "The footnote says the *glass* is a *mirror*." Flustered, I responded, "Well, it just goes to show that you can't believe everything you read." "Or *hear!*" the student declared.

Now, as a seasoned teacher and scholar of folly, I would ask the curious student what a jester could *do* with that mirror. Perhaps he talks to himself or studies his reflection or turns the glass to the audience. Who, after all, is the fool? The mirror represents duality, both union and separation. It reflects a second self, identical to yet distinct from one's self. A metonym for the jester, the glass also suggests our equivocal attitudes toward the fool. Fools intrigue us even as we amuse fools. Expecting comic relief or divertissement, we are mocked and manipulated. Seeking clarification or anticipating proverbial wisdom, we become confounded. Fools and fooling complicate perceptions, disrupt meaning, confound and compound perspective.

To follow the fool through the looking glass is to enter no-man's land. Shakespeare's fools bring topsy-turvy and play handy-dandy, leap capriciously between planes of reference, and pit one thing against another: the more far-fetched, the better. Gaily unselfconscious, innocent of intro-spection, Shakespearean fools are paradoxically self-reflexive performers. Their jester's mirror encourages speculation (*speculum* is Latin for mirror). The marotte, perhaps decorated with a miniature self-image, figures the fool's duality, depicting and mocking the fool "himself." These props, like much foolish flapdoodle, rupture the illusion of verisimilitude and rein-force the blatant artificiality. Presuming that "this world is contingency and absurdity incarnate, the oddest of possibilities masquerading momentarily as a fact,"[11] the fool revels in profusion and disarray. Exposing and perform-ing follies, the fool may be in danger of becoming respectable.

How is it possible that the last shall be first? A paradigm shift in liter-ary theory blazoned by William Empson about 1930 enables readers better to perceive, appreciate, and enjoy Shakespeare's fools and anatomy of folly. Invoking Heisenberg's uncertainty principle, the complementarity of quan-tum mechanics, relativity, and perspectivism, Empson licenses the simulta-neous validity of contradictory readings, based on reiterated words in the plays that refuse "to be read in terms of either/or."[12] One thing we know: fools produce multiple types of ambiguity. To his fools, myriad-minded Shakespeare often entrusts incongruity and contradictions. One imagines wandering around Arden with a clever fool named Empson, spouting this wisdom from *Seven Types of Ambiguity*: "The two meanings of the word, the two values of the ambiguity, are the two opposite meanings defined by the context, so that the total effect is to show a fundamental division in the writer's mind."[13] Maintaining both/and instead of either/or, fools represent Shakespeare's law of indeterminacy and the aspectuality of viewpoint.

In Empson's wake, New Critics treated Shakespeare's fools and fool-ing with invigorated attention and concern. Their preference for multiple feelings and competing attitudes made fool's play more seriously intrigu-ing. Nowadays fools enjoy greater entitlement than ever, not as entertain-ers, truth-tellers, and pathfinders but as carnivalesque lords of liminality, demons of deconstruction, and purveyors of subversion. Fools illustrate Shakespeare's hybridity and liminality, grotesque or monstrous amalgama-tions, dialectic of high and low, excess or extravagance, resistance to resolu-tion, antic discombobulation, and infinite supplementarity. *Play* fascinates poststructuralist critics alert to all sorts of folderol or hey nonny-nonny and eager to investigate the fool's *mise en abyme*. Puns, for instance, are cherished signs of deceptive multiplicity and signifiers of a word's treacherous insta-bility. Fools also gain traction for their antimimetic function and self-reflex-ivity. Reconfiguring apparent dichotomy as dialectic, fools and critics share the premise that opposites are (or should be) mutually implicated: inverted

Figure 1.1 Hans Holbein, Fool and his bauble. Woodcut engraving published in Erasmus, *Praise of Folly*.

or identified, reversed or interrogated. The postmodern decentering project has reconstructed our sense of folly as wisdom.

Perhaps the fool's hour is come round at last. My purpose is not to idealize the fool or to make another simple reversal of binary oppositions. Foolery is the dynamic, ongoing exchange between opposites such as sublime and ridiculous, everything and nothing. Fools bring us closer to the heights and depths of experience and keep both poles in play. This giddy oscillation between extremes is both a source and an effect of fooling. *King Lear* dramatizes how everything becomes nothing and how nothing becomes everything. Given "nothing" by Cordelia, Lear hears his fool ask, "Can you make no use of nothing, nuncle?" (1.4.130–31). A fool's discourse might be nonsense, blither, or babble, or it might be pertinent, insightful, even inspired. Is it gold or fool's gold, the real turtle soup or merely the mock? Fools foment the illusion that audiences are collaborators and participants in the illusion and solicit spectators face to face, as if the fool is on our side and at one with us.[14] But fools are two-faced rascals always double-dealing and sometimes saying so: *Ducdame, ducdame!* Like Jaques drawing auditors into the circle, fools ensorcell and make fools of us all.

CHAPTER 2

This Great Stage of Fools

Moria boasts, "Why should I want a temple, since the whole world, unless I am badly mistaken, is a splendid temple dedicated to me?" (Erasmus 75). Nowhere could Folly claim more dedicated disciples than in Shakespeare's England, where jesters, zanies, and harlequins capered on stages, enlivened festivals and holidays, and might live at royal courts and great houses. All sixteenth-century Tudor monarchs including Henry VIII and Elizabeth I kept jesters: Will Somers and Dick Tarlton were both household words in their day and beyond. The year 1588 was widely known not only as the year of the Armada but also as "Tarlton's time." Two centuries after Tarlton's demise, his name and image adorned signs for London pubs. Cardinal Wolsey had a fool named Patch, and King James's jester Archie Armstrong proudly bore the title *joculator domini Regis*, frolicked late nights with his monarch, and insulted Bishop Laud to his face.[1] Thomas More, to whom Erasmus dedicated *Moriae Encomium*, kept a fool named Henry Patenson, who was prominently situated in the very middle of the More family portrait.

The London theater company Shakespeare joined in the early 1590s included a gifted clown, Will Kemp, who had already been designated "vice-gerent generall to the ghost of Dick Tarlton."[2] A "vice-gerent" or vice-regent is deputy head of state—or in this case master of revels and minister of vices. Out of motley, Kemp was independently prominent and successful enough to become a principal shareholder in the Lord Chamberlain's Men. It would be several years before Will Shakespeare became as renowned as Will Kemp. For any aspiring playwright, clowns were a natural resource, and Will Kemp was a featured player from the first. Audiences keenly anticipated his arrival. Stage directions on extant actors' sheets indicate "enter Will Kemp" rather than his character Peter in *Romeo and Juliet*. Kemp *was* the Clown the way that Charlie Chaplin is the Little Tramp and Woody Allen the schlemiel. Kemp cultivated a special relationship with spectators who might see him before the show, as he mustered a crowd and collected tickets. A flamboyant figure, costumed extravagantly in an ass-eared cap and bells and multicolored tunic or motley, he would have carried a prop—an insignia of folly, probably a mirror or a wafer and perhaps a marotte or bauble.[3] Welcoming him with titters, laughter, and applause, audiences no doubt wondered, now what's he going to do with those full-blown ox-bladders on the end of a fool-stick?

Kemp's forte was calculated buffoonery. Like Charlie Chaplin, he was a dexterous dancer pretending to be a klutz. Once Kemp performed a "Nine Day's Wonder," jigging a hundred miles from London to Norwich.[4] He talked to himself in his handheld mirror or addressed the facsimile of his head on the end of his bauble. He botched language, bent his body like a pretzel, and took pratfalls. Holding the stage solo, he spoke directly to his audience, sometimes improvising or veering on far-fetched tangents, to the chagrin of the author: "And let those that play your clowns speak no more than is set down for them," counsels Hamlet, "for there be of them that will themselves laugh to set on some quantity of barren spectators to laugh too" (*Ham.* 3.2.38–42). A flagrant show-off, Kemp constantly broke boundaries and invaded the audience. He presumed their sympathy, winked in complicity as if they were all one. Kemp's antics might not have had much to do with the rest of the play, "though in the mean time some necessary question of the play be then to be consider'd. That's villainous, and shows a most pitiful ambition in the fool that uses it" (3.2.42–45), as the drama-loving Prince of Denmark complains. Irresponsible and outrageous, clowns can't stand still and won't shut up.

Shakespeare's first audiences probably appreciated the clown's shenanigans more than the playwright's artistry. The showstopper in *Two Gentlemen of Verona* is Kemp as Launce, bitching about his dog, Crab, "the sourest-natur'd dog that lives: my mother weeping, my father wailing, my sister crying, our maid howling, our cat wringing her hands, and all our house in a great perplexity, yet did not this cruel-hearted cur shed one tear: he is a stone, a very pibble stone, and has no more pity in him than a dog," and so forth (*TGV* 2.3.5–11). Well, you had to be there. Shakespeare's script merely precipitated Kemp's bawdy slapstick. Clowning is all style, its full effects available only on stage, though there's a price to be paid for the clown's premium on performance. When Launce simply disappears, unremarked and unlamented, nobody minds because the clown is a pretend person, a diverting interlude. Ephemeral and gratuitous, Launce scarcely connects with the other characters in the play, not even Crab the dog. Like the joker in the pack, conventional clowns have temporary impact but ultimately don't count. Launce's scene typifies the nature and limits of clowning. Kemp provoked laughter by appearing ridiculous and confounded. The wordplay on *shoes* and *soles*, the innuendo involving *stones, holes, staffs*, and *wands*—all are well-worn gags and grist for the mill. Puns connect unrelated things and dismantle meanings. Launce can barely distinguish *himself* from Crab:

> Nay, I'll show you the manner of it. This shoe is my father; no, this left shoe is my father; no, no, this left shoe is my mother; nay, that cannot be so neither; yes, it is so, it is so—it hath the worser sole. This shoe, with the hole in it, is my mother, and this my father—a vengeance on't! there 'tis...I am the dog—no, the dog is himself, and I am the dog—O! the dog is me, and I am myself; ay, so, so. (*TGV* 2.3.13–24)

If Launce cannot identify himself, what can he do? It doesn't matter; he will create something out of nothing. The clown's show is the efflorescence of style: "Nay, I'll show you the *manner* of it" (my emphasis).

Will Kemp's celebrity fueled Shakespeare's curiosity about clowns and fools. Shakespeare regularly borrowed plots and invented humorous characters not found in his sources. He seized any opportunity to create robust clowns and vital fools, tricksters and deceivers, gulls and victims. The word *fool* and its cognates *folly, foolish*, and *fond* appear over 600 times in Shakespeare.[5] By contrast, the Bible repeats "fool" and "folly" about 200 times. Another very early play, *Comedy of Errors*, demonstrates the theatrical appeal and dramatic potential of foolery. Adapting Plautus's Roman farce about long-separated identical twins, Shakespeare doubles the trouble and multiplies the fun with two sets of twins: clowns both named Dromio serve masters each called Antipholus. Implausible? No matter, never mind! Clowns exist to perform ridiculously, brazenly. In *Comedy of Errors*, fools are everywhere, identified by colorful nicknames and synonyms: *mome, malthorse, capon, coxcomb, idiot, patch, sot, ape, ass*, and others. Several scenes are clowns' routines, where impudent wise guys up-end unwitting straight men. Antipholus says that his slave Dromio "lightens my humor with his merry jests" (*Err.* 1.2.21). "Sportive humor" (1.2.58) is the jester's job, cheering the boss with merriment, bawdry, and a fart joke.[6] Held to "neither rhyme nor reason" (*Err.* 2.2.48), the Dromio twins are obliged only to be festive, responsible for irresponsibility. Clowns provoke people and pay the price. Dromio is incessantly slapped and pummeled, but like a true clown, he is resilient. Chaplin said that the clown "always returns again. So in a way he is a spirit—not real. And because he is always returning, that gives comfort. We know he cannot die, and that's the best thing about him."[7] With extraordinary durability, clowns bounce back from falls, drubbings, and humiliations. You can't keep a good clown down.

Comedy of Errors suggests Shakespeare's impatience with pure farce and his preference for impure hybrids. Regularly *dulce* but only accidentally *utile*, these clowns are not yet quizzical commentators, "touchstones," or shrewd observers who test and assess the perspective of others, as Shakespeare's fools will do. Contributing occasional "wise saws and modern instances" (*AYL* 2.7.156), clowns entangle their interlocutors in contradictions and expose their follies: those who think themselves wise are revealed to be fools. Shakespeare's first clowns have the deficiencies of their virtues. Restricted in capacity and efficacy, they do not challenge conventional wisdom or catalyze recognitions and revelations. Clowning is comparatively circumscribed, relatively unthreatening and unenlightening.

Quickly the young Shakespeare discovers the potential of clowning to disrupt more profoundly, to figure more prominently, and to comment more provocatively. Though *clown*, *fool*, and *jester* remain more or less synonymous in Elizabethan England, Shakespeare begins to differentiate. Conventionally, a *clown* is an ignorant rustic confounded at court or lost in the city. A *jester* is a sophisticated courtly performer such as Will Somers or Dick Tarlton, also known to Elizabethans as an *artificial fool*, who "counterfeits folly for the entertainment of others" as opposed to a "natural" fool or lunatic.[8] The first Kempian clown to deliver more than meets the eye is Bottom in *A Midsummer Night's Dream* (1595).

Bless'd Bully Bottom

Bottom's clownish antics are at first simply delightful and delightfully simple. An inverted weathervane, he signals that we should look in the opposite direction. The clown gets things ass-backward or bottoms first, confusing bombast for poetry, burlesque for tragedy, and banality for loftiness. Gradually, though, Bottom helps direct and clarify our perceptions. Though amusingly "mechanical,"[9] he provides much more than intermittent amusement. Bottom dramatizes the confusion between dreaming and waking, reason and imagination, play and reality. In this way too, Bottom embodies duality: he becomes humorously pertinent, obliviously prescient. When he volunteers to play Thisbe "in a monstrous little voice" (*MND* 1.2.52), Bottom unknowingly foreshadows his own metamorphosis into a beast.

Initially he is a lovable but ludicrous buffoon. Recognizing both his heartiness and his bossiness, his mates call him "Bully Bottom." Always demanding or commanding, he calls the shots and runs the show. Bottom is plucky, cocksure, full of himself—spectacularly what he *is*. Imperious and importunate, Bully Bottom is irresistible and unstoppable. His virtues and his foibles are intertwined. Eager to play every role in "Pyramus and Thisby," he wants all the parts, including drama critic: "A very good piece of work, I assure you" (1.2.13). Bottom always remembers the audience—presumed to be naively overawed by his talent. He is passionately dedicated to the illusion "in the true performing of it" (1.2.25). He blusters and bullies with energetic egomania and blissful unawareness: this combination he might term, if he knew himself better, "my chief humor" (1.2.28). Without discomfort, he seems delimited by the clown's part: a blunderer whose malapropisms include *obscenely* for *obscurely*, he is the least likely bloke to fathom bottomless vistas. He blithely praises himself—playing Hercules *rarely*—then comments complacently, "This was lofty" (1.2.39).

Bottom dimly apprehends the restrictions of static identity and obliquely anticipates the possibilities of metamorphosis. Though such transformation is second nature to any actor, Bottom carefully explains it to his mates: "I Pyramus am not Pyramus, but Bottom the weaver" (3.1.20–21). Addressing his peers as an audience and inventing lines to distinguish actor and role, Bottom resembles a playwright. Bottom's follies and virtues are closely associated with love of theater. He insists, "I am a man as other men are" (3.1.43–44), with just a faint foreshadowing of mystical exaltation: "My life for yours" (3.1.41–42). Instead of blowing with the wind or peeing upwind, he looks up.

Bottom experiences a truly awesome transformation on this fantastic night. Capering cluelessly, he stumbles upon the time of his life. Part of the joke is that Bottom "himself" is indifferent to his altered state. Magically "chang'd," he is stubbornly, humorously himself, an ass, blatantly idiotic. That ass's head signifies his *innate* asininity. When Bottom is transported, everything goes topsy-turvy: the lowest figure on the totem pole becomes king of the hill. Peter Quince exclaims in astonishment, "Bless thee, Bottom, bless thee! Thou art translated" (3.1.120–21). In being "translated" or transformed, Bottom is uplifted and "blessed."[10] The assification of Bottom is a comic consecration. Abased, he is exalted. Abandoned, shaken, and fearful his mates are scheming "to make an ass of me" (3.1.20–21), Bottom struts and sings without hearing or regarding himself. He sings no better than he acts.

Yet Titania is spellbound when she awakens: "What angel wakes me from my flow'ry bed?" (3.1.128–29). The incongruity between Titania and Bottom invites burlesque, juxtaposing clown and queen, beauty and the beast, goddess and mortal. This apparently unbridgeable canyon is unexpectedly crossed and crisscrossed. Instead of Bottom advancing and Titania withdrawing, the lady takes charge and the male gets taken. And rather than descend from lyric to lewd, from grand to gross, the scene elevates his Lowness to her Highness. The rude mechanical and the faerie queen share a reversal—a carnival communion. Inveterately crude, Bottom remains ridiculous yet becomes indeed "lofty." At Titania's proclamation of love, he does a double take and pronounces not inaptly: "Reason and love keep little company together now-a-days" (3.1.143–44). Titania's gorgeous response ignores the disparity between her dignity and his ludicrousness. It's not a problem! She will "purge [his] mortal grossness" and raise him to "aery spirit" (3.1.160–61). In *A Midsummer Night's Dream*, even material as intractable and unpromising as Bottom may be refined and sublimated (temporarily at least), for Bottom is graced at the same time that he is exposed. What goes up comes down and vice versa. And so it goes.

Bottom is amazingly "transported" and marvelously foolish. Caught between mundane reality and earthly paradise, Bottom goes both ways with clownish helter-skelter and boundless zig-zaggery. Flamboyantly, Bottom is dual. His goofy name has two sets of doubled letters, *o*'s and *t*'s; it even begins and ends with a symmetrical letter. And, of course, the "bottom" is a prominently dual anatomical part. Bottom is surprisingly hybrid—a brazen clown who in one brief, shining moment morphs into a sage. Directly after Hermia muses that "every thing seems double" (4.1.189), Bottom stands unsteadily on a threshold: changed back to his ordinary self, with the extraordinary night dimly present and fast fading, he struggles to remember his dream—"to translate a translation."[11] This clown is goofily inspired: humorously, fortuitously, and in spite of himself, Bottom produces a most rare vision, quick as any lightning.

Awakening from his enchantment, Bottom tries to locate himself, as if still rehearsing with his mates.

> When my cue comes, call me, and I will answer: my next is, "Most fair Pyramus."…God's my life, stol'n hence, and left me asleep! I have had a most rare vision. I have had a dream, past the wit of man to say what dream it was. Man is but an ass, if he go about t' expound this dream. Methought I was—there is no man can tell what. Methought I was, and methought I had,—but man is but a patch'd fool, if he will offer to say what methought I had. The eye of man hath not heard, the ear of man hath not seen, man's hand is not able to taste, his tongue to conceive, nor his heart to report, what my dream was. I will get Peter Quince to write a ballet of this dream: it shall be called "Bottom's Dream," because it hath no bottom; and I will sing it in the latter end of a play, before the Duke. Peradventure, to make it the more gracious, I shall sing it at her death. (*MND* 4.1.200–19)

Disoriented but undaunted, Bottom struts grandly: someone *else* must notice the star's cue. He tramples logic, mixes senses, and pontificates obtusely: "The eye of man hath not heard, the ear of man hath not seen." His confusion of bodily parts is deliciously bawdy: "His hand is not able to taste, his tongue to conceive." Blithely wacky, Bottom becomes strangely moved, uplifted: "God's my life!" Even his absurd "when my cue comes, call me," heeds a calling, as if some revelation is at hand. Sure enough and incongruously, Bottom echoes 1 Corinthians: "But as it is written, The things which eye hath not seen, neither ear hath heard, neither came into man's heart, *are*, which God hath prepared for them that love him."[12] The Geneva translation, the one Shakespeare knew best, exhorts us to reach "the *bottom* of God's secrets."[13]

This is clowning with a difference, far beyond Launce's buffoonery or Dromio's knockabout. Bottom is a great clown to whom something *happens*. Touched, *gloriously* foolish, garbling scripture, struggling to fathom and articulate his "most rare vision," Bottom is an individual responding to an experience that "hath no bottom." Catalyzed, an illiterate mechanical has a startling instinct, to make art: "I will get Peter Quince to write a [ballad] of this dream." Bumptious Bottom glimpses, as it were, the sublime: "God's my life...a most rare vision...to make it the more gracious." Ludicrously, indubitably, Bottom hits the hammer on the head. Intuiting that dreams and visions are past the wit of man, Bottom speaks in tongues. As it is written, so it shall be: the last shall be first.

Bottom's amusing gaffes, stock switcheroos, and farcical revelation indicate the higgledy-piggledy fluidity of the whole play, especially its breakdown of real and imaginary, waking and sleeping, supernatural and mortal. Bottom's "most rare vision" reflects the proximity of sublime and ridiculous. It is as if Bottom projects a hologram of himself, so that we view both the fool's body and an eerie aura or luminous emanation. Fooling inspires a double vision, alternately or simultaneously closer and more distant. It is an odd, disorienting perspective, potentially fruitful and apparently more accessible to the least of our brethren; in *A Midsummer Night's Dream*, a bottom's up, arsy-versy vision is most available to the least enabled. Bottom's metamorphosis retains elements of continuity: through his transformation, Bottom remains incorrigibly "himself." The humor depends upon his stubbornly implacable Bottomness, blustering as Pyramus or guffawing as Titania's beloved. Though Bottom boasts that he can be anything—"Let me play the lion too" (1.2.70)—he remains risibly in character, Bottom always and Bottom still. Yet Bottom is habitually double. His performance in "Pyramus and Thisbe" illustrates the power to fabricate personal identity. Bottom makes hay or a marvelous mishmash when he superfluously but reasonably insists upon the difference between himself and his role: "And for the more better assurance, tell them that I Pyramus am not Pyramus, but Bottom the weaver" (3.1.19–21).

Bottom is humorously determined to perpetuate that dual vision, that sense of being "translated" or two in one. In his return to "himself," Bottom's awakening speech seems touched by divinity. Simultaneously the first and the last, top and bottom, his dying is immortal. In his visionary moment, Bottom is the rude mechanical with a glowing nimbus, in this sense himself and not himself. He perfectly embodies that Erasmian paradox, wherein "to know oneself is to know oneself an ass, but to be an ass is not to know oneself."[14] Bottom's glorious moment is an indication of fools to come, who resist categories, elude definitions, flout singularity, and multiply doubts about identity, meaning, and value.

Prepost'rous Puck

A Midsummer Night's Dream deploys Puck to supplement and contrast Bottom. Puck defines himself forthrightly: "I am that merry wanderer of the night," he announces. "I jest to Oberon and make him smile" (2.1.43–44). Puck is, in effect, Oberon's jester, master of the "revels here to-night" (2.1.18), a carnivalesque spirit, and agent of "night-rule" (3.2.5) with a penchant for hoodwinking mortals: "A merrier hour was never wasted there" (2.1.57). The power of Puck's fooling proves his point: "Lord, what fools these mortals be!" (3.2.115). To demonstrate the ubiquity of folly is Puck's irrationale: fun for him and for us at the expense of his unhappily fooled victims. Puck is the primary denizen of disorder. Some of Puck's antics are gratuitous divertissement; others, such as leading astray "night-wanderers, laughing at their harm" (2.1.39), are more sinister. Though his natural bias is toward mischief rather than mayhem, Puck implements Oberon's "hateful" (2.1.258) scheme to "torment" Titania (2.1.147).

Variously construed as merry sprite or nightmarish peril, adorable rascal or demonic imp,[15] Puck is more flagrantly dual than Bottom: "Robin Goodfellow" and "sweet Puck" (2.1.34, 2.1.40) but also "Hobgoblin" (2.1.40) and agent of the "king of shadows" (3.2.347). Mercurial and protean, he is a trickster and a shape-shifter.[16] Like Bottom metamorphosing from clown to fool, buffoonery to bonanza, Puck expands markedly. When he discovers the workmen's rehearsal, he decides to "be an auditor," like us, and "an actor too perhaps, if I see cause" (3.1.79–80). Armed with that magical potion, Puck becomes another farce to be reckoned with. Oberon needs Puck to explain what has happened: "What night-rule now about this haunted grove?" (3.2.5). While Oberon commands, it is Puck who stages and narrates events.

One long speech, otherwise gratuitous, inverts the hierarchical arrangement of king and jester. Puck makes things happen according to providential design and virtually invokes the comic god: "Shall we their fond pageant see? / Lord, what fools these mortals be!" (3.2.114–15). Seconds later, he confirms his affection for fools and devotion to folly: "And those things do best please me / That befall prepost'rously" (3.2.120–21).

Prepost'rously is fool's diction, meaning contrary to reason or common sense; foolish, absurd, derived from the Latin for "first coming after" or "reversed." In *Praise of Folly*, *praeposterum* is the rhetorical figure translated by Chaloner as *topsy-turvy*. In 1588 George Puttenham defines the Greek trope *Hysteron, proteron* as "the Preposterous": a form of "disorder" or inversion of natural order, placing the cart before the horse.[17] In foolery, truly, what goes around comes around. *Preposterously* is perfectly Puckish.

However zestfully he delights in the preposterous, Puck establishes himself as a reliable witness by clearly explaining the volatile situation.[18] Noting the lovely changeling boy contested by Oberon and Titania, Puck immediately segues from wrath to revelry and anger to "joy." Thus Puck reiterates the theme and foreshadows the denouement. For all his insouciance, he is apposite. He is a trusted confidante of the Faerie King who addresses him warmly and intimately as "my gentle Puck" (2.1.148). Despite his privileged status, Puck remains subject to the comic law: what goes up must come down, or pride goeth before a (prat)fall. Strutting his stuff, Puck is upbraided by Oberon for "mistak[ing] quite," a dire "misprision." Humorous incapacity causes accidents or muddles. The king's chagrin puts him in his place. Puck's prodigious powers are incongruously limited: like Bottom, vaunting and swaggering, Puck wanders, muddles, and screws up royally and hilariously.

Puck revives to school Oberon: "And so far am I glad it so did sort / As this their jangling I esteem a sport" (3.2.352–53). So get with the program, Highness! Puck's lesson seems effective, for it precipitates Oberon's arbitrary decision to halt the game, clarify the confusion, and restore order: "All things shall be peace" (3.2.377). Notably, Puck's response to the king's decree is not simply to acquiesce but to take charge: "My fairy lord," he says, "this must be done with haste" (3.2.378). Puck now speaks with unexpected authority about light and night, life and death. He discourses rather like another supernatural creature, Old Hamlet's ghost marking the approach of morn when "damned spirits all" must troop home:

> And yonder shines Aurora's harbinger,
> At whose approach, ghosts, wand'ring here and there,
> Troop home to churchyards. Damned spirits all,

> That in crossways and floods have burial,
> Already to their wormy beds are gone.
>
> (3.2.380–84)

Wandering here and there, Puck consorts "with black-brow'd night," as if he too were a "damned spirit" raised (3.2.387, 3.2.382).

More than anyone in *A Midsummer Night's Dream* (always excepting Bottom), Puck has it both ways, seeing with godlike apprehension the first and the last, the beginning and the end. Leading the lovers on a wild-goose chase, up and down, up and down, he prolongs the prank for the sheer joy of fooling and as a show of force. As though he were Jehovah summoning Abraham or Christ calling Lazarus, Puck mocks Demetrius, "Come hither. I am here" (3.2.425). It's also Puck who brings the lovers together by impersonating them. The roundelay of reconciliation is a game of hide-and-seek: the cherished self is figured as a voice, an assumed role, a trick or will-o'-the-wisp. Following Lysander's "voice," imitated by Puck, Demetrius is confounded: "Yea, art thou there?... When I come where he calls, then he is gone... Where art thou now?" (3.2.412–24). Well might he wonder. Puck's enactment of Lysander is another counterfeit creation, intangibly evocative, as insubstantial as a dream: seen with parted eye, as something that is and is not. Thus, the fundamental process of fooling and being fooled represents the bifocal vision the play stages and encourages.

Puck also proclaims a second chance and more doubling: "In your waking shall be shown. / Jack shall have Jill: / Nought shall go ill: / The man shall have his mare again, and all shall be well" (3.2.460–63). Like Bottom's dream, Puck's chant recapitulates the play's tensions—waking/sleeping, true delight/confused anguish, the nature of vision, and the power of love. Apparent nonsense, "The man shall have his mare again," jostles with the comic imperative "all shall be well." Like Bully Bottom, Prepost'rous Puck seems to have caught wind of *Praise of Folly* and, Moria-like, blends prophecy and pother.

Puck attends the renewal in amity between Oberon and Titania and restores Bottom: "Now, when thou wak'st, with thine own fool's eyes peep" (4.1.84). Ultimately, wielding a broom to sweep away dangers and safeguard the dream, Puck emerges as veritable guardian of the gate, no minor service:

> Now it is the time of night
> That the graves, all gaping wide...
> And we fairies, that do run
> By the triple Hecat's team

From the presence[19] of the sun,
Following darkness like a dream,
Now are frolic. Not a mouse
Shall disturb this hallowed house.
I am sent with broom before,
To sweep the dust behind the door.

(5.1.379–90)

In his solemn invocation "In remembrance of a shroud" (5.1.378), Puck sounds magisterial, rather like Prospero gleaning the forbidden world beyond the grave. Sweeping the dust "behind the door" is a ritual purification limning a boundary between inside and outside and marking the rite of passage being celebrated in the bedrooms of the palace. It's telling that Puck's ceremony at the threshold both opens and seals the border. Fortifying the boundary and protecting the portal, he prepares the entrance for the faeries to cross. Is Puck merely negligent (again!)—or two-faced and snookering? More likely, this border figure institutes an open-door policy. Like Puck himself, the portal goes both ways: it has been well said that Puck's door "emblematizes the openness and closedness that mark the end of the play."[20] Puck has become much more than a gopher and a go-between: he links fairies and mortals, connects "real" and supernatural realms. Ultimately, the merry wanderer becomes the privileged mediator, o'er-leaping another boundary between holiday and everyday. Like Bottom in his visionary moment, Puck reverses the duke's preference for reality over fantasy and reason over imagination in this play of possibilities, reversals, and topsy-turvy.

The wonderful clowning and fooling of Puck and Bottom herald the glorious follies of Falstaff in *Henry IV* (1596–98).[21] Here is Kemp's apex and the zenith of clowning. Everything Shakespeare knew, loved, and distrusted about clowns goes into Falstaff. When "Falstaff riseth up" (*1H4* 5.4.110 s.d.) from supposed death, he makes a ludicrous resurrection analogous to Bottom's moment of glory. Yet how different! Falstaff is more magnificent than anything Bottom could dream. Though Bottom glimpses glory, Falstaff creates sublimity. Bottom's boisterous clown gets lucky with an ensorcelled goddess, whereas the awesome Falstaff, as if blessed by supernatural or magical forces, wields potent powers. Both have access to a neverland beyond the mundane world. But Falstaff makes it happen—at least temporarily. In imagination and through language, Falstaff moves nimbly between real and fantastic, sublime and ridiculous. Plucked into fairyland and returned to his ordinary self, Bottom demonstrates, willy-nilly, that the ass might be first. Asserting his will, Falstaff stages a comic redemption, at once self-dramatizing and self-mocking.

Both the clown Bottom and the great fool Falstaff perform as if their lives depend on it. Although Shakespeare's clowns *represent* representation, fools such as Falstaff reflect on their own performance and speculate about perception and perspective. Deliberately exploiting ambiguities and sowing confusion, Falstaff challenges assumptions; nothing is sacred or authentic, reliable or guaranteed—neither honor nor love, nor any verity. Falstaff raises foolish equivocation to a higher level, as if seeing matter in terms of spirit and spirit in terms of matter, as Robert Frost once characterized poetry.[22] Bottom's peep of what "eye of man hath not heard, the ear of man hath not seen" (4.1.211–12) is expanded and expounded by Falstaff, Shakespeare's "great fool" (*2H4* 2.1.195) and apostle of folly. As we will see in the next chapter, Falstaff is the King of Infinite Jest who stands for nothing and everything.

Condemned into Everlasting Redemption

Kemp's last Shakespearean role, Dogberry in *Much Ado About Nothing*, is sharply diminished: an inescapable comedown from Falstaff. Dogberry gets no respect! He is a strutting nitwit and pompous idiot. Never in contact with Beatrice or Benedick, Dogberry is largely irrelevant, thrust in belatedly to clown and caper. With his witless malapropisms, vain pretensions, and impervious stupidity, he cannot enrich anyone's perceptions nor "improve the occasion," much less precipitate any revaluation. It is tempting to write him down an ass and write him off. Always touting his wit, he loves to stand on ceremony and define protocols pointlessly. The fool loves words and abuses them mercilessly: "You are thought here to be the most senseless and fit man for the constable" (3.3.22–23). A flat humor figure, he is good for mindless *non sequiturs*—with one exception.

Dogberry discovers Don John's villainy, though only by happenstance. The watchmen overhear Borachio and Conrade bragging about the deception of Claudio and ruin of Hero. Like Bottom who demands to play all the roles, Dogberry dominates the inquiry, delivering superfluous instructions, posing irrelevant questions, and assessing their responses: "A marvelous witty fellow, I assure you" (4.2.25). Somehow the truth emerges and prompts Dogberry's indignation: "O, villain! thou wilt be condemn'd into everlasting redemption for this!" (4.2.56–57). With this glorious absurdity, Dogberry almost approaches Bottom's comic vision, "I have had a dream." Like Bottom, Dogberry manhandles the Queen's English and botches scripture.[23] Though Dogberry saves the day, his moment of triumph is short-lived and doesn't earn an invitation to the wedding festivities. At least Bottom gets his star turn even if he is denied the privilege of an epilogue!

Less lovable than Bottom, less incisive than Feste or Touchstone, Dogberry is a throwback to clowns of yore. His gestures toward self-consciousness are ridiculously vain: "Dost thou not suspect my place?" (4.2.74). His ultimate concern is that he be inscribed and commemorated as if he were a dying hero. Instead of reaching the stars, Dogberry shoots himself in the foot: "Remember that I am an ass...forget not that I am an ass" (4.1.76–78). Dogberry's longest articulation culminates in a wonderful self-annihilation; yet he gives a fleeting glimpse of pathos, a hint of interiority that Shakespeare provides for almost every character no matter how lowly or foolish. Beneath his vaunted dignity, Dogberry is "a fellow that hath had losses" (4.2.84). But Shakespeare's gentle touch is unsentimental, and Dogberry's role—or is it Kemp's part?—remains tightly limited and never recognized. In the end it is Borachio, Don John's henchman, who declares the miracle the fool hath wrought: "What your wisdoms could not discover, these shallow fools have brought to light" (5.1.232–34). The figure of Dogberry suggests the ambiguous nature of fooling in a romantic comedy in which foolery seems to be highly valued. *Much Ado About Nothing* interrogates and curtails fooling drastically.

Natural Philosopher, Material Fool

Even as the fool scales the heights of glory as Falstaff, all hell broke loose in the Lord Chamberlain's Men: Will Kemp left the theater company, of which he was part owner and star performer. What happened no one knows. Perhaps there was a "battle of the Wills" between clown and playwright.[24] By 1599 Robert Armin replaced Will Kemp. Armin was a very different kind of actor and resource for Shakespearean foolery. Not a jigger or slapstick comedian, the diminutive but ruminative Armin was also a literary critic—high calling indeed! Explicating his art in publications such as *Nest of Ninnies*, Armin distinguishes among "the fool as sinner, the fool as privileged critic of society, and the fool as merry-maker."[25] On stage, Armin's fools include Touchstone in *As You Like It*, Feste in *Twelfth Night*, Lavatch in *All's Well That Ends Well*, and Lear's Fool. These merrymakers display richer interiority and figure more substantially than Kemp's clowns—always excepting Falstaff, who is beyond category. With the arrival of Robert Armin, the fool (perhaps playing possum) "riseth up." The fool is dead; long live the fool! Armin rejuvenates Shakespearean foolery. Now foolery moves from the margins toward the center or toward "some necessary question of the play." Contriving confusion and cultivating illusions, fools may reflect cogently and speculate skeptically. Armin's fools carry out more calculated explorations of folly and wisdom; some become both the object and the source of mockery. Ingratiating but expendable clowns like Launce morph into high-wire performers instructing and perplexing audiences and rankling and threatening authorities.

In *As You Like It*, Touchstone is a court jester and the kind of artificial fool Armin terms a "privileged critic of society." Touchstone's emblematic name might also be an in-joke, referring to Armin's apprenticeship as a goldsmith. To underscore his own sophistication and mark his distance from simpler clowns, Touchstone browbeats the Arden rustics. Where Launce blathered and Bottom blundered, Touchstone discourses; instead of malapropisms, he crafts puns. "Such a one," as he jests, "is a natural philosopher" (*AYL* 3.2.32). His fooling manufactures meaning through double-talk, strained conceits, blarney, specious erudition, choplogic, and rigmarole. To be a "corrupter of words" (*TN* 3.1.36) like Feste, Touchstone is an adroit rhetorician and practiced orator. His rhetoric persuades, though, by making and unmaking meanings in a process of fusion and fission; his words split and merge. With puns, fools discredit singularity and generate excess.[26] The pun is mightier than the word! No category or ordinary distinction is safe, and no conclusion is conclusive. Touchstone loves *amphibology*, the contemporary term for ambiguity or a "figure of sence incertaine." He fattens on paradox, oxymoron, and aporia to "make doubt of things when by a plaine manner of speech wee might affirme or deny him."[27]

Consider Touchstone's articulation, "We that are true lovers run into strange capers; but as all is mortal in nature, so is all nature in love mortal in folly" (2.4.54–56). Wittily, he plays on *mortal* as both "human, subject to death, fatal" and "excessive, abundant, tiresome and prolonged."[28] That "we" is telling: Touchstone participates in the foolishness he spoofs and purports to speak from experience. The fool's puns are pithy: "The truest poetrie is the most faining, and what / They sweare in Poetry, may be said as louers, they do feigne."[29] Touchstone's pun epitomizes fooling by implying contradictory possibilities: a) love poetry expresses genuine feelings, b) love poetry artfully fashions feeling, c) love poetry deceptively contrives feeling. The issue Touchstone highlights is not whether an attitude is genuine or contrived, an emotion sincere or disingenuous, but whether the performance is well feigned, the artifice compelling. Touchstone suggests that one feigns even when one is most willing or *fain*. Apparently antithetical, faining and feigning overlap in Touchstone's foolosophy. *As You Like It* partially confirms Touchstone's conflation of feeling and fooling, faining and feigning, and exuberantly celebrates artifice. Asking whether an attitude or an emotion—what one fains—is well feigned, *As You Like It* dramatizes the limited value of sincerity and the greater significance of style. The possibility that there is no person behind the performance, no face behind the mask, is seriously entertained and happily conceivable. The fool fragments our perceptions, confusing our conceptions of reality by introducing radically different, even diametrically opposed, perspectives. Is it a duck or is it a rabbit? Fools plump for both views simultaneously, providing a double take—as in the game of handy-dandy, now you see it, now you don't! Teasing questions and entertaining divertissement become urgent issues and jocoserious jests.[30] Function follows fun. Barthes said that the Eiffel Tower attracts meaning the way a lightning rod attracts thunderbolts. Shakespeare's fools attract meaning and disseminate it.

As You Like It elaborates Touchstone's jest about faining and feigning by dramatizing the potency of fooling and celebrating the merits of artifice. Moria mentions that "fabrications of artifice" (Erasmus 52) are among her favorite projects. Style truly is the touchstone. Without artifice, feelings (however ardent) are inadequate or unavailing. Touchstone's emphasis on the contingency of feeling and the validity of fooling is (at least) partially valid. In *As You Like It*, the fool strides forth and stands for nothing—nothing but the enactment of a hypothetical, the pleasure of "performance and prowess and feats of association"[31] that Robert Frost mischievously advocates.

Even for a fool, Touchstone is remarkably mercurial. Introduced as "Nature's natural" (1.2.49), a dull simpleton or "roynish clown" (2.2.8), he is known at court for scurvy shenanigans, merely the "whetstone" of others' wit. From the well-worn bag of fool's banter, Touchstone produces stock material: "The more pity that fools may not speak wisely what wise men do foolishly" (1.2.86–87). Yet in Arden, Touchstone blossoms into a sophisticated critic and deft parodist, commanding the stage longer and more impudently than at court. Perceiving follies more perspicuously, he banters sharply and speculates impressively. When Touchstone arrives in the forest of Arden, he remarks sardonically, "The more fool I" (2.4.16). Even the jester's casual jokes make more than one kind of sense. Touchstone is indeed "the *more* fool" than he was at court or than most of Kemp's clowns were. His attitudes are more complex. He responds acutely to what he sees and hears. To lambast amorous hokum or courtly blather, Touchstone must be an acute listener and an imaginative observer. He is able to enter and appreciate the viewpoints he mocks.

Though Touchstone's progress from "clownish fool" (1.3.130) to "worthy fool" (2.7.36) clearly reflects the changing of the guard from the roustabout Kemp to the cerebral Armin, it also makes internal dramatic sense. Constrained at court, Touchstone is free to speak out and fool around in Arden. Touchstone's burgeoning also demonstrates the fool's elasticity as he adapts and improvises. Playing the sardonic exile, the maudlin lover, the condescending courtier, and the melancholy moralist, his forte is parody, the zestful imitations of highfalutin Petrarchan poetry and courtly balderdash.

Protean Touchstone masters an impressive range of styles. Touchstone is the laureate of relativity. This fool *feigns*—to show off, take advantage, give and get pleasure. He is an actor, ludic and performative, never serious or concerned about expressing feelings or defining truth. With the "pure impartiality of the mirror,"[32] he asserts nothing, maintains no position or investment; whatever is said, Touchstone reflects or reverses. Unprincipled and opportunistic, Touchstone will be anything except sincere or idealistic.[33] Touchstone plays one thing against another in an endless, silly dialectic.

In his most ludicrous guise as Audrey's suitor, a fool for lust, Touchstone's aggravating qualities become more objectionable. Ironically, the character who flaunts his verbal prowess and patronizes his rustic companions pursues an illiterate country girl. Yet when he is with her, Touchstone's jests become more intricate, his wit more flamboyantly learned: "I am here with thee and thy goats, as the most capricious poet, honest Ovid, was among the Goths" (3.3.7–9). Allusions to Ovid, puns on goats/Goths, and learned play on "capricious" (derived from the Latin *caper*, male goat) gaily ignore and merrily exploit his beloved's ignorance. That aria on *faining* and *feigning* ostensibly responds to Audrey's naive question.

Like any fool worth his bauble, Touchstone plays to the audience and flaunts his folly: in for a penny, in for a pound. Grounded and realistic, Touchstone has a single illusion—that he has no illusions. Targeting romantic love, he naturally comes a cropper, driven by carnal appetite to wed a simple girl oblivious to his cherished wit. Yet he wears his humiliation easily and becomes his own best subject, shrewd enough to regard himself humorously. He lauds Audrey's vulgarity and blazons his own carnality. Oddly, he never tries to satisfy his desire. He seems more bent on being betrayed, cheerfully proclaiming that "many a man has good horns, and knows no end of them...so man hath his desires" (3.3.53–81). Because he disrespects marriage, he plans to jump ship. If more accessibly human than most fools, Touchstone also flaunts his knavish amorality. Touchstone provides a tenable viewpoint but rarely the comprehensive picture. His "courtly wit" never fazes Corin, for instance, undismayed by Touchstone's aggressive wordplay. Touchstone regularly reverts to commonplaces of jesting ("The fool doth think he is wise, but the wise man knows himself to be a fool") and braggadocio, hectoring Audrey's hapless swain William.

In his final turn, Touchstone's flagging wit revives: "I press in here, sir, amongst the rest of the country copulatives, to swear and forswear, according as marriage binds and blood breaks" (5.4.55–57). "Country copulatives" is wickedly reductive and brazenly inappropriate for lovers on the cusp of holy matrimony; typically, Touchstone is all-inclusive and self-deprecating. Touchstone thus stakes his claim on shifting sands, swearing and forswearing, faining and feigning. Sublimely fantastic and ridiculously "material," he moves from matrimonial vows to bodily imperatives. The "blood breaks" in several senses of *breaks*: "to lay territory; rupture [the ground]; force a way through [a barrier]; to penetrate; to open up; contract or covenant; an oath, one's word" (*OED*). Adroitly, he mocks and excuses his bride, a "poor virgin, sir, an ill-favor'd thing, sir, but mine own" (5.4.57–58).[34] Again spotlighted, Touchstone reasserts himself as a witty critic and wry commentator, not the sole source of meaning and value but a reliable touchstone. Prompted to "nominate in order now the degrees of the lie" (5.4.88–89), Touchstone rises to the occasion with his charming speech about the lie seven times removed. Comically punctilious and hyperbolically pedantic, his catalog of causes is calibrated in precise sequence and slickly parodies Jaques's *pièce de résistance*. Touchstone's ultimate take on feeling and fooling is his brilliant last line: "Much virtue in If" (5.4.103). Advocating the artist's holy hypothetical, Touchstone seems to speak for Shakespeare: after all, it seems, "no man else *will*" (5.4.59; my heavy-handed emphasis).

Touchstone is wise enough not to take himself too seriously. Disillusioned but undaunted, sensible and down-to-earth, Touchstone is "a material fool" (3.3.32),[35] always plumping for physical pleasures and bodily needs, the first to say that he is tired, hungry, or horny. In the forest where there is no clock, Touchstone minds mortality and reminds us of time lost, that whatever our mortal longings we ripe *and* rot. Touchstone's mockery subjects all ideals and aspirations to the fool's touchstone. Touchstone is a lightning rod, absorbing the cynicism that threatens the romantic impulses of *As You Like It*. He allows Shakespeare "to swear and foreswear"—feeling, fooling, faining, and feigning. One of Shakespeare's best readers says, "The fool's cynicism, or one-sided realism, forestalls the cynicism with which the audience might greet a play where his sort of realism had been ignored. . . . He embodies the part of ourselves which resists the play's reigning idealism."[36] By "exorcising opposition," Touchstone underwrites the romantic comedy despite his skeptical qualms and cynical forays. The fool is at cross-purposes. Touchstone provides a crucial perspective in this play of perspectives, a point of view that is sharply articulated and valued yet weighed in the balances and found wanting. A prudent, commonsense commentator, Touchstone is also a commentary on the limits of common sense, a necessary but inadequate guide. A fool does not necessarily unmask illusions to reveal reality. Beyond the earthbound vision of the wise fool, undreamed of in his philosophy, are beauties, charms, delights, hopes—possibilities the fool does not value and cannot know. Touchstone is always fooling, and if he had his druthers, the game would never end.

Nothing That Is So Is So

Perhaps Ecclesiastes is right that it *is* better to leave the house of mirth and visit the house of mourning. The possibility seems to have occurred to Feste in *Twelfth Night*. Though one anticipates that a fool would thrive amid such festive antics, Feste's participation seems halfhearted and his meditations disheartened. His contributions are hardly festive. He is content to notice "misprision in the highest degree!" (*TN* 1.5.55). Consider Feste's talent for singing. Even the drunken carousers Toby and Andrew appreciate that he has "so sweet a breath to sing" (2.3.21) and immediately call for a "catch" (2.3.18), or song. Feste performs love songs, standard fare, urging "present mirth" and "present laughter" (2.3.48) and discouraging delay—gather ye rosebuds while ye may. Usually he sings plangently about loss and mortality: "Youth's a stuff will not endure" (2.3.52), "Come away, come away, death" (2.4.51), and "For the rain it raineth every day" (5.1.392). It is hard to envision this jester as the life of the party. When Toby bellows, "But I will never die," Feste punningly retorts, "Sir Toby, there you lie" (2.3.106–7). At pains to tell us that he wears no motley in his brain, this fool appears more comfortable in mourning. Mindful of his vulnerable status in the house, Feste only hesitantly joins the device to baffle Malvolio. Despite his jaunty name, fun always seems to leave him at a loss. He is considerably closer to Malvolio's saturnine disposition than to Toby's bacchic mentality. Rarely does Feste even pretend to be gay. When to Orsino he quietly comments, "Now the melancholy god protect thee" (2.4.73), Feste seems quite acquainted with that particular deity.

Flexing his muscles and strutting his stuff, Feste gradually plays a more pronounced role. When he ventures into the scheme to torment Malvolio, Feste's turn as Sir Topas displays his manifold talents as an actor, "dissembler," mimic, impersonator, and learned wit. Like many fools, Feste is a jack-of-all-trades, quick to improvise and capable of sustained disquisition. One thing Feste gets right: in Illyria, "nothing that is so is so" (4.1.8–9). This point he demonstrates as well as articulates. Impersonating the priest, Feste delivers obscure and grandiose taradiddle that mocks and parodies the victim's identity: "That that is is" (4.2.14) initiates a barrage of doubletalk, blarney, mock erudition, specious logic, and palaver. The fool corrupts words by exploiting ambiguities and battens on confusion; his verbal antics are performative rather than substantive, favoring surface over essence. Often the fool suggests that there is no essence, only surface, a plight that can also be disorienting and disturbing. He unfixes us, or leaves us oscillating among the possibilities of puns, innuendo, and hokum. Fundamental assumptions—such as the significance of personal identity—become unmoored; commonsense categories separating self and other become unclear, perhaps untenable.

Feste's stunt also marks the periphery of fooling and suggests its inherent disreputability. Initially reluctant, Feste enthusiastically torments Malvolio. Feste's pretense that he is exorcising the "hyperbolical fiend" or "dishonest Sathan" (4.2.25, 4.2.31) who inhabits the mad Malvolio reminds us that foolery is associated with ungodly spirits and destructive forces. The fool is perennially outside the bounds or bordering on the dark side. (Viola reconnects foolery and foreboding when she compares the fool to the *haggard*, a predatory bird.) Though Feste can "dally nicely with words," Viola adds aptly that he "may quickly make them wanton" (3.1.14–15). Feste's casual torture of Malvolio is disturbing. Only when the plot unravels and he is summoned by Olivia does Feste deliver Malvolio's letter, and even *then* he recites it so jeeringly that Olivia chastises him: "How now, art thou mad?" Feste is fool still: "No, madam, I do but read madness. And your ladyship will have it as it ought to be, you must allow vox" (5.1.293–96)

An "allowed" voice, the fool reflects the folly all around him; he can do no other. So are we fated to "read madness" and encounter resistance. Instructed to "read i' thy right wits" (5.1.297), Feste cannot or will not do so. Ignoring Olivia's emphatic disapproval, Feste launches a bravado recapitulation:

> Why, "some are born great, some achieve greatness, and some have greatness thrown upon them." I was one, sir, in this enterlude—one Sir Topas, sir; but that's all one. "By the Lord, fool, I am not mad." But do you remember? "Madam, why laugh you at such a barren rascal? And you smile not, he's gagged." And thus the whirligig of time brings in his revenges. (5.1.370–77)

Feste cannot resist vaunting his tour de force as the priest and re-creates for an unappreciative audience some of his particularly fine strokes. Mocking Malvolio's proud condescension, Feste still regards Malvolio's humiliation as justly deserved and amusing. Like so many of Shakespeare's fools, Feste repeatedly and ultimately positions himself outside the community, perched to discern the spectacle of folly, more bemused than troubled, a wily commentator, partly admirable, hardly lovable, deeply disquieting, and finally unknowable.[37]

The motley fool is more complexly divided and divisive than the particolored clown. Like Moria, the fool speaks "plain, unvarnished truth"

(Erasmus 55) yet fabricates "artifice" (53). He is simultaneously actor and role, spectator and spectacle, observer and observed: "But that's all one, our play is done," says Feste, ending *Twelfth Night* (5.1.407). Fools imply that we are all actors, perpetually playing, and spectators, ever observing—if not as you like it, willy-nilly, what you will. A clown such as Launce works solo and speaks to us directly or via his dog Crab. A fool like Feste more often addresses two audiences, within and without the fiction. In Feste's fooling, the border between real and imaginary, besieged by clowns, cracks open. Feste stresses the make-believe nature of the show: "our *play* is done." Under pressure from the fool, the dichotomy between "play" and "real" dissolves. Feste makes hay of liminality, eludes categories, and entertains mutually incompatible possibilities. Feste's last song expresses the fool's tendency to dissolve events, to resist "atoning together," by singing hey nonny-nonny. He thus sustains foolery while exposing and deriding it. Thus Feste adumbrates possibilities that he himself distrusts and mocks. While the play moves toward a degree of resolution, community, and integration, the fool remains lost in translation or outside the charmed circle, singing sadly and alone.

Holy Reasons and Superfluous Folly

Lavatch in *All's Well That Ends Well* appears to be a halfhearted or burnt-out fool, intermittently and grimly amusing, whose repertory features the conventional tergiversation, quibbles, wordplay and saucy wit, proverbial wisdom, and sour spoofs. Though he prides himself on "an answer [that] will serve all men" (*AWW* 2.2.13–14), he lacks Feste's poignancy and theatricality or Touchstone's vitality and inventiveness. Like that obnoxious scourge of folly Thersites in *Troilus and Cressida*,[38] Lavatch exposes unsavory realities and reduces everyone to bodily instincts: "I am driven on by the flesh, and he must needs go that the devil drives" (1.3.28–30). Deflating aspirations and undermining pretensions, he grounds everyone or drags them into the mire. No wonder he is so often addressed, characterized, and dismissed as a "knave." Only through lenient license and long tenure does the bitter old fool escape whipping. Countess says her late husband "made himself much sport out of" Lavatch, who remains by her husband's "authority" (4.5.64–65). She explains that service to the household is regarded by the clown as a "patent for his sauciness," so he "runs where he will" (4.5.66–67). Evidently Shakespeare felt it necessary to repeat a motive for her indulgence of his disgusting bawdry. The Countess plays along "to entertain it so merrily with a fool" (2.2.61), she says, and for the dubious possibility of instruction: "I will be a fool in question, hoping to be the wiser by your answer" (2.2.38–39).

This old jester may be past his prime, but he's not merely running out the clock.[39] Lavatch mixes obscenity and theology in a distinct parti-colored style. His mix-and-match sometimes echoes the more evocative jesting of Lear's Fool, as when Lavatch states, "To say nothing, to do nothing, to know nothing, and to have nothing, is to be a great part of your title, which is within a very little of nothing" (2.4.24–27). It is striking how frequently Lavatch professes "faith" or "holy reasons, such as they are" (1.3.32–33).[40] Despite the improper double entendre (*reasons:* raisings, erections), for someone so dispirited Lavatch seems surprisingly pious! He depicts himself as "a wicked creature, as you and all flesh and blood are, and indeed I do marry that I may repent" (1.3.35–37). To introduce a cuckoo/cuckold ballad, he calls himself "a prophet, I, madam, and I speak the truth the next way" (1.3.58–59). Never consoling and often aggravating, this fool goes out of his way to offend. Gratuitously, Lavatch remarks that the ailing Countess is "well" except for two things: "That she's not in heaven, whither God send her quickly! the other, that she's in earth, from whence God send her quickly!" (2.4.11–13). Harping upon infirmity, mortality, and iniquity, Lavatch professes service to "the prince of darkness, alias the devil" (4.5.42–45). His discourse encompassed heaven and hell, sin and grace, God and Satan.

Pointing both ways, Lavatch is not merely perverse. His "foolish" obsession with corporeal nature and bodily needs[41] emphasizes the discrepancy between the level of nature and the level of grace. In Christian theology—from 1 Corinthians, *The City of God*, and *Summa Theologica* through the sermons of Launcelot Andrews and John Donne—man is fundamentally divided. Lavatch represents himself as demonic or diabolic:

> I am a woodland fellow, sir, that always lov'd a great fire, and the master I speak of ever keeps a good fire. But sure, he is the prince of the world....I am for the house with the narrow gate, which I take to be too little for pomp to enter. Some that humble themselves may, but the many will be too chill and tender, and they'll be for the flow'ry way that leads to the broad gate and the great fire. (4.5.47–55)

Alluding to Matthew, Lavatch envisions himself in but not of this world, rather like Paul's fools for Christ—"for the house with the narrow gate." This prompts Lafew to muse that Lavatch is "a shrewd knave and an unhappy" (4.5.63), which encourages consideration of the other-wordly fool and indicates the inadequacy of Lafew's wordly wisdom.

In *All's Well That Ends Well*, fooling is reinforced by Parolles, a fool and gull who flaunts motley as brazenly as the professional "Clown."[42] The

Great Pretender Parolles figures prominently in thirteen scenes, including the long centerpiece of the play. There is little chance that such a flamboyant character will be neglected. Parolles is a coveted role often given top billing.[43] Perhaps the playwright identifies with the "upstart" parvenu sporting "motley to the view": Parolles even pens a sonnet! Yet Parolles is vociferously reviled. Apart from murderers such as Macbeth and Richard III, only Thersites rivals Parolles's bad eminence. Nobody but foolish Bertram values despised Parolles—a dishonorable liar who betrays his comrades, including Bertram, to save his miserable life. In a world of "jade's tricks," practices, double-dealing, and duplicity, Parolles distinguishes himself as *counterfeit*.[44] Lafew pronounces, "The soul of this man is his clothes" (2.5.43–44), and Helena sees him as Vice or "superfluous folly" (1.1.105). Critics as well as characters seem eager to dispatch him. Quiller-Couch wanted to cut the "whole Parolles business" because his chatter is so offensive that it degrades Helena "to remain in the room" with "this impertinent." The well-calumniated Parolles is compared to the king's fistula, an unspeakable malady. Critics tend to take at face value the Countess's view that Parolles is "a very tainted fellow, and full of wickedness. / My son corrupts a well-derived nature / With his inducement" (3.2.87–89). Of course, Bertram's mother needs to think that her son is corrupted by an evil genius.[45]

Parolles is vilified so that Bertram can be absolved and exonerated. One might dispute such severe assessments of Parolles. Most of his faults are follies: foolish excesses that are easily spotted, exposed, and punished.[46] Like Lavatch, Parolles has redeeming qualities: energetic and indefatigable, he improvises and survives; never dull or entirely inapt, he can be consciously funny. Even a victim of his scurrilous abuse might "begin to love him for this" (4.3.262). Though Parolles is no Falstaff, his assault upon virginity is comparable to Sir John's demolition of honor. Disdaining illusion, Parolles harbors no saving self-delusions. A preposterous bullshitter, he seems aware of playing a role and he castigates himself "when he begins playing it too realistically."[47] Like Lavatch, Parolles deflates aspirations and punctures convictions. Though they make it hard to affirm any saving grace or enduring value, in this play wariness is a wise policy.

There is one notable exception to Parolles's habitual contempt. Curious about the old king's miraculous recovery, Parolles is not cynical about the miracle or Helena's tender mercies. He tacitly accepts the blessings of grace. Otherwise, Parolles is immune to spiritual introspection or self-reflection. He seems to regard his harrowing humiliation not as retribution but as an unfortunate misstep. He never perceives himself as a deceiving "double-meaning prophesier" (4.3.99–100), as Bertram finally recognizes. Naturally, fools of a feather flock together. Both Bertram and Parolles are liars willing to say anything. Stalking Diana, Bertram echoes Parolles's arguments against virginity. Simultaneously, each is tricked and caught in the dark—hoist upon his own petard. Outlandish Parolles thus represents the fool within Bertram, the folly that must be "found" to be exorcised.

Eventually Parolles himself modestly recuperates. "Being fool'd," he resolves to *thrive* "by fool'ry" (4.3.338). Thus the counterfeit captain made of silk morphs into a "genuine" artificial fool. Earlier mocked and debased "for the sake of laughter," he is now treated as a reliable witness. To the astonishment of Bertram, Parolles is summoned to testify against him. Parolles the gull and scapegoat is accepted back into the fold. Truly, "the web of our life is of a mingled yarn, good and ill together" (4.3.71–72). Folly is pervasive and endemic rather than redeemed or transcended. Nor is "superfluous folly" (1.1.105) quite so disastrous or disgusting as it might be. Lavatch and Parolles are fools whose state and fate, idiom and idiosyncrasies Shakespeare highlights, elaborates with relish, and deploys with multiple and contrary purposes.

What does fooling signify? Does any fool "signify"? Moria is always praising herself and fooling us. Nothing is more contingent and provisional, kaleidoscopic and polyphonic than Moria's fooling. Motley-minded Shakespeare multiplies possibilities and complicates challenges rather than stipulates meaning and affirms value. Fools pose questions and will not stay for an answer. What can I know and how do I know it? Is this a lightning bug or lightning bolt? Shakespeare's fools are variously reliable, irrelevant, cogent, absurd, oracular, and deranged. The wise man's either/or becomes the fool's both/and. In the prestidigital fool's hands, wisdom and folly change places. Fooling might be illumination or nonsense. Shakespeare exploits the fool's confusing complexities to make it harder to distinguish between counterfeit and real, fool and gull. The fool himself becomes a fascinating, complicated subject, and fooling becomes an issue and theme. This brings us back to Falstaff and to the next chapter, "The History of Folly in the Henriad."

CHAPTER 3

The History of Folly in the Henriad

A true prince...is always exposed to public view so that he may
either promote the welfare of his people by a spotless character,
like a beneficent star, or he may, like a baleful comet, bring disaster
upon them.

—Erasmus (107)

None of the kings in Shakespeare's "Henriad"—*Richard II*, the two
parts of *Henry IV*, and *Henry V*—has a court jester, yet fools are
everywhere. The Henriad is both the sparkling crown of folly and
a stringent anatomy of folly. The vain and frivolous Richard II is, according
to his successor, a blatantly foolish king of misrule: "The skipping King, he
ambled up and down, / With shallow jesters, and rash bavin wits" and "mingled his royalty with cap'ring fools" (*1H4* 3.2.60–61, 3.2.63). Melodramatic
and histrionic, Richard discovers "the carnival nature of kingship itself"[1] by
gazing into his mirror: "Within the hollow crown / That rounds the mortal
temples of a king / Keeps Death his court, and there the antic sits, / Scoffing
his state and grinning at his pomp" (*R2* 3.2.160–63). Richard's shattered
mirror is the emblem of his fallen and fragmented state. Yielding the crown
to Bolingbroke, he deliberately plays the fool as an act of self-abasement;
yet the scene is also a spectacle of self-exaltation, flamboyantly upstaging
Bolingbroke. Though Richard's foolish "cap'ring" disgusts Bolingbroke, he
himself proves a poor player whose own turn as King Henry IV remains an
unconvincing illusion. A usurper defied as a pretender, Henry overplays the
role of monarch and never fully establishes his royal "state." The king's opening speech—"So shaken as we are" (*1H4* 1.1.1)—is highly over-elaborated;
upbraiding his son in act 3, scene 2, Henry delivers one of Shakespeare's

Figure 3.1 Durer, Fool, and King woodcut engraving published in *The Ship of Fools*.

longest speeches.[2] On the battlefield at Shrewsbury, "the King hath many marching in his coats" (5.3.25). Unfortunately, these decoys dressed in the royal colors are also inadvertent reminders that "the King himself" wears borrowed robes. The rebel Douglas insults the monarch to his face: "What art thou / That counterfeit'st the person of a king?" (5.4.27–28). Not even *the* king! Forced constantly to reaffirm his legitimacy, Henry replies, "The King himself, who, Douglas, grieves at heart / So many of his shadows thou hast met / And not the very King" (5.4.29–31). Unable to project "sunlike majesty" (3.2.79), to himself no more celestial or permanent than "a comet" (3.2.47), Henry presides warily over a realm filled with shadow kings.[3]

Foolosopher King

One such "shadow king" casts a very large shadow indeed. Falstaff holds court in the tavern, where he mimics "the very King," mocks monarchy, and questions the legitimacy of Prince Hal: "God save thy Grace—Majesty I should say, for grace thou wilt have none" (1.2.17–18). Of course, all fools pull down the high and mighty; what distinguishes Falstaff is that he goes both ways. Like Touchstone, a "material fool" immersed in physical needs and pleasures, Falstaff also has an "inexplicable touch of infinity."[4] When "Falstaff riseth up" (5.4.110 s.d.) from playing possum after Prince Hal's elegy, his comic resurrection seems the definitive triumph, "the true and perfect image of life indeed" (5.4.119). Vitally alive, Falstaff's vigorous self-assertion is inspired fooling enhanced by what Moria terms "divine afflatus" (Erasmus 24). This great fool is more profoundly sublime and spectacularly ridiculous than any other fool, saving perhaps Don Quixote. If Falstaff is not exactly a holy fool, he is Shakespeare's foolosopher king.

Notice for example how, left to himself, Falstaff moves divergently as he indignantly rejects the honor of being embalmed: "Embowelled! if thou embowel me to-day, I'll give you leave to powder me and eat me too tomorrow. 'Sblood, 'twas time to counterfeit...The better part of valour is discretion, in the which better part I have sav'd my life. 'Zounds" (5.4.111–21). Blasphemously, he transforms the embalming ritual into cannibalization. "Eat me too tomorrow" evokes the communicant eating the body and blood of Christ. Then there is the Falstaffian twist, abasement turned into exaltation: the exclamations *'Sblood* and *'Zounds* (His blood, His wounds) reinforce the resurrection motif. Falstaff brazenly remakes himself from an emboweled corpse into the Savior. This "great fool" (*2H4* 2.1.195) not only asserts life but also vindicates himself with "counterfeit" or bogus scriptural idiom. His facetious denial notwithstanding, he is always the "double man" (*1H4* 5.4.138).[5]

A favorite Falstaffian routine is a form of doubling he terms "damnable iteration" (1.2.90). Like the pick-purse Autolycus, that "snapper-up of unconsider'd trifles" (*WT* 4.3.26), fools shamelessly filch material. (A playwright who customarily appropriates plots might see this as a venial offense.)

Anything from casual chitchat to Erasmian erudition is ripe for pilfer. Impersonating authority in borrowed idiom, Falstaff's "damnable iteration" has contradictory effects. We must wonder: Is Falstaff *always* fooling, disingenuously avowing sincerity or piety? Amphibious, he tacitly divides himself ("in the which better part") through puns, paradoxes, and amphibology. Falstaff sits on a crapper joking of redemption; dying, he babbles of green fields. Falstaff refines quibble to comic epiphany: "I am no counterfeit... but the true and perfect image of life indeed" (*1H4* 5.4.115–19). Scriptural allusions enable Falstaff (like Erasmus's Moria) to strut in borrowed robes, to magnify himself, and to mock authority. "Counterfeit" fool's play blurs illusion and reality by affirming and negating simultaneously.[6] Yet repeating that word *counterfeit* like a talisman, Falstaff addresses the audience directly as if he were real. He distinguishes himself from the mere characters on the stage by stressing his fictiveness. Falstaff is an actor's "counterfeit of a man who hath not the life of a man" (5.4.116–17).

Falstaff's mingle-mangled divinity contends that it is the fallen Hotspur, not the cowardly sham, who is the facsimile of life. "To die," he insists, is "to be a counterfeit; for he is but the counterfeit of a man who hath not the life of a man: but to counterfeit dying, when a man thereby liveth" is "life indeed" (5.4.115–19). Surely Falstaff has a good point. But Falstaff's fooling also makes fun of itself: "I lie," he says (5.4.115). Any line between fantasy and reality, genuine and counterfeit, what is *true* and what is "perfect image" wavers. In the Henriad, the fundamental difference between true and false is less "sure and certain" than the "real" king or "true Prince" recognizes.

Deceptions spread far beyond tavern antics. Prince John offers amnesty to the defeated rebels—and promptly executes them. Falstaff, who counterfeits to live and lives to counterfeit, is no more dishonorable than a host of intriguers and deceivers. Is not Hal the prince of pretense? Even in his moment of glory, newly baptized in blood as the true prince, Hal plays along with the monarch of make-believe: "For my part, if a lie may do thee grace" (5.4.157), he will "gild" Falstaff's preposterous claim to have killed Hotspur. Grace is still something contrived, enacted, feigned, just as Falstaff always says. Everyone in the Henriad from kings to clowns is counterfeit. In Moria's proverbial wisdom, recapitulated by Rabelais, kings and clowns have the same horoscope. Is it coincidental that *majesty* encompasses *jest*?

Falstaff's artful sophistry is not as simply bogus as the devil citing scripture, though it's true that he does so a lot: "'Tis no sin for a man to labor in his vocation" (1.2.104–5), "By this fire, that's God's angel" (3.3.35), et cetera. Disgraceful or blasphemous as Falstaff's "iterations" are, they persistently indicate his true vocation: that of foolosopher king. Both Hal and Falstaff constantly harp on redemption, metaphorically linking folly with divinity or associating sacred and profane. Though Falstaff cites scripture to spoof piety and mock Hal, he confidently professes the faculty of foolery for some time: "A good wit will make use of any thing. I will turn diseases to commodity" (*2H4* 1.2.247–48). He terms his annihilation of honor "my catechism" (*1H4* 5.1.141) and defines addiction to sack as "the first humane principle I would teach" (*2H4* 4.3.123). To hear Falstaff tell it, he is graced with extraordinary powers, as when he joyously boasts, "The brain of this foolish-compounded clay, man, is not able to invent any thing that intends to laughter more than I invent or is invented on me" (*12H4* 1.2.7–9).

Falstaff's creed is self-delighting and self-generating, as he fashions himself from scratch (or clay), much as Shakespeare created the great fool who doesn't exist in his source material. His ephemeral incarnations are a series of roles: like those "men in buckram" Falstaff conjures, they have no essence but a fantastic multiplicity. All the world's a stage for his witty invention, multiple metamorphoses, and playful pluralism: "Marry, then, sweet wag, when thou art king, let not us that are squires of the night's body be call'd thieves of the day's beauty" (*1H4* 1.2.23–25). Falstaff characteristically translates reality (literally, the *body*) into a more appealing illusion (figuratively, *beauty*), a magical sovereignty via the pun on the thieves' "booty." Performing before the prince who moments later swears to "imitate the sun" (1.2.197), Falstaff dubs himself one of "Diana's foresters, gentlemen of the shade, minions of the moon, and let men say we be men of good government, being govern'd, as the sea is, by our noble and chaste mistress the moon, under whose countenance we steal" (1.2.25–29). The selves proliferate like the phases of the moon, that fitting sign for the fool's metamorphoses. Fabulous Falstaff can be what he will and as he likes it, if only provisionally. He tries out various honorific titles: Diana's forester, gentleman of the shade, minion of the moon. He also sports several names and a host of epithets: Sir John, Falstaff, Jack, "that huge bombard of sack, that stuff'd cloak-bag of guts...that reverent Vice, that grey Iniquity" (2.4.451–54), et cetera. No Shakespeare play provides more ways to identify someone, for this great fool is no one thing and virtually everything.

The paradox of "infinite jest" is massively evident in Falstaff's girth and discourse. Invariably, Falstaff expresses the fool's double standard by juxtaposing words with similar sounds and disparate meanings. Puns constitute the Fool's Standard Reversal: "I would it were otherwise, I would my means were greater and my waist slenderer" (*2H4* 1.2.142–43), or "O, give me the spare men, and spare me the great ones" (3.2.269–70). When Falstaff mocks the Hostess as "neither fish nor flesh, a man knows not where to have her" (*1H4* 3.3.127–28), Mistress Quickly takes the bait and indignantly proclaims that "thou or any man knows where to have me, thou knave, thou!" (3.3.129–30). Falstaff's jest demonstrates foolish fission: beginning with a single, simple word—*have*—he builds comic confusion and individual duality, "neither fish nor flesh." The Hostess falls victim because she is literal and single-minded, bamboozled by Falstaff's cunning ambidexterity.[7] Double trouble for the auditor doubles the fun for the punster. In the fool's utterances, words invariably split, suggesting incongruities that may or may not "reamalgamerge."[8]

A variation is the two-step, as when Falstaff claims that were it not for the corrupting influence of the young prince, he would be known for "pure and immaculate valor" (*2H4* 4.3.37–38). At its best, Falstaff's wit is fluently adaptable and wondrously free, like his girth that is "out of all compass" (*1H4* 3.3.20). Logic and reason are mundane, confining categories that Falstaff blithely ignores or giddily trammels: he is the epitome of contradiction and the master escape artist. The Chief Justice notes that he is "well acquainted with your manner of wrenching the true cause the false way" (*2H4* 2.1.109–11). Prince Hal anticipates the fool's slipperiness when he springs his trap to catch Falstaff lying about the robbery: "What trick? what device? what starting-hole? canst thou now find out to hide thee from this open and apparent shame?" (*1H4* 2.4.262–64). And here is the fat fool's nimble escape—how quickly he recovers! "By the Lord, I knew ye as well as he that made ye. Why, hear you, my masters, was it for me to kill the heir-apparent? Should I turn upon the true prince?" (2.4.267–70). As is here apparent, even Falstaff's self-serving chicanery underscores the issue of identity and majesty.

Unable to conceive how far the fool lives from the strictures of conscience, the Chief Justice regularly underestimates Falstaff's freedom from reality and empowerment by folly. Falstaff habitually outfoxes his adversaries by accepting their opprobrium and celebrating his deficiencies. Invited to mock him, we laugh with him. Falstaff revels in folly everywhere, especially in himself—in contrast, as we'll see, to satirists like Thersites or Jaques, who rail at vice *ex cathedra*. Not only witty in himself, Falstaff is also "the cause that wit is in other men" (*2H4* 1.2.10).

Gamboling and cavorting, "only" playing or fooling, Falstaff incessantly appeals to the audience to woo us and fool us. Falstaff regularly soliloquizes or directly addresses the audience; perhaps this is because he does not know what his feelings are or what he is, as if he strives for validation in performing. With just one exception, we do not see Falstaff asleep or supine but busily at work with words, directly in our faces, his eyes moving in anticipation of the response he might elicit, and perspiring from ardent effort. Asserting his real presence yet underscoring his own cock-and-bull nature, the fool plays to two audiences: the one within fiction and the one outside of the fiction. Falstaff's toy-like "dagger of lath" (*1H4* 2.4.137)[9] is thus figurative: never *really* used, it is hacked to simulate strenuous activity in the Gadshill scam; it is another prop in that long-running show, "Falstaff's Follies." Falstaff, Rex Ludens, makes the world his stage and presides over the kingdom of Never-land. Descriptions of Falstaff as a "stuff'd cloak-bag" and "a creature of bombast" (2.4.451–52, 2.4.327) magnify the disorienting sense that this figure onstage is actually an actor in costume and greasepaint enacting lines from the playbook.[10] When "Falstaff riseth up," the resurrection of the fool reminds us that the really dead Hotspur and Blunt will also revive, wash off their makeup, hang up their costumes, and mull the afternoon's production over ale. In his great set pieces, annihilating honor or celebrating sack, Falstaff is an actor playing an actor, yet he is somehow capable of stepping out of the play to assert independent life.

What it means to consider something (a sentiment, desire, lament) real or "true" is surely another "question to be ask'd" (2.4.410) in contemplating fools like Falstaff, whose extravagance flaunts the artificiality of his art. As I will elaborate in chapter 4, the words *feign* and *counterfeit* resonate throughout *As You Like It.* What, if anything, does the playful, histrionic fool *feel* beneath those crocodile tears? Hath not a fool senses, affections, passions? If you prick him, does he not bleed? Consider, for instance, Bradley's marvelous empathy for Falstaff, informed by the conviction that Shakespeare's language conveys the feeling and meaning directly from the playwright to the reader's heart. Bradley enters Falstaff's joy: "Happy" is "too weak a word; he is in bliss, and *we share his glory,*" for his enjoyment is "*contagious.*"[11] Following Bradley, some readers regard Falstaff as not merely a privileged but also a sanctioned figure, with a gravity "quite interior to his physical poundage: he lards the earth not merely with his sweat, but covertly with a Christian spirit as wise as serpents and as harmless as doves."[12] Harold Bloom conceives Falstaff as "a comic Socrates," inspired and inspirational, "who is free, instructs us in freedom," comparable in charisma to Hamlet; both are "*in* their plays, but not *of* them. . . . Falstaff is a person, while Hal and Hotspur are fictions."[13] Even Dr. Johnson, no friend to folly and habitually wont to kick the rock, apostrophizes Falstaff as though he were not a literary invention but a real presence: "Unimitated, unimitable *Falstaff,* how shall I describe thee?"[14] Hence the fool offers—along with his self-reflexive, skeptical *Verfremdungseffekt* (alienation effect)—an alternative authenticity: he inspires foolish faith.

Falstaff's gospel of folly also provokes skeptics and makes him a scapegoat. J. Dover Wilson designates Falstaff's stock repertory as "mock-repentance" or "mock-maudlin" and disbelieves even his love for Hal: "The old humbug's professions of affection are no more to be credited than his offers of marriage."[15] Alert to the danger of being hoodwinked by the maestro, Wilson discredits everything Falstaff says or does as bogus. Similarly, John

W. Draper—constructing Falstaff in the narrowest sense as "a Fool and Jester"—finds nothing but mock-moralizing proverbs, sophistry, and fake syllogisms, a rodomontade of "moralistic shreds and patches."[16] One man's holy fool is another man's humbug.

Fools such as Falstaff provoke wildly differing reactions to basic questions: Is this wise or nonsensical, lovable or despicable, prophetic or antic, sincere or disingenuous? Given that Falstaff will say or do anything for a laugh, one can never determine with confidence what the fool is or signifies, for he means only what he is now playing. "Sincerity" and "fooling" are as riotously entangled as "purpose" and "play." In foolosophy, these are false dichotomies; to confound them is the fool's mission. Falstaff has no true colors but motley; he is *always* fooling, ardently sincere about fooling us. The fool would fain *feign*. More confusingly, Falstaff makes his own feelings the main subject, grist for the mill, and the springboard for endless sallies, pirouettes, and high jinks. Foolery is in this sense comprised of the fool's guts: as Joyce's Shem writes, "over every square inch of the only foolscap available, his own body."[17]

Falstaff as joker is the wild card in any game: he can be anything and trump everything. Fools are professionally invested in counterfeit goods, the making of make-believe: forgeries are Falstaff's stock in trade. Improvising freely and unfettered to reality, he makes it up as he goes along: two men in buckram become four, then eight…Though his deconstruction of honor and his celebration of sack are unabashed sophistry, his performances have purchase and punch. *Flyting* with "the true prince," burlesquing the "real" king, or feigning feelings, Falstaff produces compelling impersonations and reality effect. Thus Falstaff's fooling becomes second sight to test the validity of heroism, valor, honor, majesty, and authority. In Falstaff's seriocomic sleight-of-hand all are exposed as counterfeit, illusions, and delusions. Foolery surmounts or demolishes any boundaries between feeling and fooling, real and imaginary.

Falstaff robustly embodies the power of folly and dimly, occasionally, perceives its limits. "Thou seest," Falstaff comments, "I have more flesh than another man, and therefore more frailty" (*1H4* 3.3.166–68). The jest is also comically orthodox: if Jesus was right in saying that the spirit is willing but the flesh is weak, then Falstaff correctly concludes that the more flesh, the more frailty. Falstaff's "therefore" distinguishes himself from other fools by suggesting a sizable degree of self-knowledge. Like *King Lear*, the Henriad licenses folly to explore the intimate, necessary relationship between fool and king, though it differs markedly in that it continually tests and ultimately contains folly by revealing its apparently make-believe, ephemeral nature. Surprised and seduced by folly, we are released and clarified—only to then find ourselves in a hall of mirrors, lost in the funhouse. Hal's solution, so "resoundingly" avowed at the end of part 1, dissolves in part 2.

For Falstaff, fooling is an end in itself, whereas it serves ulterior purposes for Hal. In Freudian terms, Hal's play is tendentious even when it appears inconsequential. The "play extempore" (2.4.280) displays and dissects folly. At first, we delight wholeheartedly in Falstaff's improvisations, gathering props and incorporating Mistress Quickly's prattle, all in "royal" blank verse and with suitably solemn demeanor. The fool's first rule: to be funny, stay serious. Falstaff's sententious and moralistic discourse caricatures regal rhetoric by blending pompous inflation ("a question to be ask'd") and burlesque reduction: "That thou art my son I have partly thy mother's word" (2.4.402). One of the fool's major projects is to expose the *counterfeit* king. Right after Hal so devastatingly "takes off" Hotspur and just before Hal vows to take out the Percies for real and for good, Falstaff puns fruitfully on the name of the clan: "Shall the son of England prove a thief and take *purses?*" (2.4.409–10; my emphasis, i.e., "Percies"). Second rule: two meanings, preferably contradictory, are more than twice as good as one.

"Deposing" the mock king to play the king in earnest, Prince Hal also reveals the self behind his antic persona. Falstaff, however, continues to ignore or misread what Hal presents as "open and apparent" (2.4.264): that holiday will give way to workaday, that play must yield to responsibility, and that make-believe is subordinate to reality. When Falstaff majestically declares, "This chair shall be my state, this dagger my sceptre, and this cushion my crown" (2.4.378–79), the prince instantly corrects Falstaff's jest by changing the fool's "shall be" to his own actor-king's "as if": "Thy state is taken for a join'd-stool, thy golden sceptre for a leaden dagger, and thy precious rich crown for a pitiful bald crown" (2.4.380–82). Like the play extempore and the whole drama, Hal's revision moves us from participation in folly to detached contemplation—both in and out of folly. Playing, he stresses the provisional, tentative nature of the game and underscores the disparity between the Falstaff Game and Hal's Reality Show: the mock-king's "precious rich crown" is *really* "a pitiful bald crown"! Enacting the king, Hal ruthlessly excoriates folly and denounces Falstaff as "a devil...that reverent Vice, that grey Iniquity, that father ruffian...worthy, but in nothing" (2.4.447–59). Often in the Henriad, the fool is associated with his traditional companion or double, the devil, and that word *ruffian*—like the terms *riot* and *dishonor* (1.1.85)—was then a considerably stronger insult.

Falstaff's remarkable reply, the "banish not him thy Harry's company" speech (2.4.466–80), crystallizes the fate of folly in this play. The speech is another astonishing recovery: once again the great fool seems to have "'scap'd by miracle" (2.4.165–66). But the resounding climax, "banish plump Jack, and banish all the world" (2.4.479–80), is not the last word, as everyone but Falstaff must realize. Hal's devastating reply, "I do, I will"

(2.4.481), accomplishes several things simultaneously: besting Falstaff in the battle of wits (for once!), Hal decrees the fool's ancillary, dependent status; reaffirms his own command of language, situation, and self; progresses from the level of humor ("I do") to the plateau of duty ("I will"); contemplates that future state as forthcoming and a field for continued mastery; and concludes the "play extempore" by announcing that as king he will, indeed, stop fooling. Ironically, Hal's pronouncement sunders kingship and folly in the very scene that had seemed to affiliate them most intimately. The knock on the door signaling the sheriff's arrival ends the game despite Falstaff's desperate attempts to maintain the illusion. "I'll to the court in the morning," Hal declares (2.4.543–44), while Falstaff might as well murmur, "And I'll go to bed at noon" (*Lr* 3.6.85). Although Falstaff does not yet disappear like Lear's Fool, the reign of folly is over. The prince's time is come and that of Falstaff, "that vanity in years" (*1H4* 2.4.454), most assuredly passed. The struggle between folly and reality is great theater but no contest.

Even in his decline, however, the fool endures, jeopardizes the prince's "mastery," and throws a spanner in the works. Consider how Falstaff migrates in and out of the military-political world of the Henriad. Egregiously, hilariously displaced at Shrewsbury, he is inexplicably accepted within the king's inner circle afterward. Ludicrously, yet with apparent success, he claims credit for defeating Hotspur, for in *Henry IV, Part 2*, he enjoys the benefits of his "good service" (1.2.61–2), and Coleville, upon hearing his name, surrenders without a fight. Such wacky inconsistencies figure the fool as an inveterate hybrid, dual or split every which way. Shadow-like, the fool confounds our sense of "truthiness," no matter how resolutely it is reiterated by Prince Hal. Evidently not all there, the fool sometimes seems to be all we have. Despite the Prince's personal triumph and the royal victory, Falstaff certainly doesn't just fade away.

Yet in *Henry IV, Part 2*, Falstaff, obviously enfeebled, becomes more the object than the source of humor. From his first entrance, a Renaissance star turn, he regards himself as an institution, full of comic hubris, short on self-irony, and still enacting but no longer anatomizing folly; at times he resembles the vainglorious and strutting Pistol, that disabled fool in *Henry V* full of bluster and void of power. Falstaff the Carnival King or Counterfeit Monarch becomes, like Richard, "a mockery king of snow" (*R2* 4.1.260). If Falstaff's credo in part 1 is the exhortatory celebration, "Give me life" (5.3.59), in part 2 his motto becomes the elegiac lament, "We have heard the chimes at midnight" (3.2.214). Now, Falstaff appears asking his page for the doctor's diagnosis of his urine, and the boy's jesting rejoinder, like so many jokes in this play, is not cheering.

So pressing is mortality in part 2 that Falstaff no longer asserts or pretends to believe that he is exempt from nature's law. "Well," he concedes to his adversary the Chief Justice, "I cannot last ever…I am an old man, you should give me rest" (1.2.213–17). Often, as with Doll Tearsheet, he scarcely tries to be amusing, simply lamenting, "I am old, I am old" (2.4.271); frequently his jokes limp or backfire. Falstaff's vaunted wit deteriorates to merely mechanical inversions or what comics call the old switcheroo, as when the Chief Justice declares, "God send the Prince a better companion," to which Falstaff dutifully responds, "God send the companion a better prince!" (1.2.199–201). Surveying his pathetic recruits, he relies on wordplay that would once have been too obvious to utter: "Is thy name Mouldy?…'Tis the more time thou wert us'd" (3.2.104–6). Worse, the very joke rehearses the corruption of time, finishing the fool like all men. Falstaff thus embodies another paradox of folly: full of life, he is closer to death. Gleefully burlesquing the king's grace, Falstaff finds that ultimately the joke is on the fool. The inescapable fact is that the infinitely jesting Falstaff is only temporarily spared or provisionally licensed. A liminal figure, he lives at the border, in closer contact with the pleasures and the liabilities of the body. Even the way he formulates his outrageous hopes when he learns of the old king's death reminds us of the death's-head staring Falstaff in the face: "I know the young king is sick for me" (5.3.135).

Madcap Prince of Wales

It is a truth universally acknowledged that every king is in want of an heir. Shakespeare's Foolosopher King adopts the "nimble-footed madcap Prince of Wales" (*1H4* 4.1.95), as Hotspur memorably dubs Hal. Falstaff's "heir apparent" is a boon companion who indulges in folly and yet remains wary of it: "Well," muses Hal, "thus we play the fools with the time, and the spirits of the wise sit in the clouds and mock us" (*2H4* 2.2.142–43). The prince, playing the fool yet heeding the wise and implying that the fool's days are numbered, locates himself simultaneously in and out of time. Like Falstaff, constructing his identity as dual, Hal is less complexly amphibious: his sportive self enacts folly, but behind it is the "true prince" (*1H4* 2.4.270), biding his time. Confident that he himself has a true and essential identity—the words *true* and *false* reverberate throughout the Henriad—Hal assumes that Falstaff has one as well: "How might we see Falstaff bestow himself to-night in his true colors, and not ourselves be seen?" (*2H4* 2.2.169–70), he asks Poins. The prince is sure that Falstaff's fundamental nature is "open, palpable" (*1H4* 2.4.226) but that he himself can remain securely disguised. Hal tellingly positions himself vis-à-vis folly: "Well then, once in my days," Hal says, "I'll be a madcap" (1.2.142–43). Dr. Johnson's definition of *madcap*—"either taking the *cap* for the head, or alluding to the caps put upon distracted persons by way of distinction"[18]—underscores the ambiguity of Hal's role: it can be seen as either "put upon" or intrinsic, or some varying mixture, anticipating the "antic disposition" of another young Danish prince.

In soliloquy (1.2.195–217), Hal envisions himself as folly's sovereign and scourge, not unlike the Hebrew prophets, intimidating in his authority. He knows us all, understands himself, and controls everything. Hal only rarely speaks for the exclusive benefit of the audience, and even when he does, his discourse has the quality of set speech or memorized performance. The speech, beginning "I know" and ending "I will," resounds with regal certitude and subordinates Falstaff's folly to its antithetical adversaries: righteous virtue, reality, time, and truth. Some of Hal's wise saws could fit seamlessly in the Book of Proverbs: "If all the year were playing holidays, / To sport would be as tedious as to work" (1.2.204–5). Hal's regal blank verse follows and subsumes the foolery begun when Falstaff inquired the time. Now, alone, Hal makes time his subject, himself its master: "I know you all, and *will a while* uphold / The unyok'd humor of your idleness . . . I'll so offend, to make offense a skill, / *Redeeming time* when men think least I will" (2.2.195–217; my emphasis). Hal's soliloquy announces—"foreshadows" is too tepid for such a spectacular substantiation—his mystical ascent from mortal body to sacred monarch. Already Hal imagines a future perspective from which he regards "the thing I was" (*2H4* 5.5.56), a creature immersed in error.

Hal's radiant self-image as "the sun" (1.2.197) recalls Falstaff's inventive characterization of his gang as "gentlemen of the shade, minions of the moon" (*1H4* 1.2.26) and reifies the providential hierarchy, for the moon, waxing and waning, depends for its luster on the splendid, powerful sun. When this son becomes "the sun," he will illuminate everything truly and brightly. Falstaff's illusion melts under the harsh rays of the sun-prince, no slouch at interpreting a trope or enforcing his will; Falstaff's "I wish" is the opposite of Hal's oft-repeated formulation, "I will."

Hal's scruples trump Falstaff's fooling. Hal plays the fool but will not *be* the fool. If Hal's repertory is less dazzling than that of the old maestro, it is compensated by his magisterial command of timing. For Falstaff the show must go on, for life is always and only a performance; the prince knows better when to play and what parts. Like Falstaff, Hal is a prodigious player but with the crucial difference that Falstaff can only play at being something. When his cue comes, Hal (unlike Bottom!) is ready. He already realizes that even kingship is a spectacle so that he will "*imitate* the sun" and "*show* more goodly and attract more eyes / Than that which hath no *foil* to set it off" (1.2.197, 1.2.214–15; my emphasis). In his apprenticeship to Falstaff, Hal learns how to "yoke" folly and make it work. Hal comprehends Falstaffian folly, while

Falstaff neglects royal reality and disdains princely purpose. The prince's play is both parti-color and many-minded. The prince's performance, like that of any good actor, is in part an illusion designed to fool the audience: "I *falsify* men's hopes…Redeeming time when men *think least* I will" (1.2.211–17; my emphasis). To become kingly is to counterfeit or enact royalty, which differs from the fool's premise that nothing is more than a construction.

Though the king fears and resents his son's "vile participation" (3.2.87) in "riot and dishonor" (1.1.85), the prince pointedly repudiates serious misconduct: "Who, I rob? I a thief? Not I, by my faith" (1.2.138). Although he pretends to join Falstaff's gang of thieves in a game of trick the trickster, Hal avoids direct "participation" and ultimately returns the stolen booty with interest—"The money shall be paid back again with advantage" (2.4.547–48)—and assures us that "the money is paid back again" (3.3.178). The repetition guarantees Hal's honor. Hal's self-definition as a madcap is spot-on. Shakespeare turns to advantage the audience's awareness that this prodigal son *will* repudiate his follies and become a true king.

A striking demonstration of Hal's madcap capacity to play while working and work while playing is his impersonation of Hotspur: "I am not yet of Percy's mind," he proclaims (2.4.101–2), suggesting that he can also "do" that part when he "will." He knows and sees beyond Hotspur. The fierce warrior is just another role that Hal will perfect when the time comes; until then, there is time to "play Percy" (2.4.109) as an object of mockery and to expose Hotspurious honor as a sham. Hal does something quite similar in the tomfoolery with Falstaff following the Gadshill caper. Habitually, he invokes reality to counter vainglorious pretenses: "Mark now how a plain tale shall put you down" (2.4.254–55). Brilliantly, Falstaff replies, "By the Lord, I knew ye as well as he that made ye" (2.4.267–68). But Jack's wondrous dodge—bouncing back from being "put…down"—boomerangs, for it recognizes that this "heir-apparent" (2.4.269) is incontrovertibly "the true prince" (2.4.270). The pattern of appealing illusion succumbing to irresistible actuality is reinforced by Falstaff's triple repetition of the phrase "the true prince."

The submission of make-believe to reality is staged in the play extempore, where Falstaff's plea for folly—"banish not him thy Harry's company" (2.4.478)—is characteristically unsentimental, quickly sacrificing his cronies Peto, Bardolph, and Poins. He provokes the prince to "depose" the mock king and to play the king himself. Falstaff's game becomes a rehearsal of the time Hal will proclaim the truth obscured by "the base contagious clouds" (1.2.198). Though these ultimate realities are discernible even amid the carnivalesque masquerade, Falstaff fails to read the writing on the wall. From their opening banter—"Thou judgest false already" (1.2.66)—to

Hal's elegy for the shamming Falstaff, "O, I should have a heavy miss of thee / If I were much in love with vanity" (5.4.105–6), the great fool constantly ignores or misreads Hal's signals. Much virtue in If! Unless we are as self-deluded as Falstaff, we know what's coming.

The King's Farced Title

At the coronation, Falstaff is a sorry figure, "stain'd with travel," disheveled, and "sweating with desire to see [Hal]" (*2H4* 5.5.24–25). At this point perhaps more than anywhere else, the fool conveys genuine feelings, not unmixed with grasping greed and self-aggrandizing posturing, but (as he says to Shallow and Pistol) expressing "the zeal I had to see him" (5.5.14): "It shows my earnestness of affection... My devotion... as if there were nothing else to be done but to see him" (5.5.16–27). Though he has often indicated his love for Hal, the way Falstaff now addresses his old friend seems not only winning but also alienating. Thrusting himself into the coronation procession and exclaiming, "God save thy Grace, King Hal! my royal Hal!" (5.5.41), Falstaff exposes his squint-eyed belief that the divinely graced king is still just "Hal," Falstaff's own possession; the same proprietary diminution is implicit in "My King, my Jove! I speak to thee, my heart!" (5.5.46).

Falstaff is incapable of conceiving Hal's ritual ascent and symbolic transformation. A coronation celebrates the mystical translation of mortal man to divinely sanctioned king. Interrupting the ceremony, Falstaff violates decorum, desecrates a sacred ritual, and stages Hal's worst nightmare: the return of the repressed. Hal has many reasons to be worried about his legitimacy or the perception of his divine majesty. A conspicuous scapegrace and heir to a usurping regicide, he is suddenly, publicly accosted by his grotesque alter ego. It must remind Hal of those medieval paintings of devils dragging the horrified soul to hell. In response, the new king stresses his conversion or transformation: "Presume not that I am the thing that I was, / For God doth know, so shall the world perceive, / That I have turn'd away my former self" (5.5.56–58).

The challenge confronting Hal is daunting. He must "reconstruct a symbolic order of monarchy out of the most diverse and unpromising materials: residues of the dying political theology of the king's two bodies; chivalric protocols of the court and battlefield; magisterial rhetoric."[19] Repudiating Falstaff, he renounces follies like the prodigal son. The Hal who teased Francis, romped with Poins, and clowned with Falstaff has said good-bye to all that. Hal's divine exaltation is Falstaff's debasement: "I know thee not, old man, fall to thy prayers. / How ill white hairs becomes a fool and jester! / I have long dreamt of such a kind of man, / So surfeit-swell'd, so old, and so profane" (5.5.47–50). In effect, Hal forsakes his own humanity: the fool is disgraced because the king is *graced*. A prodigious caesura underscores their disparity: "Make less thy body (hence) and more thy grace"; the only touch of wit mocks fat Falstaff: "Know the grave doth gape / For thee thrice wider than for other men" (5.5.52–54).[20] Hal's utterance moves from fool's first person to the royal we, forbidding Falstaff from "our person" (5.5.65).

The banishment of Falstaff is harsh and, to many, shocking. Exuberantly enacting folly in part 1, Falstaff liberates life from fact in defiance of reason and pursuit of joy. Drawn into his field of force, we deplore his humiliation and loss. Of course Falstaff has no hope of fulfilling Henry's condition for reconciliation—"And as we hear you do reform yourselves" (5.5.68)—for that would require extirpating folly, which for Falstaff means death. The fool cannot change; he must remain a fool.

Falstaff survives in *Henry V* only in traces and in the memories of the Hostess and his cronies. Fooling is a poor thing, relegated to the likes of Pistol or contemplated nostalgically. The Hostess's account of Falstaff's death reminds us that the nearly irresistible charisma of the fool—his power to bewitch—competes with Shakespeare's imperative: the necessity to subordinate folly to that higher authority that Falstaff temporarily eludes and foils. The Hostess highlights the fool's innocence, as though he were "any christom child" (*H5* 2.3.11–12), a creature of nature who "babbl'd of green fields" (2.3.17). Our final image of Falstaff is both ludicrous and affecting, as Mistress Quickly describes feeling his cold feet "and so up'ard and up'ard, and all was as cold as any stone" (2.3.25–26). Even yet we might fool ourselves into believing that he descends "up'ard," for like his regal counterparts, this "great fool" (*2H4* 2.1.195) remains indelibly all-too-human and larger-than-life. It is poignant to speculate that Shakespeare remained of two minds about the demise of his "great fool," for he succumbed to the temptation to stage yet another resurrection, though most lovers of foolosophy regard the "Falstaff" who frolics gamely through *The Merry Wives of Windsor* as an impostor or counterfeit fool, as it were, "superfluous folly" (*AWW* 1.1.105). This facsimile "Falstaff" suffers indignities worse than death.

To the new king, his youthful follies are an insubstantial pageant or perhaps viewed "with parted eye, / When everything seems double" (*MND* 4.1.188–89). Hardly has the curtain risen on *Henry V* when the Archbishop of Canterbury rehearses Hal's miraculous translation, rendered by the archbishop as a type of resurrection:

> The breath no sooner left his father's body,
> But that his wildness, mortified in him,

> Seem'd to die too; yea, at that very moment,
> Consideration like an angel came
> And whipt th' offending Adam out of him.
>
> (*H5* 1.1.25–29)

Lo the divinely sanctioned king, "his body as a paradise / T' envelop and contain celestial spirits" (1.1.30–31). Immediately immersed in the rough-and-tumble ecclesiastical politics and heroic banditry, Henry V remembers his own folly but rarely and only in the past tense. He remarks the Dauphin's jibe, "How he comes o'er us with our wilder days, / Not measuring what use we made of them" (1.2.267–68). Such acknowledgment is exactly what he withholds from grasping Falstaff at the coronation and only very rarely expresses henceforth.

The night before Agincourt, Henry V maintains that "the King is but a man...all his senses have but human conditions" (4.1.101–4), but only to himself in soliloquy can he contemplate the antic within. He continues to separate the counterpart king and fool: "Twin-born with greatness, subject to the breath / Of every fool" (4.1.234–35). He envisions himself as harassed, not inhabited, by folly. His "hard condition" (4.1.233) is not to be foolish but to be plagued by the follies of *others*. Yet in private, Henry sees ceremonial, sacred kingship as pretense and delusion. Like Richard before him, Henry discovers that

> 'tis not the balm, the sceptre, and the ball,
> The sword, the mace, the crown imperial,
> The intertissued robe of gold and pearl,
> The farced title running 'fore the king,
> The throne he sits on, nor the tide of pomp
> That beats upon the high shore of this world...
>
> (4.1.259–65)

Henry realizes the twin-born condition of kingship and the illusory nature of his "farced title." *Farced*, signifying "to stuff," suggests artificial grandeur or ceremonial puffery and appears in *Praise of Folly* as well as *Finnegans Wake*.[21] "Farced title" was the way Falstaff would mock monarchy. Perhaps memories of Falstaff precipitate Henry's excessive guilt for "the fault / My father made in compassing the crown" (4.1.293–94). As late as the battle of Agincourt, Hal is still "Imploring pardon" (4.1.305) for his father's complicity in Richard's murder. Perhaps the murdered mock-king Richard conjures the unquiet spirit of Falstaff. Though Henry V perceives folly from on high, he can neither truly scourge it nor ever transcend it. Folly retains stubborn intractability, persistent power, and haunting capacity. The fool is dead; long live the fool!

CHAPTER 4

Fools for Love: Fooling and Feeling

> Clowns and storytellers have an almost magical ability to manipulate things and situations so as to make seem possible what is impossible and false what is true.
>
> Dario Fo, *Tricks of the Trade*[1]
>
> The lunatic, the lover, and the poet
> Are of imagination all compact.
>
> (*MND* 5.1.7–8)

How do I fool thee? Let me count the ways. Foolery has many guises, and, as we have already seen, the word *fool* has different denotations and competing connotations. We began with artificial fools or jesters who make merry to entertain, using jokes, banter, and wordplay for fun and enlightenment. This chapter focuses on three romantic comedies staged between 1598 and 1602 in which the predominant form of fooling is to deceive or trick, to fool someone unaware of the pretense: *Much Ado About Nothing*, *As You Like It*, and *Twelfth Night*. Here many lovers resemble natural rather than artificial fools because, of course, anyone in love is a fool for love. Amorous idiocy or mad love involves many types of foolery, including contests of wit, masquerades, festivals, rituals, holidays, staged performances, and, most important for our purposes, trickery and subterfuge. As Moria stresses, "This deception, this disguise, is the very thing that holds the attention of the spectators" (Erasmus 43). Chaloner's 1549 rendition, "the feignyng and counterfaityng is it, that so delighteth the beholders,"[2] provides two terms that figure egregiously in Shakespeare's anatomy of folly: feigning and counterfeiting.

Figure 4.1 Henry VIII (1491–1547) as a musician with his fool Will Somers, ca. 1530–47. Reproduced with permission of the Bridgeman Art Library International.

My particular concern is the differing and developing relations between fooling and feeling in these romantic comedies: How do we comprehend and why do we care about characters who are either fooling or being fooled? Perhaps we should follow Puck, who permits audiences to enjoy the spectacle and to laugh at the characters: "Lord, what fools these mortals be!" (3.2.115) In *A Midsummer Night's Dream*, feelings lack weight or purchase and change rapidly. Hurt feelings, pain, suffering, and humiliation dissipate. Is Oberon abusive? Monstrously. How Titania feels about her husband's trick—outrage? disgust? resentment?—we cannot tell, for she is emphatically mute. It is as if her feelings hardly matter. Later Shakespearean comedies treat feelings very differently. Although the plays continue to percolate with fooling, they also regard feelings (especially the heroines' attitudes and aspirations) more substantially and sympathetically. Beatrice, Rosalind, and Viola are exponentially more compelling than the relatively uninteresting Helena and Hermia or the apparently indistinguishable Demetrius and Lysander. Again *Praise of Folly* helps frame the tension between feeling and fooling. In his introductory letter to Thomas More, Erasmus stresses the ludic nature of his "jeu d'esprit" (2).[3] Moria's potpourri mixes effervescent wit, bemused tolerance, ironic eulogy, serious umbrage, earnest indignation, and jaunty whimsy to delight and instruct, illuminate and confound. As she unhelpfully reiterates, "I may seem to be saying all this merely as a joke" (95). Or again, "But unless I am completely deceived by '*Selflove*,' my praise of Folly is not altogether foolish" (4). Moria stresses the purely performative or rhetorical quality of the discourse: it is an act, a role, a guise put on for a particular occasion and purpose. The frequently repeated word *festivus*—festive, companionable—prompts us to have fun. To make sense, readers must be highly selective, using stable ironies and straight reversals to elucidate the rest. For instance, Huizinga concludes that the "lasting value" of *Praise of Folly* "is in those passages where we truly grant that folly is wisdom and the reverse."[4] Moria's zig-zaggery is rarely this straightforward. So disconcertingly is Moria "betweene game and earnest" (209) that Chaloner proposed marginal notes to guide readers. Irony Alert   Beware Fooling Author!

The difficulty of ascertaining meanings and keeping abreast of metamorphoses is compounded in Shakespeare's romantic comedies, in which role-playing and make-believe, fooling, and being fooled raise serious questions about deception, duplicity, and deceit. How do we understand the flow of fooling in *Much Ado* or *As You Like It*? How do rapid changes, tricks, illusions, and self-swindling reveal their characters' feelings and shape our attitudes? The tension between feeling and fooling galvanizes Shakespeare's romantic comedies, which celebrate the efficacy of fooling even as they critique fooling and test its adequacy.

The Career of Humor: Much Ado, Mirth, and Matter

A shared talent for foolery is the telltale sign that Beatrice and Benedick are made for each other, though fooling is also the major obstacle to their union. Both are skilled verbal jousters, Benedick a "quick wit" (*Ado* 2.1.383) and Beatrice "so swift and excellent a wit" (3.1.89). Each quibbles, construes words in bawdy or ridiculous senses, exaggerates fancifully, and elaborates "comparisons."[5] They perform fool's routines as set pieces for general delectation. Like Falstaff or Touchstone mocking honor, Beatrice avidly spoofs "wooing, wedding, and repenting" (2.1.73). Benedick extravagantly pontificates; to say that he would go anywhere to escape Beatrice, he generates nine lines of ingenious hyperbole. Their peers regularly prompt them as if they were indeed entertainers. Their playful foolery is largely endearing—and provides reason to cherish and admire them, care about their relationship, and wish them well. Yet their "skirmish of wit" (1.1.63) is also counterproductive, self-evading, and self-defeating.[6] *Much Ado About Nothing* weighs fooling in the balances and measures its limits. The play shows how fooling constrains and misleads both Beatrice and Benedick.

Beatrice's witty jesting utterly dominates the discourse, though in his absence she refers constantly to Benedick, dubbed "Signior Mountanto" (1.1.30)—a fencing term suitable for a soldier and sparring partner.[7] Her humor, provoked by "Signior Mount On To," is saucy and bawdy. High-spirited, Beatrice mocks Benedick relentlessly, fervidly, and sometimes grotesquely: "I pray you, how many hath he kill'd and eaten in these wars? But how many hath he kill'd? for indeed I promis'd to eat all of his killing" (1.1.42–45). She associates Benedick with challenge and competition, folly and love, killing and eating. Though Leonato discourages his niece's banter, Beatrice persists. Jesting conveys her preeminent intelligence and vitality and reveals her animated interest in "the Benedick" (1.1.89–90).[8] Beatrice insults Benedick directly: "I wonder that you will still be talking, Signior Benedick, nobody marks you" (1.1.116–17). Well, perhaps *someone*! Yet even in ridiculing love, Beatrice suggests their affinity: "I thank God and my cold blood, I am of your humor for that" (1.1.130–31).

Like any jester worth his bauble, Benedick makes himself a figure of fun by belaboring female infidelity: "That a woman conceiv'd me, I thank her; that she brought me up, I likewise give her most humble thanks; but that I will have a rechat [call sounded on a hunting horn] winded in my forehead, or hang my bugle in an invisible baldrick [belt or girdle], all women shall pardon me" (1.1.238–42). Benedick almost gaily envisions himself as the cuckold, flaunting his foibles and his humiliation "vildly painted...in such great letters": behold "Benedick the married man" (1.1.264–68). Professed tyrant of the fair sex, Benedick harps on horns obsessively, even for a charter member of the Men's Club of Messina,[9] that "college of wit-crackers" (5.4.100–1) vaunting masculine bravado.

Less inclined to rail against marriage generally, Beatrice prefers to mock Benedick specifically and usually bests her "overmaster'd" (2.1.61) opponent. His repertory is too narrow. Though both rely on "reciprocations of smartness and contest of sarcasm,"[10] her wit is broader and sharper. She jests to resist constraints and to assert her independence: "Freedom begets wit and wit begets freedom."[11] Conveying an irrepressible gaiety and teeming mind, her jests flow perpetually and abundantly. The other characters tolerate and commend her sarcastic aggression. "Merry as the day is long" (2.1.49), Beatrice was "born to speak all mirth and no matter" (2.1.330).[12]

Yet Beatrice's fooling, however clever and amusing, bespeaks naive illusions and vain self-delusions. She fools herself seriously enough to merit correction. "Mastered" not only by the patriarchy but also by a misconception of herself, she *needs* comic chastening to become more fully human. In Shakespearean comedy, renunciation of marriage is repudiation of humanity. When Beatrice brightly announces, "No, uncle, I'll none. Adam's sons are my brethren and truly I hold it a sin to match in my kindred" (2.1.63–65), she violates the comic imperative: *all* Adam's sons and daughters are bound to "match in [our] kindred" and fated to be "wooing, wedding, and repenting" (2.1.73). Another formulation by Beatrice—"lest I should prove the mother of fools" (2.1.286)—is humorously telling. Only by sequestering herself, refusing marriage and motherhood, can Beatrice avoid being "the mother of fools," for as Moria preaches, we are all fools, most of all those who deny it. Beatrice's exceptionalism is a form of comic hubris or foolish pride. In this play, willful isolation invites retribution, here termed *requital*.

Much Ado examines the effects of fooling on various bystanders as well as victims. In Messina, female intransigence and scorn "naturally" disturb males. Beatrice's uncle frets, "Thou wilt never get thee a husband if thou be so shrewd of thy tongue" (2.1.10–19), and Leonato's brother agrees: "In faith, she's too curst" (2.1.20). Benedick says Beatrice is "possess'd with a fury" (1.1.191) and designates her "the infernal Ate" (2.1.255–56)—Homer's goddess of madness or irrational behavior, whose name is usually translated as "folly," "ruin," or "madness." Beatrice's inapt jokes and insistent demands threaten the patriarchal order, as when she urges Hero, that model of modesty and obedience, to "say 'Father as it please *me*'" (2.1.55–56; my emphasis). Fancy free, without father or husband, Beatrice is alarmingly unrestrained and will please herself. Of Benedick, she proclaims, "Why, he is the Prince's jester, a very dull fool; only his gift is in devising impossible slanders. None but libertines delight in him, and the commendation is not in his wit, but in his villainy, for he both pleases men and angers them, and then they laugh at him and beat him" (2.1.137–42). Targeting his fooling and flyting (that wonderful old word for rebuking and abusing an adversary), Beatrice exposes Benedick. Describing her birth under a dancing star (2.1.335), Beatrice seems almost sublime: she is a force—and a danger.

Benedick's humors, more serious liabilities than Beatrice's, require more rigorous "anatomy" and radical procedures. As defensive and proud as Beatrice, he indignantly resents her ridicule: "The Prince's fool! hah" (2.1.204–5). He maintains that he is no fool but a "merry" spirit misperceived or unappreciated by Beatrice's "base, (though bitter) disposition" (2.1.207–8). Methinks the gent doth protest too much. Beatrice scores a palpable hit, as Benedick partly senses. "But, that my Lady Beatrice should know me, and not know me!" (2.1.203–4) refers to his disguised state and defines his confused ambivalence. Denying that he credits her opinion, Benedict admits that "every word stabs" (2.1.248). Behind the persiflage, just visible, is a man capable of dissecting his own folly and possibly growing from a tiresome joker to a wiser man—if he can breach his tomfoolery, "huddling jest upon jest with such impossible conveyance" (2.1.244–45).[13]

Though they are both too clever by half, it is Beatrice who breaks the cycle of antagonistic jesting and defensive raillery. To the prince's comment that she has lost the heart of Benedick, Beatrice responds *not* with a clever rejoinder but with a surprising revelation: "Indeed, my lord, he lent it me awhile, and I gave him use for it, a double heart for his single one" (2.1.278–80). This quibble resonates beyond glib banter or ferocious *flyting*: "Marry, once before he won it of me with false dice, therefore your Grace may well say I have lost it" (2.1.280–82). Beatrice reveals a grace beyond the reach of jest. Herself "a double heart," with more facets and aspects than the simpler comic heroines of *A Midsummer Night's Dream*, Beatrice might also make herself the source *and* object of critical scrutiny—if she can overcome her self-protective barriers.

The mixed virtues and limitations of Beatrice's foolery are dramatized in a surprising exchange with the prince. Ebullient, she declares, "Good Lord, for alliance! Thus goes everyone to the world but I, and I am sunburnt. I may sit in a corner and cry, 'Heigh-ho for a husband!'" (2.1.318–20). The prince, misconstruing Beatrice's tone, replies, "Lady Beatrice, I will get you one" (2.1.321), sustaining the joke—if it is a joke—testing the waters if it is not. Remarkably, she continues to fool and flirt boldly: "I would rather have one of your father's getting. Hath your Grace ne'er a brother like you? Your father got excellent husbands, if a maid could come by them" (2.1.322–25). Wit, whither wilt? Beatrice's coyness is thoughtless. Jesting brashly, like one of the boys, with bawdry and double entendres on "getting" and "coming," she is fooling recklessly.

To the prince's unexpected overture, "Will you have me, lady?" (2.1.326), Beatrice responds, "No, my lord, unless I might have another for working-days" (2.1.327–28). Whatever the prince's intentions—fooling, flirting, or courting—Beatrice tactfully extricates herself and spares him, with an elegant complement and self-deprecating humor: "Your Grace is too costly to wear every day. But I beseech your Grace pardon me, I was born to speak all mirth and no matter" (2.1.328–30). The prince takes her meaning, and so should we: *all mirth and no matter*. Following her hint, he says gallantly, "To be merry best becomes you, for out a' question, you were born in a merry hour" (2.1.331–33). Mirthfully and deftly negotiating a charged situation,

Beatrice again gainsays the prince, so gracefully, so lyrically, that not even he could wish it otherwise: "No, sure, my lord, my mother cried, but then there was a star danc'd, and under that was I born" (2.1.334–35). Beatrice contradicts ("No, sure") and complicates ("but then"), clearly yet courteously. The playful wit that carried Beatrice away also rescues and redeems her: she has the defects of her virtues and vice versa.[14] She rejects Don Pedro because she recognizes the uncertainty of his proposal and realizes he is too proper to be her husband—not because she is "all mirth" but because she comprehends more matter beneath or beyond mirth. The prince, recognizing her intellectual superiority, realizes that Benedick is the proper mate for this bright, particular star. Inspired by his glimpse of Beatrice's attributes, Don Pedro launches the scheme to unite Benedick and Beatrice. But their match requires each to move beyond the vanity of detachment and pride of wit. In their "merry war," fooling and feeling are also at odds.

Both hero and heroine are amusingly reductive, Benedick more blatantly than Beatrice. "Misprising what they look on" (3.1.52), each rides a hobbyhorse.[15] In soliloquy, Benedick is pleased to see "how much another man is a fool" to laugh "at such shallow follies in others" (2.3.8–10). Prating proudly, Benedick invites comic undoing. Naively presuming he can outfox feelings, Benedick muses "that one man" will "become the argument of his own scorn by falling in love" (2.3.7–11). Benedick unwittingly illustrates his own principle. His mind recognizes and resists an impulse that will flourish into a feeling. He has enough mother wit to observe in others follies he will later laugh at in himself.

Benedick is ripe for transformation. Aware that Claudio's plight might bear on his own, he wonders, "May I be so converted and see with these eyes? I cannot tell; I think not" (2.3.22–23). In acknowledging the possibility of perceiving differently, Benedick seems less stubbornly adamant. The joking way he expresses his resistance is also promising: "I will not be sworn but love may transform me to an oyster, but I'll take my oath on it, till he have made an oyster of me, he shall never make me such a fool" (2.3.23–26). Still regarding love categorically as folly, he now includes himself as part of that infinite company of fools. His self-image as an "oyster" doesn't suggest intractability. At the height of his bravado are signs that Benedick remains foolishly blinkered yet not irretrievably lost. Among his litany of rare female virtues—wisdom, virtue, wealth, fairness, nobility—he includes "good discourse" (2.3.33–34), Beatrice's forte. Manifestly, Beatrice displays all the qualities Benedick prizes, except of course mildness; and Benedick needs the stab of words to challenge his complacent self-regard. When cocksure Benedick concludes, "But till all graces be in one woman, one woman shall not come in my grace" (2.3.28–30), we realize that one woman will.

Precisely because the obstacles obstructing our hero are entirely internal, it is appropriate and necessary that Benedick be *fooled* into love, gulled to glory. Two revelations in the staged conversation precipitate Benedick's conversion: that Beatrice adores him and that his friends deplore his "contemptible spirit" (2.3.180–81). The prince's stratagem triggers Benedick's modest self-realization that he is "unworthy so good a lady" (2.3.208–9). His second soliloquy recognizes that he is beloved *and* deficient, a discovery that is significant yet incomplete, serious but amusing. Risibly, he attempts to accommodate his sudden change of heart rationally; he is determined to be *logically* in love. Clinging to the pretense of self-control, he worries how his friends, accustomed to his recitals against marriage, will respond. Still cherishing his own voice, however compromised its authority, he rehearses his defense.

Benedick makes a remarkable renunciation, forsaking his erstwhile identity. Like Prospero drowning his magician's staff and book, Benedick discards his jester's persona and script. The "career of his humor" (2.3.241–42) has taken a miraculous turn, surprising yet fitting. Frankly conceding that loving him is "no addition to her wit," he resolves to make her feeling "no great argument of her folly, for I will be horribly in love with her" (2.3.233–35). (A great gift to an actor, that *horribly*.) Man's "paper bullets" are unavailing against the force of love: "Shall quips and sentences and these paper bullets of the brain awe a man from the career of his humor? No, the world must be peopled. When I said I would die a bachelor, I did not think I should live till I were married" (2.3.240–44).

With no diminution of power to amuse himself, Benedick refocuses his antic disposition to encompass and express feelings. Gleefully, he rehearses his preposterous argument and becomes more self-deprecating, accommodating without regret his own folly: "Happy are they that hear their detractions, and can put them to mending" (2.3.229–30). He inches from social critic to self-critic. Still, Benedick remains smugly conceited: resolved to integrate unfamiliar feelings into his outmoded persona and asking new questions that he answers to his satisfaction, he is only partially transformed in this comic apotheosis. He pays lip service to the compromises and contingencies envisioned more seriously by Beatrice when she responds to a similar challenge only moments later. Even in the sanctuary of soliloquy, presenting himself ironically, Benedick quite reluctantly sees himself as a subject for mockery. If the scornful bachelor has died, or at least withdrawn, the loving husband has not yet been born. Benedick's conversion and the "career of his humor" remain works in progress.

To what extent must the heroine also change from mocking humorist to loving partner? Does she perceive her own folly? We've seen that Benedick overreacts to Beatrice's chiding because he senses that he is ridiculous. Compared to Benedick, Beatrice seems marginally more disposed to introspection and self-revelation. Having cryptically acknowledged that painful past history with Benedick makes her a "poor fool" (2.1.314), Beatrice heeds Hero's pointed criticism:

> O god of love!...
> But nature never fram'd a woman's heart
> Of prouder stuff than that of Beatrice.
> Disdain and scorn ride sparkling in her eyes,
> Misprising what they look on, and her wit
> Values itself so highly that to her
> All matter else seems weak. She cannot love,
> Nor take no shape nor project of affection,
> She is so self-endeared.
>
> (3.1.47–56)

Speaking more confidently and aptly than ever before or after, Hero pinpoints Beatrice's "misprision," the blindness of her cousin's superior intelligence. Benedick and Beatrice both overhear staged conversations contrived to trick them into acquiescence, and each practices humor that "values itself so highly" that "all matter else seems weak" (3.1.53–54). The latter formulation reinforces Beatrice's distinction of "all mirth and no matter," fooling and feeling. Their comic epiphanies subtly contrast heroine and hero. Beatrice is less flamboyantly given to histrionics or humor. Revealing her (genuine though amusing) confusion and capacity for reflection, Beatrice poses questions instead of making assertions; she is focused, succinct, and cogent. Disinclined to Benedick's self-irony, she constructs a deliberate and articulate response. Heretofore brashly vocal and quick off the mark, Beatrice is now stunned into introspection. Strikingly, the heroine is subjected to more pointed critique than the hero, for "such carping is not commendable" (3.1.71) in a lady. Female wit seems especially worrisome even to the women of Messina. Hence the prince and Claudio characterize Benedick as stubbornly proud, while Ursula and Hero depict Beatrice as proudly *unkind*, meaning both unsympathetic and dangerously unfeminine.

More so than Benedick, though, Beatrice is changed, changed utterly and suddenly as if by magical metamorphosis: "What fire is in mine ears? Can this be true? / Stand I condemn'd for pride and scorn so much? / Contempt, farewell, and maiden pride, adieu! / No glory lives behind the back of such" (3.1.107–10). In a relatively prosaic play, the blank verse signifies enhanced dignity; Beatrice relinquishes "maiden pride" in order to confront painful truths. Unlike Benedick, Beatrice emphasizes the change she will make in herself:

> And, Benedick, love on, I will requite thee,
> Taming my wild heart to thy loving hand.
> If thou dost love, my kindness shall incite thee
> To bind our loves up in a holy band;
> For others say thou dost deserve, and I
> Believe it better than reportingly.
>
> (3.2.111–16)

In turning her thoughts and opening her heart, Beatrice moves like a flower toward the sunlight. Wonderfully, they "require" and echo each other: "Love me? Why, it must be requited" (2.3.224) anticipates Beatrice's "And Benedick love on, I will requite thee" (3.2.111). Now collaborating rather than competing, they bid fair to become ideal lovers bound "up in a holy band" (3.1.114). Instead of pride fueling mockery, "kindness shall incite" both. No longer maintaining her own jealously guarded jurisdiction, Beatrice subordinates herself—let me stress—*not* to Benedick's despotic jurisdiction but to his "loving hand," their "holy band" of marriage, and claims of community: what "others say" she is now willing to "believe" and affirm. Her vaunted humor—talking for victory in verbal contests, that ostentation expressing itself in stylistic exuberance—may no longer be an insuperable obstacle to happiness; heroine and hero recognize the need to curtail foolish jests as a condition of mature, reciprocal love.

Contemplating the shortcomings of jesting and the pull between feeling and fooling in *Much Ado About Nothing* highlights two oddly positioned and curiously ephemeral fools. One fool suddenly blazing forth is Margaret, the gentlewoman who attends and inadvertently ruins Hero. Rather meagerly motivated, Margaret is usually regarded as a simple foil—a lusty, bawdy contrast to Hero's maidenly reticence and a pawn in Don John's nefarious plot. Yet instead of dispatching her business and disappearing, Margaret twice reappears, prominently, and is gratuitously mentioned twice more in act 5. Why does Shakespeare permit Margaret to carry on so extensively with Beatrice? A hint is Hero's remark to Margaret, "my cousin's a fool, and thou art another" (3.4.11), suggesting that Margaret is not merely the lesser light reflecting the heroine's greater glory. When Beatrice decides to leave the house of mirth and get serious, Margaret steps up. Insolently but saliently, she makes fun of Beatrice, objecting to a particular "illegitimate construction!" (3.4.50); her phrase is a virtual subtitle for this play about "noting" and misunderstanding. Strutting her stuff, astutely punning on

Benedictus, Margaret calls attention to her own humorous elevation: "Doth not my wit become me rarely?" (3.4.69–70). Then Margaret deftly dances away from consequentiality: "I have no moral meaning....I am not such a fool to think what I list" (3.4.79–83). She casts Beatrice in the unaccustomed role of second banana, beats her at her own game, and for good measure gets the last word in their miniature skirmish of wit. No wonder Beatrice calls Margaret "the fool": the latter takes over the role of household jester abdicated by the former Lady Tongue. Surprised and impressed by Margaret's resourceful fooling, Beatrice asks, "How long have you profess'd apprehension?" (3.4.67–68)—that is, made jesting your vocation. Beatrice's edginess indicates some lingering propriety about turf; as in, I'll do the jokes, Margaret, you mind Hero's wardrobe! Thus Margaret, who unwittingly and disastrously stood in for Hero, shockingly upstages Beatrice and replaces the heroine as the featured funny girl.

The fate of fooling in *Much Ado* is determined when Beatrice and Benedick avow their love and enter a different galaxy of discourse. Benedick has been stunned nearly speechless by the wedding debacle. His most significant response is what he does *not* say or do: join the male diatribes against Hero and exit with Don Pedro and Claudio. Instead, following Beatrice into the chapel, Benedick conveys his sympathy unambiguously: "Surely I do believe your fair cousin is wrong'd" (4.1.259–60). Their quick, intense exchanges, under the pressure of terrible circumstances, differ radically from the "merry war" of yore. Now Benedick speaks forthrightly and plainly and is amazed to discover, "I do love nothing in the world so well as you—is not that strange?" (4.1.267–68). Heartfelt passion is expressed not by fanciful flourishes or jocose comparisons but by unmistakable clarity.

At first Beatrice stammers in tumultuous confusion: "As strange as the thing I know not. It were as possible for me to say I lov'd nothing so well as you, but believe me not; and yet I lie not: I confess nothing, nor I deny nothing. I am sorry for my cousin" (4.1.269–73). Halting language dramatizes her difficulty moving beyond the wit that sustained and protected her. The seesaw rhythm indicates the profundity and intensity of her anguish for her cousin Hero. She is not ready to meet Benedick in candor and ardor, not until he passes a crucial test. Yet it is a trial for *both*: Beatrice, like Benedick, needs to divest herself of the verbal defenses precluding commitment and preventing reciprocity.

In this sense, both Benedick and Beatrice are Bergsonian humor characters with mechanical humor encrusted upon their vital spirits. Because these "blocking forces" are internal obstacles, not merely external impediments, they prove more substantial than disapproving fathers or arbitrary laws; only gradually do these qualms and concerns yield to rapprochement. Benedick entreats her to aver love, "And do it with all thy heart," to which Beatrice comes halfway with a qualification or hedged commitment: "I love you with so much of my heart that none is left to protest" (4.1.285–87). Until she can trust him fully, she cannot—she will not—open herself.

Benedick's first response to her demand, "Kill Claudio," is horror. But he *listens* to Beatrice, who expresses her case with crystalline directness: "Sweet Hero, she is wrong'd, she is sland'red, she is undone" (4.1.312–13). The decisive exchange comes when Benedick, in unambiguous language, asks, "Think you in your soul the Count Claudio hath wrong'd Hero?"—to which Beatrice responds, "Yea, as sure as I have a thought or a soul" (4.1.328–30). Her pellucid reply is an avowal. To Benedick's question she makes one significant addition, from "soul" to "thought or soul." For Beatrice, love must be the marriage of true minds.[16]

In effect Benedick converts. Metaphorically, Beatrice asks Benedick to kill the Claudio within, to sacrifice or exorcise his worst aspects. Benedick accepts the challenge, (again) in terms of betrothal: "Enough, I am engag'd" (4.1.331). Forcefully, he plights his troth in two successive "I will" formulations: "I *will* challenge him. I *will* kiss your hand" (4.1.331–32; my emphasis).[17] Words buttress deeds as passion replaces play. The urgency of the moment and the power of their love preclude disingenuousness, coyness, self-protective mockery, or sophisticated wit. Hero and heroine achieve a communion based on common purpose, shared regard, and mutual trust.

The limits of fooling and the diminished value of wit are vividly dramatized when Benedick challenges Claudio. Claudio's reaction is appalling: instead of mourning Hero's demise or asking what Benedick knows, he and the prince rail about Leonato and his brother, "two old men without teeth" (5.1.116). Not even mention of Hero's grieving father troubles the blithe and bonny bachelors, seeking Benedick's bonhomie: "Wilt thou use thy wit?" (5.1.124). As a rule, whenever characters *invoke* wit—some twenty times in the play, a third of them in this scene—their own wit is suspect. Not all sounds of woe can be, or should be, converted into hey nonny-nonny, despite the song. Sometimes it *is* better to visit the house of lamentation than the house of mirth.

Accordingly, Benedick rejects banter: "I pray you," he entreats his brothers in arms, "choose another subject" (5.1.136–37). Undeterred, they proceed obliviously and callously, puzzled by Benedick's archness. Blandly assuming their old clowning comrade is joshing as usual, they are amazed to discover that "he is in earnest" (5.1.194). Finally Benedick confronts Claudio in no uncertain terms. "You are a villain. I jest not; I will make it good how you dare, with what you dare, and when you dare. Do me right; or I will protest your cowardice. You have kill'd a sweet lady, and her death shall fall heavy on you" (5.1.145–49). Notable here is the stark, plain style, the blunt, unmistakable purport of Benedick's declaration. Now is no time for humor, wordplay, or quibbles: "I jest not." The erstwhile prince's jester has learned the importance of being "earnest" (5.1.194), reiterated incontrovertibly as "most profound earnest" (5.1.195).

Still the prince, who seems not to hear this "aside" to Claudio, misses Benedick's tone and purpose; prince and Claudio caper about capons. Benedick's ironic dismissal, "Sir, your wit ambles well, it goes easily" (5.1.158), encourages Don Pedro to revert to the jest played on Benedick. The anecdote rehashes the stale subject of wit and what Beatrice supposedly said about Benedick's wit, and so on and on for fourteen tedious, embarrassing lines. Predictably, the Men's Club of Messina recycles their favorite jape and every husband's dire peril: "But when shall we set the savage bull's horns on the sensible Benedick's head?" (5.1.181–82). It is as if the prince and Claudio accidentally ambled from *Love's Labor's Lost* into *Much Ado*. Benedick will have none of it. "Fare you well, boy, you know my mind. I will leave you now to your gossip-like humor" (5.1.185–86).

Margaret now accosts Benedick in the garden. With Hero presumed dead does Margaret lament her ostensibly deceased mistress? If Margaret knows Hero lives, does she confess or regret her participation? Hardly. Instead, she offers bawdy banter reminiscent of the Men's Club, foolishness Benedick politely parries. When she tries to continue verbal fencing, Benedick gently dissuades her and abandons the game: "A most manly wit, Margaret, it will not hurt a woman." His thoughts are now elsewhere: "And so I pray thee call Beatrice; I give thee the bucklers" (5.2.15–17)—that is, I give up this skirmish of wit.[18] There is fine symmetry here. In her last appearance, Margaret underscored Beatrice's abnegation of folly; here she precipitates Benedick's renunciation of humor.

Henceforth, though not without some momentary backsliding, Benedick tempers wordplay and speaks "plain and to the purpose like an honest man" (2.3.18–19). Left to his devices, he struggles to compose a poem, expressing his feelings "in festival terms" (5.2.41). It is *hard* to "woo" without shopworn wit and hand-me-down idiom! Happily, words plain and to the purpose— salted with a dash of vigor and an ounce of verve—will serve. As though belated, born too late to deploy Renaissance tropes and Petrarchan conceits, Beatrice and Benedick are learning to express themselves and communicate in new-made and heartfelt language. In acts 1 and 2, Claudio and Hero conveyed their feelings for each other self-consciously, briefly, and ineffectively; Beatrice and Benedick, exploring unchartered territory, sometimes stumble. When Beatrice inquires about Benedick's exchange with Claudio, characterized by Benedick as "only foul words" (5.2.50), she momentarily reverts to the ornamental elaboration Benedick forsakes: "Foul words is but foul wind, and foul wind is but foul breath, and foul breath is noisome" (5.2.52–53).

Now, because each can help the other, Benedick rights their course: "Thou hast frighted the word out of his right sense, so forcible is thy wit. But I must tell thee plainly, Claudio undergoes my challenge" (5.2.55–57). Instead of self-aggrandizing oneupsmanship, the lovers express mutual respect, their reciprocity calibrated by the exact division of lines in both length and weight. The process of requiting each other is ongoing. They abjure callow humor but not wit entirely, lest they dwindle, dully, into domesticity—or become altogether earnest.

> *BENEDICK*: Thou and I are too wise to woo peaceably.
> *BEATRICE*: It appears not in this confession; there's not one wise man among twenty that will praise himself.
>
> (5.2.72–75)

The denouement of *Much Ado*, despite one's queasiness about the reunion of Hero and Claudio, is a triumph for Benedick and Beatrice—a victory over cutting, exuberant, but insouciant fooling. Their repartee had been a "battle of wits," each seeking supremacy, striving to possess the other's words to make them fit their own prescribed, egocentric meanings. Cavalierly taking liberties with each other's language was a kind of irresponsible appropriation and a preemptive strike upon feeling. Now they mutually celebrate wise love. Benedick has left behind his former friends, who are still feebly jesting about the savage bull: "Tush, fear not, man, we'll tip thy horns with gold" (5.4.44). Benedick sports buoyantly yet pertinently—even his quibbling double entendre cannot obscure his purpose: "But, for my will, my will is your good will / May stand with ours, this day to be conjoin'd" (5.4.28–29). It is the sort of manic wordplay, punning on his own first name, the playwright rarely resisted in his earlier comedies and his sonnets.

Benedick thus recapitulates his progress from glib equivocator to plain speaker, from humorist to husband, from mocking jester to candid helpmeet; subordinating himself, he is "conjoin'd" with his beloved, and together they enter the community. Instead of competition, their conversation conveys complementarity, mutuality, and parity. They learn that humor in measured doses at appropriate moments is invaluable but that there are feelings deeper than fooling. Kissing Beatrice, Benedick rejects banter publicly and renounces fooling emphatically: "I'll tell thee what, Prince: a college of wit-crackers cannot flout me out of my humor. Dost thou think I care for a satire or an epigram?" (5.4.100–2). When Benedick playfully pronounces that "man is a giddy thing, and this is my conclusion" (5.4.108–9), foolishly wise and wisely foolish, he does not except himself from giddy contradiction. He publically declares his affinity with fools. In a final flourish, he gaily urges the prince to wed and parodies his former, cuckold-crazed self.

Certainly the fooling of Beatrice and Benedick has real appeal—expressing charm, cleverness, and vitality—and substantial benefits seemingly without cost or consequence. Self-assertive and self-protective, their rampant fooling as default mode insulates them from the claims and liabilities of feeling: such Bergsonian anesthesia of the heart blocks intimacy, hinders communication, precludes understanding, and discourages kindness. Beatrice and Benedick learn to discipline their antic jesting and curtail derisive mockery. Benedick and Beatrice are characters we laugh with and laugh at. Both are seriously "self-endeared," and each is fooled into love scornfully disdained as folly. In a play about mistakes and mistaking, "strange misprision" (4.1.184), the protagonists are tricked into happiness. With comic justice and romantic blessing, both become love's fools.[19]

Faining and Feigning in As You Like It

> feignyng and counterfaityng…delighteth the beholders
> —Chaloner's Erasmus (38)

C. L. Barber construes wit in *As You Like It* as language that gives us "something for nothing." *Much Ado About Nothing* renders foolery much more warily, skeptically, and critically. *As You Like It*, probably produced just after *Much Ado About Nothing*, stages the "alliance of levity and seriousness"[20] in a uniquely satisfying fashion, both interrogating and cherishing foolery. This play really does seem to be as good as it gets for everybody, lovers and exiles, a ruminating melancholic, rustic clowns, and jaded jesters. In Arden, a "natural philosopher" such as Touchstone is keen to debate for the fun of thinking and feeling. Here too the jester pretends to be a "true lover," and the truly true lovers Rosalind and Orlando are fooling or fooled, according to Touchstone's principle: "As all is mortal in nature, so is all nature in love mortal in folly" (2.4.55–56).[21] What is the connection between feeling and fooling in a play bursting with feigning and counterfeiting? Rosalind elaborates upon "counterfeit" (4.3.166–82), a synonym for deception and performance. Of course, Rosalind is disguised as a boy pretending to be herself. Her many-minded, sustained fooling raises the question: Can there be a person without a "well-counterfeited" role? Perhaps to lack a guise is to want a self. This theatricality—sympathetic to the imaginary of fooling, favoring artifice over essence and style over substance—undergirds *As You Like It*. To what extent does

Figure 4.2   Rosalind and Touchstone, Act III, Scene 2, in *As You Like It*, by William Shakespeare (1564–1616). Reproduced with permission of the Bridgeman Art Library International.

this romantic comedy affirm the possibility of supposedly real feelings, sincerity, and authenticity? In a world of feigning, is there a principle of verification, or is it all much ado about nothing, as you like it, hey nonny-nonino? The issues implicit in *Much Ado About Nothing* are staged very differently here. *As You Like It* scrutinizes fooling rigorously, sympathetically, and comprehensively in Shakespeare's apotheosis of foolery. In this play of ideas, Rosalind is the foolosopher queen and Touchstone is her catalytic jester. When a fool performs, one always wonders whether all the sophistry, absurdity, and patter really *matter*; so often foolery merely dallies with perceptions and impersonates attitudes. Many of Touchstone's reflections and responses are contrivances to generate enjoyment or provide a spectacle. When Touchstone woos and weds Audrey, the quality of their discourse and the authenticity of their feelings are incidental considerations, whereas Rosalind's emotions and feelings matter immensely to her and to us. Yet to test and confirm crucial feelings, this heroine devises and sustains an elaborate pretense; deception is her means of validation. Like Hamlet's antic disposition or Falstaff's counterfeiting, Rosalind's "holiday foolery" (1.3.14) is deft and discombobulating, seriocomic and problematic.

Besides Lear, Rosalind is the Shakespearean protagonist most intimately connected to the jester, a heroine who truly would "rather have a fool to make me merry than experience to make me sad" (4.1.27–29). Rosalind combines the folly of love and the love of folly; she exudes merriment and radiates mirth. Contemplating her initial disguise as strategic protection, Rosalind relishes an opportunity to "suit me at all points like a man" with a "swashing and a martial outside" (1.3.116–20). She enjoys playing, both performing and observing: spying Silvius and Phebe, she decides, "I'll prove a busy actor in their play" (3.4.60). In such metatheatrical moments, an actor plays a woman playing a lover playing a romance watching a "pageant truly play'd" (3.4.53).[22] For Rosalind as for Hamlet, the distinction between acting and doing or being, feigning and feeling, is blurred and perhaps moot. Acting out her love for Orlando, for instance, Rosalind stages a make-believe wedding ceremony that under English common law is legally binding. Implicitly trusting or risking foolery, unlike cautious Celia, Rosalind dances near the edge. In love, she can be fetchingly silly, "mortal in folly" (2.4.56). Excited by the presence of her infatuated admirer, Rosalind puns and blithers manically. Yet she also sees through and beyond romantic hallucinations to determine whether her besotted poet is or might become a true lover.

She knows she needs a touchstone to test language and authenticate feelings. Thus Rosalind's "foolery" is fundamentally purposeful and consequential. She synthesizes elements of Touchstone's humor[23] and Jaques's satire to develop an Erasmian foolosophy distinctly her own. When "Ganymede" proclaims that "love is merely a madness, and I tell you, deserves as well a dark house and a whip as madmen do; and the reason why they are not so punish'd and cur'd is, that the lunacy is so ordinary that the whippers are in love too" (3.2.400–4), she echoes Jaques. Yet Rosalind's denunciations differ from Jaques's self-indulgent diatribes. She is too robustly high-spirited to "forswear the full stream of the world, and to live in a nook merely monastic" (3.2.419–21). The power of her feelings is evident in her reaction to Orlando's bloody napkin. When she hears how Orlando "fainted, / And cried in fainting upon Rosalind" (4.3.148–49), she swoons and vainly pretends she was pretending, as if Ganymede were keeping character as Rosalind. Thus Rosalind feigns feigning, or feigns Ganymede feigning feigning. Pointedly, Oliver is not deceived: "This was not counterfeit, there is too great testimony in your complexion that it was a passion of earnest" (4.3.169–71). Struggling to maintain her dissembling, Rosalind reassures Oliver, "I shall devise something; but I pray you commend my counterfeiting to him" (4.3.181–82). The reiterated term *counterfeit* ironically underscores that Rosalind is never more herself than now, when her feelings burst her disguise. As the napkin is the token of Orlando's true love, so is her swoon an involuntary affirmation, it seems, of Rosalind's true self: indeed, as Oliver suspects, "testimony…that it was a passion of earnest" (4.3.170–71).[24]

Earnest passion beneath or beyond counterfeit, fooling, and role-playing fulfills romantic comedy's promise of correction, clarification, and verification. The time for "sober meanings" (5.2.69) is at hand and Rosalind is its diviner.[25] To indicate that everything is illuminated and authenticated, Rosalind reiterates several times that she *knows*. When her question for Orlando—"If you do love Rosalind so near the heart as your gesture cries it out" (5.2.61–63)—is resolved to her satisfaction, she declares, "Now I speak to some purpose" (5.2.52–53).

Left unresolved is the question implicit throughout *As You Like It*: How does one know that someone else speaks to some purpose? If this play shows anything, it is that sincerity is beside the point—at best, a distraction. To vouchsafe "with all my heart" matters not if the speech is sodden and foolish, like Phebe's urgent professions of devotion to "Ganymede": "I'll write it straight," Phebe proclaims. "The matter's in my head and in my heart" (3.5.137–38). "Straight," heartfelt ardor proves inadequate, unavailing, and debilitating. The problem with Orlando's love poetry is not the poet's insincerity but the poem's simplicity: a failure of style indicates a lack of self-awareness. Borrowing language and staging poses, Orlando is ingenuous and inane. Perhaps if he did not regard his feelings so seriously, he could produce more resourceful, joyful play of language, the kind of writing Robert Frost touts: "I like to fool—oh, you know, you like to be mischievous.…The whole thing is performance and prowess and feats of association."[26]

It is almost always assumed that Orlando lacks sophistication and that Rosalind's disguise fools him. Rosalind is the heroine as we like it, strong, smart, and lovable.[27] Marjorie Garber emphasizes, "Her disguise as Ganymede permits her to educate him about himself, about her, and about the nature of love." Garber's Orlando is sadly uneducated, pathetically in-articulate, immature and self-absorbed, witless and imperceptive—a bit of a buffoon, "too dense" to recognize his beloved. "Determined to be love-sick," he is the butt of humor, "extremely funny on the stage—but funny at Orlando's expense."[28] Orlando has been called "as silly as one of Rosalind's sheep," the "least conscious of Shakespeare's unconscious heroes," and "a sturdy booby."[29] Edward Berry compares Orlando to Orsino in *Twelfth Night*, two "fools under the watchful eyes of women they will marry but do not know."[30]

Tempting as it may be to envision the heroine on top for once or at last, zeal to lionize Rosalind and deprecate Orlando may overlook a game-changing possibility that Orlando is *also* fooling—or feigning. In addition to redeeming the hero's tattered honor, this hypothesis sets up an elaborate hall of mirrors, magnifying reflection and self-reflection, as suggested by that encounter between Jaques and Touchstone: "holiday foolery" (1.3.14) with vertiginous effects and high stakes.

Rosalind as Ganymede accosts Orlando with a flimsy pretext and draws him into a fool's scene—or rather, a fool's show in which "Ganymede" discourses wittily and at length. Ganymede, like Touchstone and Jaques, mocks idealistic pretenses, exposes "material" motivations, and quibbles and puns. This jester's performance piques Orlando to play the straight man, asking nine consecutive questions of this frisky, playful youth. Perhaps the symmetry—his number of inquiries mirroring her nine questions to Celia—suggests they are made for each other.

Is Orlando so foolishly imperceptive that he does not notice that this sophisticated shepherd boy strangely resembles his beloved and has endless time to play make-believe? If so, Rosalind faces a daunting challenge to transform this pig's ear into a silk purse. More likely, Orlando sees through Rosalind's disguise, plays along, and fools Rosalind. The speculation has some attractive implications. Redeeming Orlando makes *As You Like It* more compelling. Several hints imply that Orlando recognizes Rosalind and pre-tends to be deceived. He addresses "Ganymede" as *"pretty* youth" (3.2.334; emphasis mine)—signifying "cunning, crafty," and "ingenious, artful, well-conceived." Artful himself, Orlando notices and admires the quality in Rosalind's role-playing. The secondary meaning of *pretty*—"of a person, esp. a woman or child: attractive and pleasing in appearance; good-looking, esp. in a delicate or diminutive way"—further indicates that Orlando knows a hawk from a handsaw. Orlando has ears as well as eyes, remarking that the shepherd has an unusually tony "accent" (3.2.341) for a rustic.

Rosalind probably realizes Orlando recognizes her. This might account for her coyly female-inflected language, when Orlando asks the "pretty youth" where he dwells: "With this shepherdess, my sister; here in the *skirts* of the forest, like *fringe* upon a *petticoat*" (3.2.335–37; my emphasis). Though *skirts* means "border" or "rim," it nicely anticipates "an underskirt or petticoat" and develops a trope more likely to occur to a girl. Ganymede's comment, "I thank God I am not a woman" (3.2.347–48), is virtually a wink at Orlando, not a heavy-handed nudge-nudge but a sly gesture of complicity, as if they are collaborators on a mutually beneficial, reciprocally satisfying project. So she cites "a beard neglected" (3.2.375) as another sign of love, drawing attention to her own disguise and lack of a beard.[31] When she adds, gratuitously, "But I pardon you for that, for simply your having in beard"—that is, what you have in the way of a beard—"is a younger brother's revenue" (3.2.376–8), she practically pinches Orlando in antic glee. Why else would she say, "You may as soon make her that you love believe it, which I warrant she is apter to do than to confess she does" (3.2.387–89)? The first half is double entendre spoken by "Ganymede" to a make-believe lover but directed at the audience; the second half of the line, moving from fooling to feeling, can only be Rosalind in earnest addressing Orlando.

Both Rosalind and Orlando maintain the fiction that she is a he and he is a dolt. Rosalind's motives are consistent with her "real" character, more forthright and nearly candid: she tells Orlando she would like to meet "that fancy-monger" hanging odes on trees and "deifying the name of Rosalind" to "give him some good counsel" (3.2.363–64). Orlando's motives are implicit: acutely aware that he lacks education and breeding, he identifies himself as "he that is so love-shak'd" (3.2.367) and willingly subordinates himself to Rosalind's curriculum, "the art of love." Orlando thus acquiesces in another fool's scene on that old hobbyhorse, the elusiveness of personal identity, said by fools to be always only jest and asserted by fools for love to be essential, eternal, and transcendent. Hence, this is fooling with profoundly serious purpose. Rosalind needs to know "are you so much in love as your rhymes speak?" (3.2.396–97). Orlando needs to "make thee believe I love" (3.2.385–86). The extent of the task is evident when Orlando responds to Rosalind's crucial question, "Are you so much in love," with a proverb: "Neither rhyme nor reason can express how much" (3.2.398–99). He must learn to probe his feelings more deeply and to express them convincingly. That's why Ganymede's catalog of the lover's traits includes "an unquestionable spirit, which you have not" (3.2.374–75), in the sense of *unsociable, unwilling to talk*. Rosalind specifies what Orlando conspicuously lacks, as far as she knows, and a lover needs. Joking that Orlando (unlike the tongue-tied, dumbstruck wrestler) indicates no such deficiency, she sets the agenda with the tact of a master teacher. See, she hints, you can do this! Playing a lover enables a true lover to overcome reticence, shyness, and crippling self-consciousness.[32] Like a stutterer, Orlando might be able to sing what he cannot say.

Their game of joint pretense and counterfeit unawareness enables them to explore and develop their best selves in harmony with the beloved other. Each rehearses sympathetic and empathetic love by anticipating what the other needs to *get* as well as *be*. The skill and subtlety of each validate their match, not only because Orlando learns to style himself more effectively but also because both have the wit and heart to be true lovers and genuine mates. Such a consummation, devoutly to be wished, requires more than a commanding heroine; it calls for self-discipline and subordination, mutual sensitivity, and regard by both lovers. Instead of a virtuoso performance by a goddess, we see a romantic comedy imagined by two gifted people. My conception of feigning in *As You Like It* sees fooling as highly purposeful, a means of certifying feelings—not sidestepping, suppressing, or mocking feelings. Rather than regard the play as a zero-sum game that exalts Rosalind and abases Orlando, my reading resurrects the hero and rewards the heroine with a more suitable mate. I like to think that Orlando read *Praise of Folly* and is wise enough to take Moria's cue: "To pretend to be foolish when the case requires it is the highest wisdom" (Erasmus 117).

Counterfeit, I Assure You

The supposition that Orlando and Rosalind both play roles by pretending to be fooled focuses the issue: Is fooling the wisest way to determine the reliability and authenticity of feelings? Considered pragmatically rather than morally, the benefits of sustained fooling are compelling. As Ganymede, Rosalind enjoys her suitor's company, prolongs the pleasures of courtship, and receives her lover's adoration; she also discovers his mettle, tests his faith, gauges his qualities, and plumbs his depths. She can assert herself, enacting elements of her character discouraged by decorum. She is actor as well as stage manager, director, and producer of her own show—a veritable maestro! Wonderfully—as you like it—she is the master-mistress of a conventionally female agenda and a spunky male project. Thus Rosalind can mock love and make love, fooling and feeling in jocoserious simultaneity.

If Orlando as much as his "Rosalind of many parts" (3.2.149) is pretending, he is a less dim-witted, more many-minded hero, truly dedicated to a "noble device" (1.1.167). If so, Orlando indicates a characteristically Shakespearean duality: ironic and sympathetic, dialectical and dialogical. In this prismatic view, both Orlando and Rosalind are impressive deceivers and foolish lovers, making a marriage of true minds. They partly are made for each other and partly *become* better mates for each other. My notion of requited deception helps explain another puzzling response by Orlando when he arrives and hears Rosalind as Ganymede dispatch Jaques: "I had rather have a fool to make me merry than experience to make me sad" (4.1.27–29). What ensues could only exacerbate Orlando's concern that *he* is being cast as Rosalind's fool and might well multiply his qualms about this strange and marvelous woman. I've argued that Rosalind's congeniality with Touchstone, her appreciation for the fool's perspective, and her willingness to participate (within reason) in folly are all manifestations of her charismatic prowess. These enabling attributes should not obscure her problematic tendencies: to suffer fools reluctantly and irritably, position herself always as the ultimate arbiter, yet rush to judgment. Dominating and commanding, Rosalind can be imperious, acerbic, cocksure, and egocentric. To a young man of genteel origins but no training or experience, she might appear frighteningly bossy. Every brief line Orlando utters prompts Rosalind's elaborately witty commentary—and some alarming attitudes. She pronounces that a husband's "destiny" is to be cuckolded. Is she kidding? Even so, Ganymede's "holiday humor" is alarming. Rosalind's "No, faith, die by attorney" (4.1.94) speech exposes the vacuity of romantic idiom and is probably intended as homeopathic remedy, a dose of skepticism to inoculate the naive lover against inevitable disappointment and more virulent cynicism: "Men are April when they woo, December when they wed; maids are May when they are maids, but the sky changes when they are wives" (4.1.147–49).

Ganymede's pungently antifeminist catalog of wives' faults might well foment Orlando's apprehension and confusion. He would surely have some mixed feelings, awe at Rosalind's authority and wariness of her assurance. If she is educating Orlando, this teacher is no Socrates: "You shall…you must…you must say…now tell me…say" (4.1.124–46). Even a voluntary disciple or modest ephebe might feel a bit badgered or intimidated by such powerful imperatives. Orlando does not hear Rosalind confess to Celia "how many fathom deep I am in love" (4.1.206–7). More disturbing than Rosalind's bossy streak is her association of "wit" with infidelity. She seems to conceive female intelligence, independence, and spirit as adultery, betrayal, and deception. Is that what she means, or is this an excess of fooling? What Ganymede *says* is that husbands become cuckolds and fools: "You shall never take her without her answer, unless you take her without her tongue. O, that woman that cannot make her fault her husband's occasion, let her never nurse her child herself, for she will breed it like a fool!" (4.1.172–76). As they say on *Saturday Night Live*, "Oh, *really?*"

We return to the question: What is the relationship of Rosalind's foolery to reality? If it is true that in disguise and deception, "the real personality of the woman in love is able to reveal itself far more completely and with much greater originality and tenderness,"[33] Orlando must be terrified. One might disagree that Rosalind's wit is "like the sunshine, cheerful, beaming full of life, and glow, and warmth, and animation. We are apt to shrink from wit of Beatrice; we *bask* in that of Rosalind."[34] Perhaps that "we" is problematic, for Rosalind's "foolery" seriously discomfits and understandably disturbs Orlando. No wonder he breaks off the game; he's had enough, maybe more than enough, to ponder. As Rosalind would surely agree, life's not *just* a cabaret, old chum. It is difficult to imagine what response, however courtly or composed, would satisfy Ganymede. Orlando has already insisted unambiguously that he trusts Rosalind implicitly. Is he being asked to cede his wife-to-be carte blanche to do what she will? Ganymede's aphoristic "the wiser, the waywarder" (4.1.161) would shake any man's resolve; it approaches Iago's insinuation that all Venetian ladies are jaded debauchees and sophisticated tricksters. One wonders exactly what Rosalind thinks she is doing.

As You Like It interrogates feeling and explores fooling far more deeply than audiences of romantic comedy expect. What you are (or think you are), what you feel, may be well and good but remains *insufficient*; the ideal is not a self that *feels* but a role that *performs* artfully. Hence the denouement features fabulous artifice, including symbolic serpents, English lions, coincidental encounters, miraculous conversions, and instant betrothals. Instead of stripping pretenses, abandoning masks, and revealing essences, the resolution reinforces artifice, exaggerates incredibility, and flaunts feigning. The play in a sense calls into question "Shakespeare's faith in comedy resolutions."[35] Rosalind seems quite reluctant to cease feigning. The lovers' vows scripted by Rosalind rather weirdly recognize that "it is to be all made of fantasy" (5.2.94). That startling description of holy matrimony also characterizes the strange figure conscripted by Rosalind to consecrate the marriages. Who or what is Hymen? A "real" spirit or a "counterfeit" deity? A shepherd hired to play the role? Hymen's faint echo of Rosalind may hint that she wrote the lines he delivers.[36]

Obliged to make strange bedfellows and contrive gerrymandered sense of "these most strange events" (5.4.127), Hymen cobbles together perfunctory verse: "Whiles a wedlock-hymn we sing, / Feed yourselves with questioning; / That reason wonder may diminish / How thus we met, and these things finish" (5.4.137–40). Recognizing that people are perplexed, Hymen prescribes "wonder." Like Touchstone, Hymen produces ambiguity and exposes the permeability of boundaries. Hymen provokes a concatenation of conditionals from Duke Senior, Orlando, Phebe, and thrice from Rosalind herself, who (ostensibly) runs the show. "If there be truth in sight... If there be truth in sight... If sight and shape be true" (5.4.118–20) is echoed by the heroine, in emphatic reiteration: "No father, if you be not he... no husband, if you be not he..." nor "ne'er wed woman, if you be not she" (5.4.122–24). So many hedging *ifs* prompt Hymen to interject, "Peace, ho! I bar confusion"— only to compound the confusion with yet another gratuitously conditional phrase: hypothetical Hymen will make a conclusion, "If truth holds true contents" (5.4.130).[37]

If? If the god doesn't know, does anyone? Into the breach rush puzzled commentators. Samuel Johnson's notes construe the line as "if there be truth in truth, unless truth fails of veracity."[38] Johnson views Hymen's zany artic- ulations as merely ornamental tautologies, self-evidently true. One won- ders if truth is so evident. Johnson's truth is more confident than Hymen's conditionals or Touchstone's inspired "much virtue in If" (5.4.103). Surely Hymen's fractile formulations, the "pleasure of a divided truth," are less coherent and reassuring than Johnson's "truth in truth," which we fain to affirm and feign to believe.[39] The play seems to me less than conclusively concluded, more contingent and provisional, as when Rosalind pronounces, "Believe then, if you please, that I can do strange things" (5.2.58–59). What "strange things," and how? No wonder Orlando remains mystified: "I some- times do believe, and sometimes do not" (5.4.3). Orlando's faith in doubt, requiring perpetual readjustments of focus and perspective, may be the best one can muster or justify. Largely shepherded by Rosalind, *As You Like It* investigates the nature of feigning and queries the efficacy of counterfeit. She is Shakespeare's foolosopher queen, synthesizing fooling and wisdom in glorious triumph. Playfully confounding real and counterfeit, Rosalind is sufficiently convinced and sufficiently compelling to persuade us that there is indeed, as her fool contends, "much virtue in If." It doesn't seem entirely foolish to entertain reasonable hopes for happiness and measured faith in love, if not entirely as you like it, maybe more than you expect.

Whirligig of Foolery in Twelfth Night

Twelfth Night exhibits the jester's mantra that fools are everywhere: folly rampant! In this romantic comedy, less than six years after *A Midsummer Night's Dream*, virtually everyone appears to be deranged, over the top, and beyond the pale. Dimly suggesting "deliria," Illyria is a cockamamie Land of Cockaigne populated by the besotted and the befuddled.[40] In Illyria, "midsummer madness" (3.4.56) abounds; nearly every character enacts, perceives, or fears lunacy. It is a discomfiting spectacle that measures the perimeters and dramatizes the perils of foolery.

Orsino's opening speech invokes "excess" and "fancy" that are "high fantastical" (1.1.1–15). Both his unrequited dotage for Olivia and her obsessive mourning for her brother are borderline craziness. In Illyria, people reckon on lunacy. Olivia orders Cesario, "If you be not mad, begone" (1.5.199). Viola finds in Olivia's denials "no sense, / I would not understand it" (1.5.266–67). Smitten, Olivia identifies her passion for Cesario as insane: "Even so quickly may one catch the plague?" (1.5.295). Feste considers everybody cracked: "Foolery...shines every where" (3.1.38–39), he says, insisting that he is not insane for saying so: "I wear not motley in my brain" (1.5.57). Awakened by the revelers, Malvolio exclaims, "My masters, are you mad?" (2.3.86). Duped and self-deluded, Malvolio pauses to assure himself that he is not barmy: "I do not now fool myself, to let imagination jade me; for every reason excites to this, that my lady loves me" (2.5.164–65).

Even the laboriously merry pranksters Toby and Andrew are constantly asking each other for their "reasons," as though they vaguely intuit their inanity. When Maria tells Olivia that Malvolio is "tainted in's wits," she remarks (oddly were she anywhere else), "I am as mad as he, / If sad and merry madness equal be" (3.4.13–16). Feste's reiterated title for his lady Olivia, Madonna, suggests lunacy as he punningly implies, "He is but mad yet, madonna, and the fool shall look to the madman" (1.5.137–38). No wonder Olivia suspects "very midsummer madness" (3.4.56)! Sebastian, mistaken for his twin, exclaims, "Are all the people mad?" (4.1.27). Orsino's officer accuses Antonio of being daft. Rescued and propositioned by Olivia, Sebastian naturally wonders, "Or I am mad, or else this is a dream" (4.1.61). In his ecstatic state, Sebastian must convince himself, "Yet 'tis not madness," and struggles with the reasonable apprehension "that I am mad, / Or else the lady's mad" (4.3.15–16). The propinquity of folly and madness is a point that this play makes with special impetus, far more so than comparably farcical but less problematic earlier plays such as *Comedy of Errors* and *A Midsummer Night's Dream*.

The appeal of foolery is notably lessened. Sir Toby Belch is a less resourceful and less beguiling Falstaff, fallen on evil days, pursuing his old pleasures, drinking, cavorting, jesting, and cracking wise. More like the depleted Lavatch, Toby propounds a ragtag or hand-me-down repertory. He expresses no feelings or concern for anyone or anything: "I am sure care's an enemy to life" (1.3.2–3). Toby simply rejects seriousness—propriety, dignity, decorum, "the modest limits of order" (1.3.9). In obedience to Moria's law, "everything suddenly reversed" (Erasmus 43), he flaunts topsy-turvy, capering all night and sleeping all day. Toby is something of a feckless trickster, his eye always on the main chance; hence he endures the company of idiotic Andrew Aguecheek, who is amply endowed, an easy butt and gull for

Toby's pranks. With no purpose other than amusement, Toby labors lamely to sustain the jollies with sodden quips and strained puns. His idea of wit or cleverness is dispiriting. Toby's fooling reveals a grim determination and bilious disposition: less Falstaffian than a tiresome Lord of Misrule, it's been said, who has seen better nights. Left to their meager devices, Toby and Andrew soon exhaust their clowning reserves. It is after all *twelfth* night, the tail end of the holiday festivities, when carnivalesque vitality loses its luster and pales. As Charney notes wryly, "The *last* day of the Christmas festivities finds one sated. One more party, and then thank God for work."[41] Too many drinks and late nights take their toll, what you will. Illyria's merrymakers are at wit's end as holiday runs its course and yields inexorably to everyday. Inadvertently exposing the limits of folly, Toby and the gang move from harmless indulgences to elaborate tricks to malicious antics—the kind of thing that gives fooling a bad name.

We've seen in chapter 2 the efflorescence of the fool in *Twelfth Night*. Though Feste is hardly the cause of wit that is in other men, he inspires speculation, such as Viola's musing: "This fellow is wise enough to play the fool, / And to do that well craves a kind of wit. / He must observe their mood on whom he jests, / The quality of persons, and the time" (3.1.60–63). She discerns that Feste is observant, and she casually connects folly and wisdom: "This is a practice / As full of labor as a wise man's art; / For folly that he wisely shows is fit" (3.1.65–67). Respectful of the fool's "labor," Viola may also be a bit chary of the jester's "practice"—play-acting but also chicanery. And she is roused to generalize quite like a jester: "But wise men, folly-fall'n, / quite taint their wit" (3.1.68). This conventional wisdom indicates that folly is food for thought if not nourishing.

Viola's appreciative interest in fools contrasts Hamlet's impatient chagrin with those intrusive off-book clowns. Her empathy is characteristic and suggests latent affinities with Feste's character, situation, and attitude. Both are servants and go-betweens moving between households: peripatetic, mobile figures. Perhaps because neither is "known," each is properly named only rarely—"Feste the jester" (2.4.11) once, Viola not until 5.1.253. As "Cesario," Viola's main job is to be Orsino's ambassador to Olivia, whereas Feste, formally affixed to Olivia's house, spends as much time at Orsino's household. Both accept socially marginal status and subordination to nominal "superiors," not without stress or regret but with relative equanimity. Reliant on the good offices of a master or mistress, both heroine and fool are required to sing for their supper. Feste "*must* observe their mood on whom he jests" (3.1.62; my emphasis), lest he (like Cesario) overstep, presume, offend his betters. Both are "suitors," importunate actors dependent on favor for livelihood and validation.

Heroine and fool are thus simultaneously central and liminal characters. Striving to avoid trouble, they are implicated in the follies so pervasive in Illyria; despite their circumspection, they are receptive to influence. Despite a predilection for frankness, both hide themselves. Feste and Viola each adopt disguises, that of Sir Topas and Cesario respectively. They are adroit actors, evincing impressive range. The very term *viola bastarda* means "a highly developed idiom that involved frequent changes of register," suggesting Viola's ability to speak "in many sorts of music" (1.2.58). Both are exceptionally verbal, fluent as well as witty. "Corrupters of words" and, as Moria says, "word-jugglers" (50), they pun and parody others—further forms of double entendre; they both eschew yet thrive at what Feste calls "double-dealing" (5.1.29).

Each can be canny as well as candid. Relatively powerless, Feste and Viola are privileged commentators, apparently disinterested, who wield power through language. Free of responsibility, they observe moods and inspect and evaluate others; they frequently measure the intemperate follies of the higher-ups. Noting prolific idiocy, both are touchstones, but neither advocates pure rationality. Neither one preaches (except when Feste impersonates Sir Topas), or presumes to judge generally, each remarks specifically on local, immediate situations. Insightful, seeing through pretenses, neither seems tormented by recognitions and perceptions. Too knowing to be simply comic, too amused to be reductively satiric, without illusions, each is sad but not morose or self-pitying. Unmaskers, they are deceivers, with that faint hint of disreputability and danger associated with tricksters and manipulators: "They that dally with words may quickly make them wanton" (3.1.14–15). They are borderline characters in several particulars.

Each appreciates the other's cleverness; Viola respects Feste's vocation, "for folly that he wisely shows" (3.1.67). The realization is, to an extent, reciprocal. Each gleans an implicit kinship, though Feste remains too clinical, too detached from human suffering to appreciate Viola's depths. On the contrary, he seems strangely impervious to Viola's charm, as though he sees through her act, perhaps realizing that Cesario is female or noticing in her manipulations something uncomfortably familiar.[42] Like most jesters, Feste is unmoved by anybody's subjectivity or interiority—he is content to echo and mock others and to regard them as *others*. Feste's somewhat chilling detachment is more pronounced than that of slightly more humane fools like Touchstone. Viola senses this lack of warmth: "I warrant thou art a merry fellow and car'st for nothing" (3.1.26–27). Admiring Feste's artful turn as Sir Topas the curate, Toby comments, with unusual appositeness, "The knave counterfeits well; a good knave" (4.2.19). In associating counterfeiting and knavery and in noting Feste's prowess, Toby underscores Feste's heartless disingenuousness. Often "double-dealing" (5.1.29), Feste wants it both ways—to extract whatever he can, "but I would not have you to think that my desire of having is the sin of covetousness" (5.1.46–47). Not even the adorable Viola, whose ingenuous ardor and plucky spirit melts hearts, moves wary Feste. He conspicuously lacks the compassion of Lear's Fool or the vitality of the "mortal in folly" Touchstone.

Ultimately, "a world of revelry, of comic festivity, fights a kind of desperate rearguard action against the cold light of day."[43] Anne Barton does well to emphasize the desperation as well as the transience of Illyrian antics. So many bones stick in the throat. Consider Antonio's fate. Arrested on account of his beloved friend Sebastian, Antonio is bewildered by the disregard of Viola, whom he mistakes for Sebastian. Amid the cascade of nuptials, Antonio is simply forgotten. Sebastian marries a beautiful woman he does not know and forsakes the tried and true Antonio. There are more things to worry about despite the celebrations. Another misguided, forlorn figure is Andrew Aguecheek, tricked, cheated, pummeled, and pathetic: "For the love of God, your help!" (5.1.177). In such flashes, feelings do seem to matter—at least to the audience. Toby, without love or pity, calls him fool every which way: "an ass-head and a coxcomb and a knave, a thin-fac'd knave, a gull!" (5.1.206–7). Asinine Andrew is rather endearingly "amenable to the power of words, which is one of the most charming indications of his childlike natural folly."[44] A harmless foil to the objectionable gull Malvolio, Andrew reinforces the pathos of Malvolio. Undone, he too vanishes.

Nearly all the characters enjoying the festivities should think twice but continue to fool themselves. Surely spunky, witty Maria deserves better than Toby, an alcoholic buffoon, last heard muttering, "I hate a drunken rogue" (5.1.201). Sebastian and Olivia exchange barely a dozen words and make a match based on Olivia's ridiculous misperception. Follies compound foolish errors. Whether Viola fares much better is dubious. Orsino expresses only faint, sporadic signs of growth. In the mistaken belief that Cesario betrays him, Orsino threatens mayhem. He marries someone he calls "Cesario," whom he ultimately addresses as "Orsino's mistress, and his fancy's queen" (5.1.388). Orsino's bombastic egocentricity seems unabated, his reliability dubious. Anyone less smitten than Viola might wonder, and pause. As Moria asks in *Praise of Folly*, "To be deceived, to be blind to his vices, to imagine them away, even to love...surely this is not far from folly?" (31).

Productions of *Twelfth Night* often maximize the fooling and minimize feelings, as if it were farce. Perhaps on stage the rush toward comic closure can overwhelm compunctions and second thoughts. But the pell-mell proliferation of hasty marriages occludes unspoken regrets and discomfiting ramifications. The conclusion exposes its own implausible contrivances to suggest the intractability of what Moria calls "amorous idiocy" (48); some confusions are clarified, but foolishness abounds. The stubborn recalcitrance of folly accounts for the highly unusual choice of the fool to deliver the epilogue, and what he sings is not consoling.

I Swear I Am Not That I Play

Like Rosalind and Beatrice relatively protected from mockery and somewhat less susceptible to folly, Viola is nevertheless a fool for love and an effective "practiser." She is disinclined to be disingenuous: naturally candid, Viola seeks refuge in disguise and expresses no pleasure in deceit. Unlike the commanding Rosalind, who revels in role-playing, Viola is perplexed and pathetic; she may feel inauthentic speaking "in many sorts of music" (1.2.58). Unlike imperious Beatrice, Viola is reluctant to make a spectacle of herself or to play the fool. Nothing of the trickster and instinctively guileless, she strains to continue the "con." Viola cannot help hinting, "I am not that I play" (1.5.184).

Yet Viola is highly adroit at fooling others. Paradoxically, authenticity or sincerity is the active ingredient in her performance because Viola herself suffers "contemned love" (1.5.270), she truly pities Orsino and *hence* speaks beautifully. Addressing Olivia in the guise of "Cesario," Viola abandons the speech she has "taken great pains to con" (1.5.174) and improvises. Viola's lyrical invention, "Make me a willow cabin at your gate" (1.5.268) centers upon Olivia's name, "'Olivia!' O, you..." (1.5.274). Her name melts into the "O" of the lover's anguish. Here Viola dramatizes feelings Orsino himself could never articulate and probably never experiences. Beginning "make me" and ending "pity me!" (1.5.268–76), this lyric effusion expresses Viola's touching loneliness and ardent passion. Viola conveys not what she means to say but what she would not say, her own yearning and devotion, in the most gorgeous language: "What I am, and what I would are as secret as maidenhead: to your ears, divinity; to any others, profanation" (1.5.215–17).

There's a similar two-step between confession and concealment in her most intimate conversation with Orsino: "I am all the daughters of my father's house, / And all the brothers too—and yet I know not" (2.4.120–21). Notably, as with the veiled and remote Olivia, Viola's imaginative projection and lyric force awaken her interlocutor out of debilitating vanity; for once, Orsino considers something besides his own unfounded, hyperbolic, and unrequited feelings! Again, though, fooling and feeling are hard to distinguish, for Viola is both confounded and confounding. Speaking from the heart, of herself, Viola is "there" only obliquely, ambivalently. Struggling to be or not to be herself, she illustrates once more how "the lunatic, the lover, and the poet / Are of imagination all compact" (*MND* 5.1.7–8). In *Twelfth Night*, this triangulation of desire links and entraps three fools for love. As if they were made for each other, Olivia and Orsino have names beginning with O, comprising the same number of letters and syllables, and ending in vowels; and the women's names are virtual anagrams for each other.

Twelfth Night, like *A Midsummer Night's Dream*, dramatizes love's follies—with quite different effects. Though all the lovers in both plays are mistook and mistaken, no one is more persistently misapprehended or bewildered than Viola. Disguised nearly from the outset and unto the last, Viola's identity *remains* surprisingly contingent, perceived quite variously "as a figure for the desire that circulates in the play."[45] Viola's resolution is far less confident, clarifying, or certain than that of Rosalind or Beatrice. Not until she reunites with Sebastian and never afterward is her proper name spoken. Even in the recognition scene with her brother, Viola is strangely reticent and literal-minded, citing her father's mole upon his brow and oddly postponing the revelation "that I am Viola" (5.1.253). Why Viola requires elaborate verification and delays gratification bears upon another puzzle, her tardy realization that Sebastian is alive and in Illyria. She heard Antonio refer to Sebastian by name and registers its significance: "Prove true, imagination, O, prove true, / That I, dear brother, be now ta'en for you!" (3.4.375–76). In fact, she repeats her perception just four lines later: "He nam'd Sebastian...O, if it prove, / Tempests are kind and salt waves fresh in love" (3.4.379–84).

Possibly, Viola plays dumb to play it safe until she knows for sure. Her sluggishness might reflect her hesitant recognition that love is folly. Maybe she is reluctant to marry a bombastic boob who has never "known" her as a woman and persists in addressing her as "Cesario." Whether or not Viola is a "mercurial performer whose gender remains tenuously constituted, adaptable to circumstance—and to the 'whirligig of time,'"[46]—she is sufficiently sensible to feel ambivalent about marrying such a fool. Viola's reiterated formulation, "Prove true, imagination, O, prove true...O, if it prove true," contrasts sharply with the happy hypothetical of *As You Like It*: "much virtue in If." Viola is warier because the follies in *Twelfth Night* are more troublesome—rooted, tenacious, and enduring.

CHAPTER 5

Folly Is Anatomiz'd

*P*raise of Folly* is a treasure trove of foolish conduct regarded sympathetically by a remarkable dramatic character. Moria is a model of the fool with her tricks and turns, unstable ironies, and confounding metamorphoses. Initially a benign, tolerant, bemused defender of folly, Moria suddenly changes into a veritable scourge of abominations and heresies. Then, just as abruptly, she reverts to the genial friend of folly. Finally Moria becomes a "fool for Christ" and apostle of folly. The strange affinity between advocate and adversary of folly must have intrigued Shakespeare, whose stage of fools dramatizes similarly incongruous connections.

In *Henry IV*, the fool achieves his apotheosis and meets his match when the madcap heir apparent becomes England's true king. Falstaff and Hal, fool and scourge of folly respectively, are contending forces with comparable powers. Self-designated foes of folly figure crucially in many plays besides the Henriad, from *Romeo and Juliet* through *As You Like It* and *Twelfth Night* and most prominently in *Troilus and Cressida*. To four charismatic and obnoxious figures we now turn: Mercutio, Jaques, Malvolio, and Thersites. Drawn irresistibly to follies, simultaneously attracted and repelled, these "anatomists" strangely resemble the fools they mock, including the jesters with whom they jostle and compete. Like court fools flaunting their *lèse majesté*, Shakespeare's scourges enjoy a sort of sanction to say anything, however irreverent or reckless, vile or disturbing. Invoking the fool's "license to declare the truth without offense" (Erasmus 123) so often affirmed by Moria, these scourges abuse heroes, mock their betters, satirize lovers, and insult the authorities. These are the wise guys "who can find nothing in all human life," as Moria says, that they do not "condemn and ridicule as madness" (46).[1]

The importance of Shakespeare's fools and scourges of folly is underscored by the fact that such characters rarely exist in Shakespeare's source materials: he creates out of whole cloth and with phenomenal gusto Juliet's Nurse and Mercutio, Touchstone and Jaques, and Falstaff, for example. Shakespearean fools and anatomists tend to appear in tandem, arranged and juxtaposed for dramatic effects. Twinned or sibling-like, they share traits and compete for precedence: Mercutio vies with both Romeo and the Nurse, Feste torments Malvolio, Touchstone fascinates Jaques, among other tag-team *tumlers* and other paired comic performers.[2] Shakespeare's fools are notably adhesive, prone to mirror and echo other's characters. Foolish gemination persists throughout Shakespeare's career. In *All's Well That Ends Well*, Lavatch is the wise fool and Parolles the ludicrous gull. Pandar and Thersites divide responsibilities for comic and ironic commentary in *Troilus and Cressida*. Though estranged or marginalized, Shakespeare's scourges are astute observers and surrogate spectators, capable of saying the unsayable.

Pox of Such Antic

Mercutio the cynical mocker and Romeo the foolish lover make an odd couple, apparent opposites engaged in adolescent banter, masculine bravado, attacks, and counterattacks. So-called *flyting* figures prominently in jesting and foolery and is still going strong when athletes talk trash, rappers perform the numbers, or Tony Soprano "breaks your balls." In the rich tradition of mockery, Mercutio's abuse is extraordinarily inventive because this voluble performer is also an acute listener. He mirrors Romeo's looniness by imitating romantic hyperbole:

> Romeo! humors! madman! passion! lover!
>
> .....
>
> I conjure thee by Rosaline's bright eyes,
> By her high forehead and her scarlet lip,
> By her fine foot, straight leg, and quivering thigh,
> And the demesnes that there adjacent lie,
> That in thy likeness thou appear to us!
>
> (2.1.7–21)

Courtly lover and mocker are two ends of a ladder, high and low, from the lady's "bright eyes" to her "quivering thigh."

Mercutio's parodic language, a form of doubling, is also inclined to echo itself: "If love be rough with you," he reiterates, "be rough with love; / Prick love for pricking, and you beat love down" (1.4.27–28). Whenever Romeo

Figure 5.1 Albrecht Durer, Fool and his double, woodcut engraving originally published in Sebastian Brandt's *The Ship of Fools*.

takes amorous flight, the scourge of folly takes deadly aim. Mercutio is a formidable antagonist, a devastating denier whose very first word, "Nay" (1.4.13), contradicts Romeo's "Ay, me" (1.1.162). Anatomist of folly and fool for love are codependents. As Moria says, everything is reversed: sublime and ridiculous, exaltation and degradation. Mercutio's levity, like Falstaff's wit, seems to defy gravity. He is a reliable geyser of smut. Though Mercutio is relentlessly prosaic, rarely rhyming, he is irresistibly quotable and not just for the dirty bits. He might be the character in *Romeo and Juliet* most capable of writing a Shakespearean sonnet. Making himself "a motley to the view" (*Son.* 110.2), Mercutio expresses the skeptical doubts, cynical anxieties, erotic energies, and manic wordplay common to Shakespeare's sonnets and Shakespeare's clever fools. Obnoxiously overweening, he is disturbingly on-target, as in this virtuoso performance: "Without his roe, like a dried herring: O flesh, flesh, how art thou fishified! Now is he for the numbers that Petrarch flow'd in: Laura to his lady was a kitchen wench (marry, she had a better love to be-rhyme her), Dido a dowdy, Cleopatra a gipsy, Helen and Hero hildings and harlots... Signior Romeo, *bon jour!*" (2.4.37–44). Romeo "without his roe" is "me-oh," a variant on the conventional lover's lament, "Ah, me!" With the jester's instinct for the *jongleur* and intimate familiarity with his subject, Mercutio debases Petrarchan aspirations and burlesques romantic heroines.

There are many weapons in this antic's arsenal. Mercutio's disquisition on Queen Mab displays theatrical exuberance as well as surprising visionary capacity.[3] Like Theseus conflating lunatics, lovers, and poets, Mercutio musters lyric fecundity to debunk imagination. Demonstrating extraordinary expressive power in language matched only by Juliet at her best, Mercutio ranges from high to low, colloquial mirth to glorious myth. Positioned as a scoffing gargoyle, Mercutio has a lofty vantage point whence he articulates essential themes and underlying tensions of the play. A creature of daylight, this "prick of noon" (2.4.113) intuits that night is the realm of interiority, the id or appetitive, imperious "self." Mercutio's Mab speech also queries dreams and poetry. Mercutio has a joker's quirky inspiration and takes Puckish pleasure in mischief, confusion, and nastiness. Like Falstaff, he reacts creatively and incessantly to his best friend with oscillating affection and aggression.

Mercutio displays the fool's prodigious power and heightened vulnerability; fools are sanctioned and suffer sanctions. Licensed *provisionally*, jesters are subject to punishment, as King Lear warns his fool: "Take heed, sirrah— the whip" (1.4.110). Like the jesters, Mercutio is both a source of absurdity and a critic of the preposterous. Mercutio's badinage routinely proffers foolish insights. When Romeo renews his banter with the boys, Mercutio encourages him: "Why, is not this better now than groaning for love? Now art thou sociable, now art thou Romeo; now art thou what thou art, by art as well as by nature" (2.4.88–91). Punning on *art*, Mercutio underscores the artificiality of Romeo's romantic posturing. Implicitly Mercutio asks who is the real Romeo and what is the relation between artful style and authentic selfhood. Pertinent in some ways he doesn't comprehend, Mercutio is also patently ridiculous: "I will not budge for no man's pleasure, I" (3.1.55). This line, beginning and ending with the first-person singular, indicates what is both daunting and daft about Mercutio's egotistical sublime. In equal measures, Mercutio is "not to the purpose" (2.4.43), prismatic in his perspective and marginal in his utility. Mercutio perceives only what he habitually sees and cannot appreciate how much Romeo changes—no longer "art thou what thou art...by nature" (2.4.90–91). The hero becomes someone Mercutio cannot recognize or imagine.

We saw how Falstaff's foolery waxes and wanes as folly itself is weighed in the balances and found wanting. In his little world of the tavern, the great fool reigns supreme; in the larger world of politics and warfare, his powers are radically curtailed. Mercutio's story has a similar arc or parabola. Initially, he commands the stage and upstages Romeo. Upon "the prick of noon" (2.4.113), Mercutio casts a very long shadow. In the larger world of love and death, Mercutio's force ebbs, loses pertinence, and is abruptly terminated. As with Falstaff in *Henry IV, Part 2*, dazzling foolery diminishes into increasingly predictable, tedious jive. The game is nearly up, as Mercutio gleans, when such small beer passes for wit. He's right: "I am done" (2.4.71–72). As the fires of love consume Romeo, Mercutio's flames flicker. Even Benvolio tires of Mercutio's manic discourse: "Stop there, stop there" (2.4.94). But Mercutio, like a player piano with a single program, performs yet another "prick-song" (2.4.21), disdaining feminizing love and foreign fashion: "The pox of such antic, lisping, affecting" coxcombs, "these new tuners of accents!" (2.4.28–29). Knowing nothing of Romeo's marriage, Mercutio is stuck in a drama that is no longer playing, unable to catch the tone or fathom the purpose of his dearest friend. In the fatal fight scene, Mercutio misconstrues Romeo's gentle rejoinder as "dishonorable, vile submission!" (3.1.73). Drawing first, Mercutio takes it upon himself to defend Romeo's honor; he identifies with Romeo. Mortally wounded, Mercutio rallies for a strong curtain, bitterly damning everybody: "A plague a' both your houses!" (3.1.106). The scourge's dying curse comes true almost literally when plague prevents Romeo from receiving the friar's crucial message. With insouciant gumption, Mercutio dies, punning: "No, 'tis not so deep as a well, nor so wide as a church-door, but 'tis enough, 'twill serve. Ask for me to-morrow, and you shall find me a grave man" (3.1.96–98). Horseplay and horror are one.

Mercutio's dying words are typically double and aptly equivocal. Quiet, dignified, his language is functional, "like the wound itself," notes Calderwood, "content to be 'enough,' to 'serve' rather than run riot."[4] Yet

Mercutio's quibbling also seems jarringly macabre, more histrionic than human. Unto the last, Mercutio remains irrepressible, unregenerate, and ludicrous. A lightning rod for our compunctions, Mercutio was always likely to be struck. Mercutio the doomed scourge is—to speak oxymoronically—the central liminal figure in a play much about boundaries: among romance, comedy, and tragedy, between Montagues and Capulets, night and day, life and death, dreams and reality. Crucial scenes occur at or on borders—dawn, the walls of Verona, the Capulets' balcony, that tomb where the heroine lies apparently lifeless, actually alive, at death's door. Mercutio's death is the fulcrum on which everything turns from comedy to tragedy, marked by a grave pun. Like his many jester cousins, Mercutio is an avatar of liminality.[5]

Mercutio's fate is often regarded as appropriate or necessary, reflecting the limits of clowning and fooling in a play that wants to become tragic and romantic. As Dryden remarked, Shakespeare was "forced to kill him in the third act, to prevent being killed by him."[6] Characterizing Mercutio as "dangerously eloquent," one of Shakespeare's "rancid ironists," an "unbeliever in religion of love," Harold Bloom maintains faith in the religion of love or its imaginative possibility in lyric language and contends that Mercutio is "victimized by what is most central to the play, and yet he dies without knowing what *Romeo and Juliet* is all about."[7] A vital figure—infectious in both senses—he brazenly threatens the romantic pinnacle Bloom envisions. As much as the hero and heroine, Mercutio is sacrificed. The ultimate realist becomes a commentary on the inadequacy of realism. If Mercutio is not the devil incarnate, he is a demonic tempter, *memento mori: ego in Arcadia*.[8]

Coleridge's observation that Mercutio is "truly Shakespearean...full of such lively intellect" and "possessing all the elements of a poet" is apt.[9] Mercutio, I've suggested, is the most imaginative and creative character in the play. Caustic, flippant, and vulgar, he is anything but shallow, and he can be astonishingly lyrical. Mercutio's voice—always mocking, always shrill, ultimately stilled—resonates. Challenging romantic attitudes, a potent counterforce, Mercutio advocates the skeptical realism, loss of which proves irreparable.[10] Mercutio expresses the scourge's vision in all its power and precariousness. He is more than a lightning rod absorbing doubts. He leads the insurgent movement or disloyal opposition within the play. Resisting the simple pieties and strained purity of romantic discourse, he offers a compelling alternative to the style of Romeo and Juliet. Yet Mercutio remains "permanently stationed on the outer side of the orchard wall, as oblivious to the existence of their love as they are to him."[11] This makes it possible for us to perceive Romeo and Juliet not merely as fools for love but as true lovers in a world well lost, despite the best thrusts of the scourge of folly.

O That I Were a Fool!

The encounter between Jaques and Touchstone in *As You Like It* dramatizes the affinities between fool and scourge and crystallizes the multiple facets of foolery. Shakespearean foolery begins but never ends with a singular viewpoint. Notably, we do not see Touchstone meeting Jaques; rather, we hear Jaques's excited account: "A fool, a fool! I met a fool i' th' forest, / A motley fool. A miserable world!" (*AYL* 2.7.12–13). The "motley fool" Jaques depicts is the familiar dispenser of platitudes and paradoxes, supercilious nonsense, and bawdry quibbles on whores and venereal disease: "From hour to hour, we rot and rot" (2.7.27). But Jaques fails to recognize that Touchstone's half-baked puddleglummery deftly parodies Jaques himself. Shakespeare juxtaposes versions of folly: a fun house hall of mirrors that offers and withdraws a fixed vantage point—the scourge of folly fools himself.

Both intruders in Arden, Jaques and Touchstone are skeptical orators, intelligent, spirited, amusing figures, regarded respectfully but warily. Each performs brashly, regularly entertaining and occasionally illuminating their auditors. Though Jaques and Touchstone are salient commentators, neither is unimpeachable. They reject idealism and idealization, mock love and lovers and remain foolishly misguided. They are both sources and critics of folly:

> When I did hear
> The motley fool thus moral on the time,
> My lungs began to crow like chanticleer,
> That fools should be so deep contemplative;
> And I did laugh sans intermission
> An hour by his dial. O noble fool!
> A worthy fool! Motley's the only wear.
>
> (2.7.28–34)

Mesmerized by his double, Jaques only partially discerns Touchstone's perspicuity and totally disregards his own foolishness. "O that I were a fool!" he proclaims in an amusing subjunctive contrary to fact, "I am ambitious for a motley coat" (2.7.42–43).[12] He conceives himself as a wise man playing the fool and misperceives Touchstone's ironic mimicry. Their chance meeting is thus a parable of fooling. When Jaques says, "Give me leave" to play the fool (2.7.58), he reveals himself a fool and speaks for all of us. Touchstone exposes Jaques's delusions. Coolly, he decapitates him—and leaves his head precariously in place.

Jaques conceives himself as a courageous, misunderstood satirist devoted to the *anatomy* of folly. To "cleanse the foul body of th' infected world"

(2.7.60), he claims the fool's "liberty" (2.7.47) to speak his mind and tell the truth (to him they are one and the same). Because folly is everywhere (except, he thinks, within himself), he presumes he is mistakenly regarded as a fool. Only fools would think him a fool! Touchstone and Jaques represent two connected, competing attitudes, Motley and Melancholy. Touchstone is less stringent, less disturbed; his satiric sallies are grist for the mill, for to him nothing really matters. Touchstone focuses on harmless follies, Jaques on iniquitous vices. Touchstone is the parodist, partly loving what he laughs at, Jaques the cynic, repudiating what he deplores.[13] Still, Jaques's commentary is persistently savvy, as when dismantling Duke Senior's pastoral idealism or remarking poetry's palliative illusions: "Nay then God buy you, and you talk in blank verse" (4.1.31–32). To pastoral panegyric, Jaques adds a corrective, enticing his audience with the invocation "Ducdame, ducdame, ducdame!" (2.5.54) into a circle of fools, so everyone—courtiers onstage, viewers, readers—inhabits the *dukedom* of folly.

Solitary by choice, Jaques is incessantly invoked by his peers, though nobody takes him seriously: ridiculously solemn, he is beyond the pale, indulged as a crank. A little of Monsieur Melancholy goes a long way. He's considered an entertaining divertissement, a jester without portfolio, whose "sullen fits" are "full of matter" (2.1.68–69). Jaques is theatrically morose, sentimentally cynical, and humorously sad—hardly ever angry, mean, or cruel. Encountering Orlando the ludicrous lover, Jaques is positively solicitous, inviting his company. Rebuffed, his parting shot is a gentle jest. Never frightening, he is generally engaging. Was ever any misanthrope so congenial or any sadness so ebullient? Even his antagonist Orlando dubs him "*good* Monsieur Melancholy" (3.2.293–94; my emphasis). The faultfinder's genial tolerance indicates that Arden must be a safe place for fools and lovers!

As You Like It highlights Jaques's sour notes and cacophony.[14] Like many satirists, Jaques sounds *inordinately* disgusted, as if intimate with the vices he denounces, a suspicion encouraged by the Duke, who erupts uncharacteristically: "Most mischievous foul sin, in chiding sin: / For thou thyself hast been a libertine, / As sensual as the brutish sting itself" (2.7.64–66).[15] By now long past his gaudy nights, Jaques seems content to stand on high and mock the spectacle: "All the world's a stage, / And all the men and women merely players; / They have their exits and their entrances, / And one man in his time plays many parts" (2.7.139–42). This familiar trope is very close to *Praise of Folly*: "What is it but a sort of play, in which various persons make their entrances in various costumes, and each one plays his own part until the director gives him his cue to leave the stage" (44). Splendidly oratorical, Jaques's speech is blithely reductive, neglecting life's richly varied texture. From the "whining school boy" (2.7.145) to "second childishness, and mere oblivion" (2.7.165), no one is seen by Jaques from inside or close-up; individuals are conventional types, devoid of whatever makes experience unique, pleasant, or purposeful. We briefly glimpse "a soldier" (2.7.149), not Pistol or Fluellen, and "the lover" (2.7.147), not Romeo or Orlando. Surely we are not *fully* defined by roles and stages in the life cycle. Jaques offers vivid generalizations, not the thick texture of individual human experience.

Such tunnel vision proves inadequate. Jaques with a flourish characterizes man's final act as devoid of teeth, eyes, taste, sans everything—then, lo, old Adam arrives, as feeble and pathetic as Jaques would anticipate yet lovingly supported by his young master Orlando. The tableau, recalling the Virgilian picture of Aeneas carrying his father from burning Troy, exemplifies what Jaques's virtuoso performance neglects: the significance of individual endeavor and mutual feeling. Once more we notice the incompatibility of fooling and feeling. Jaques sees everyone as isolated and hopeless as himself and disregards connection or community. Once Orlando is made "truly welcome hither," warmed and fed, the duke recognizes him for who as well as what he is and declares himself and their "kinship": "I am the Duke / That lov'd your father" (2.7.195–96). Social bonds and kinship are ties that bind; however fragile, they matter greatly. This Jaques ignores or does not know.

Characteristically, Shakespeare spotlights an enabled spokesman to challenge the play's predominant mood. This naysayer is often resonant, articulating skeptical doubts and cynical compunctions powerfully. Such characters as Jaques and Touchstone are—it has been said—lightning rods, absorbing charges that might jeopardize the comic/romantic enterprise. Thus the play goes about its irrepressible business, as we like it. Jaques, like Mercutio, is the debunker, the bubble-burster or disabler, marked but unheeded. Arden subsumes satire. One recalls Dr. Johnson's old school chum apologizing, "I have tried to in my time be philosophical; but, I don't know how, cheerfulness was always breaking in." In *As You Like It*, as its title promises, grim and grumpy "philosophy" yields to cheerful and hopeful foolosophy.

In yet not *of* this world, marginalized by choice, Jaques is often termed a "kind of comic Hamlet."[16] Compared to Hamlet, Jaques's melancholy is more sentimental than substantial, more euphoric than harrowing: he represents the folly of melancholy. If Denmark is a prison, Arden is free play, beyond Jaques's jurisdiction. His effects upon others are nil, except for briefly delaying the marriage of Touchstone and Audrey. Even that one intervention backfires when they become part of Rosalind's celebratory extravaganza: four couples, divine visitations, magic, and merriment! Accordingly, Jaques refuses to join in the final festivities and announces his withdrawal from the newly constituted and healthier society that is so marvelously, implausibly reborn. Near the final curtain, Jaques delivers a valediction. Surprisingly, he is not prevented nor even teased. Speaking uninterruptedly and with uncontested authority, less risible and more compelling, Jaques magnanimously evaluates everyone's "merit" and judges their good fortune as "well-deserved" (5.4.188–90). But comic equanimity yields to satiric detachment: "I am for other than for dancing measures" (5.4.193). Unlike Touchstone, Jaques is unchangeable and implacable, both fool and foe of folly. In this play at least, the only thing more foolish than being in love is disbelieving in love.

Geck and Gull, Fool and Knave

The resident antagonist of folly in Illyria is surprised that Olivia indulges the fool Feste: "I marvel that your ladyship takes delight in such a barren rascal" (*TN* 1.5.83–84). Malvolio cannot imagine any pleasure or value in "these set kind of fools no better than the fools' zanies" (1.5.89).[17] Unlike Jaques, the melancholic killjoy, Malvolio bitterly resents folly; unlike Arden, Illyria is a world where "the whirligig of time brings in his revenges" (5.1.376–77). Massively fortified against folly, Malvolio is willy-nilly implicated, uncomfortably linked with the fool in *Twelfth Night*. When Feste's catechism mocks her foolishly protracted mourning, Olivia asks her reliable steward what he thinks of "this fool" (1.5.73). Malvolio's characteristically pompous put-down sounds very like Feste: "Infirmity, that decays the wise, doth ever make the better fool" (1.5.76–77). Immediately sensing affinity with his adversary, Feste retorts in kind: "God send you, sir, a speedy infirmity, for the better increasing your folly!" (1.5.78–79).

Malvolio is exasperated to be drawn even marginally into foolishness, for he regards himself as a keen monitor and vigilant censor. Like Olivia distinguishing among various types of fools, Malvolio has apparently listened carefully to their exchanges. He continues to mind Feste closely but pronounces judgments ineffectively. Olivia explains why: "O, you are sick of self-love, Malvolio, and taste with a distemper'd appetite" (1.5.90–91). Malvolio lacks Feste's license and leverage, as Olivia makes clear when she denies Malvolio the prerogative of "an allow'd fool" (1.5.94) to rail without slander and encourages her household jester. Against his will, Malvolio participates in the folly in Illyria, and even prompts Olivia to "speak'st well of fools!" (1.5.98).

Oddly, as if competing with a sibling on his own ground, Malvolio increasingly simulates "an allow'd fool," quibbling, playing, and discoursing wittily. In jester's language reminiscent of Touchstone or Feste, Malvolio describes Cesario: "Not yet old enough for a man, nor young enough for a boy; as a squash is before 'tis a peascod, or a codling when 'tis almost an apple. 'Tis with him in standing water, between boy and man. He is very well-favour'd and he speaks very shrewishly. One would think his mother's milk were scarce out of him" (1.5.156–62). An ass but no idiot, Malvolio senses Cesario's in-between state, delicately positioned on the threshold. Indeed perceptive, Malvolio is no worse than smugly off-putting here, though he soon crosses another threshold to become downright nettlesome. Dispatched by Olivia to "return" the ring, he tosses it to make poor Cesario stoop. Viola's response, a charming soliloquy, underscores Malvolio's churlishness. With obnoxious characters, Malvolio manages to be even more antipathetic. He interrupts the nocturnal revels of Toby and company with sublimely tone-deaf indignation: "My masters, are you mad? Or what are you? Have you no wit, manners, nor honesty, but to gabble like tinkers at this time of night? Do ye make an alehouse of my lady's house, that ye squeak out your coziers' catches without any mitigation or remorse of voice? Is there no respect of place, persons, nor time in you?" (2.3.86–92).

Gratuitously, Malvolio pontificates in patronizing and pretentious diction ("without any mitigation or remorse of voice," whatever that means). Incapable of laughter or delight, a classic *agelast*, Malvolio takes exception to anyone else's delight. Here he irreparably crosses a line. Never mind that he would squelch the boisterous revelers. Worse, he jeopardizes the fun promised to the audience by the play's title, *Twelfth Night; or, What You Will*. Discrediting make-believe and suppressing pleasure, Malvolio commits an affront the play will not abide.[18] Hence we feel validated as well as amused by Toby's indignant rejoinder, "Sneck up!" (2.3.94). Toby's rude response provokes Malvolio to a grave error, exceeding his authority to restore order. Going beyond Olivia's express intentions, Malvolio delivers an ultimatum: unless Toby separates himself from his "misdemeanors" (2.3.98), he will be ejected. For good measure, Malvolio berates Maria's (quite minor) contribution to "this uncivil rule" (2.3.123), thus precipitating Maria's revenge, to "gull him into a ayword" (2.3.134–35).[19]

Only such a drolly self-deluded fool could be deceived. The gull is self-swindled, hoist on his own petard. No wonder that duping Malvolio is "sport royal" (2.3.172), which engages so many (otherwise aimless) characters and delights audiences, at least for a while. Hence, or *thus*, Malvolio's goose is cooked. He becomes Shakespeare's "most notorious geck and gull" (5.1.343), at least until Othello.[20] Maria insists, compellingly, that Malvolio deserves comeuppance. Is he not "a time-pleaser, an affection'd ass, that cons state without book... the best persuaded of himself, so cramm'd (as he thinks) with excellencies, that it is his grounds of faith that all that look on him love him; and on that vice in him will my revenge find notable cause to work" (2.3.148–53)? Malvolio surely makes a fat target. In soliloquy, he fantasizes about status or perceived power. The height of his bliss is not love, not the favors of a beautiful young woman, but "to be Count Malvolio!" (2.5.35). His fantasy lavishly depicts his ascension, "sitting in my state" (2.5.45), with only oblique reference to sex.[21] Lo, a letter! Deciphering (as he thinks) Olivia's hand, Malvolio happily spies, "These be her very c's, her u's, and her t's, and thus makes she her great P's" (2.5.86–88). If the actor properly (but improperly) delivers "and her t's" as N her T's, the bawdy joke is inescapable. To make sure no one misses it, Andrew reiterates the line and asks, "Why that?" (2.5.89).

While Toby sputters that such ridiculous aspirations beyond his station are "overweening" (2.5.29), Malvolio envisions his apogee, patronizing his tormenters, with bombastic elaboration: "And after a demure travel of regard—telling them I know my place as I would they should do theirs" (2.5.53–54). Most delicious is the prospect of subjecting his "kinsman" Toby: "I extend my hand to him thus, quenching my familiar smile with an austere regard of control" (2.5.65–66) and gravely ordering him to amend his drunkenness. Malvolio's unrestrained grandiosity certainly makes him fair game and ripe for derision.[22] Maria's forged letter, archly stylish nonsense, is a Rorschach test exposing the depths of Malvolio's egocentricity and self-love. He strains mightily to bend the evidence, to translate M. O. A. I. into something meaningful and hopeful: "And yet, to crush this a little, it would bow to me, for every one of these letters are in my name" (2.5.140–41).[23] The inspiring exhortations, to "put thyself into the trick of singularity" (2.5.151–52), seal Malvolio's fate. Jubilantly he responds, "I will be proud, I will read politic authors, I will baffle Sir Toby, I will wash off gross acquaintance" (2.5.161–63). A kind of innocence irradiates Malvolio's joy. What loser has not dreamed that the last will be first? Let him without foolish fantasies cast the first stone!

The spirit of carnival reaches its apex when Malvolio is gulled into playing the fool. The basher of revels becomes the clown, cross-gartered, yellow-stockinged, and smiling goofily. Mavolio becomes what he most disdained.[24] Obediently appearing in jester's garb and behaving bizarrely "with this ridiculous boldness" (3.4.37), Malvolio astonishes Olivia, who sees the mote in his eye but not the beam in her own: "Why, this is very midsummer madness" (3.4.56). To Malvolio, it all makes perfect sense: "Why, every thing adheres together, that no dram of a scruple, no scruple of a scruple, no obstacle . . . Nothing that can be can come between me and the full prospect of my hopes" (3.4.78–82). If only!

It is fitting that someone so rigidly officious and ludicrously vain awakens the imp of irony. The bane of foolery is fooled by a "device" that exploits his self-delusions and renders comic justice. As the jest continues, however, it curdles and sours. The "geck and gull" becomes a scapegoat suffering disproportionately for his transgressions. It is an unsettling exhibition and unabashedly so. *Twelfth Night* tests the boundaries of fooling, dramatizes its careless excesses, and exposes our misguided acquiescence. First we laugh, then we chuckle nervously until we wince.

Malvolio's foolish pride and vain pretensions are treated, as Toby says, "for our pleasure and his penance" (3.4.137–38). In the harrowing scene in which Feste plays "Sir Topas the curate" and interrogates the incarcerated "lunatic" (4.2.22), Malvolio pathetically implores, "Fool, there was never man so notoriously abus'd; I am as well in my wits, fool, as thou art" (4.2.87–88). Feste replies sagely but heartlessly, "Then you are mad indeed, if you be no better in your wits than a fool" (4.2.89–90).[25] Surely "as well in my wits as any man in Illyria" (4.2.106–7), Malvolio's plain language rings true: "Sir Topas, never was man thus wrong'd. Good Sir Topas, do not think I am mad; they have laid me here in hideous darkness" (4.2.28–30).

Even the obtuse ringleader Toby grudgingly acknowledges that the joke has spoiled: "I would we were well rid of this knavery" (4.2.67–68). Toby reiterates the word used earlier to praise Feste's ability to deceive: "The knave counterfeits well; a good knave" (4.2.19). The slippage typifies the protean nature of "folly"—that term variously attached to crimes or sins, mindlessness or carelessness, amusements or entertainments. The fooling in *Twelfth Night* begins as good knavery and naughty fun and turns cruel and nasty. The treatment of Malvolio is difficult to ignore amid the supposedly festive denouement.

It's worth remembering that until 1623, the play was performed under the title *Malvolio*. Great thing of us forgot! Amid the nuptial felicities, Olivia suddenly recalls her afflicted steward, whose letter Feste has prudently or unkindly withheld. Though Feste continues to mock Malvolio, his letter— read in full—is dignified and compelling. The celebrations are interrupted by his appearance, announcing that he has been done "notorious wrong" and entreating Olivia, "Tell me, in the modesty of honor, / Why you have given me such clear lights of favor?" A fair question: "Why have you suffer'd me to be imprison'd, / Kept in a dark house, visited by the priest, / And made the most notorious geck and gull, / That e'er invention play'd on? Tell me why!" (5.1.335–44). The ordinarily imperceptive and rarely empathetic Orsino notes, "This savors not much of distraction" (5.1.314).

Olivia responds compassionately, speaking for everyone except the most adamantly hard-hearted jesters: "Alas, poor fool, how have they baffled thee!" (5.1.369). Olivia now sees him as a "poor fool," someone obviously objectionable but "notoriously abus'd" (5.1.379). Like Lear referring to the dead Cordelia as his "poor fool" (*Lr* 5.3.306), Olivia employs the term *fool* as endearment and says *thee* instead of *you*, a suggestion that "her insight into her own folly has prompted a feeling of empathy with the plight of the 'other.'"[26] What Fabian lamely condones as "sportful malice" (5.1.365) Feste more candidly calls the pranksters' "revenges" (5.1.377). Not even Malvolio's coldly furious vow—"I'll be reveng'd on the whole pack of you" (5.1.378)—shakes Olivia's regret or Orsino's resolve to "pursue him, and entreat him to a peace" (5.1.380), however futile. That Malvolio is not incorporated into the charmed circle underscores the partial and only partially satisfying closure. Malvolio's exit line would cast a pall over any party; it certainly sticks in one's craw. Whatever laughter we have enjoyed at his expense has long since faded or echoes to haunt us. Countervailing forces jeopardize the merrymaking and exhaust the laughter. Shakespeare's most notorious geck and gull, Olivia's poor fool, remains a victim of follies run amok.

Thersites's Curses

> What is the whole subject matter of that revered poem the Iliad but "the broils of foolish kings and the foolish populace"?
>
> —Erasmus (118)

Praise of Folly mentions an obscure Homeric character named Thersites as well as the well-known goddess Até. Primed by Moria, Shakespeare must have read George Chapman's 1598 translation, *Seven Books of the Iliades*, with keen interest in the divine "ruinous Folly" and in Thersites, a common Greek soldier. Thersites witnesses Agamemnon's fatal quarrel with Achilles. Much later, in book 19, the Greek king naturally blames Até for his folly or delusion. To Thersites, Agamemnon's rhetorical question is highly provocative. Brazenly, Thersites excoriates Agamemnon's follies and suffers the consequences of telling truth to power. Thersites is a scourge of folly and a scapegoat. Pathetic and ridiculous, ugly and reviled, Thersites is just the sort of strange motley figure to seize Shakespeare's imagination:

> A man of tongue whose ravenlike voice a tuneles jarring kept,
> Who in his ranke minde coppy had of unregarded wordes
> That rashly and beyond al rule usde to oppugne the Lords,
> But what soever came from him was laught at mightile.
> The filthiest Greek that came to Troy, he had a goggle eye;
> Starke-lame he was of eyther foote; his shoulders were contract

Into his brest and crookt withall; his head was sharpe compact
And here and there it had a hayre.[27]

Even Erasmus is disgusted by this puzzling grotesque: "Homer satisfied
his hatred of Thersites by composing a devastating poetical sketch of him."[28]
Astonishingly, this hideous figure publicly "upbraids" Agamemnon, insults
his comrades, denounces the war, and urges withdrawal. Who *is* this "man
of tongue"? Not even Homer seems to know. He is the single character in the
Iliad who delivers an extended speech without being identified by rank, pat-
ronymic, and place of origin. What information we get is odd: that Thersites
is the ugliest man at Troy, uniquely repulsive among his glowing, glowering
peers. Given that only one other Iliadic figure is individuated by appearance[29] and hardly any are rendered physically, the elaborate depiction of
an apparently minor, fleeting figure is striking. His looks are emblematic,
for Thersites harbors "much anger and disease" against the leaders, and the
Greeks hold him "in vehement hate / And high disdaine."

Despite his remarkable disqualifications and at a particularly inoppor-
tune moment, reviled Thersites seizes the stage and delivers a considerable
speech, some sixteen lines, to the entire assembly. He asks Agamemnon what
he complains about and why he covets more booty and plunder, won by the
troops and awarded to the general. Could he really want still more Trojan
captives for ransom? Or does the greedy Agamemnon want another "wench
fild with her sweets of youth, / Which thou maist love and private keep for
thy insaciate tooth?" After denouncing his king and general and violating all
principles of rhetoric, Thersites spurts venom upon his audience:

O mindes most impotent!
Not Achives but Achaian gyrles, come, fall aborde and home!
Let him concoct his pray alone, alone Troy overcome.

Unruly, impertinent, and insolent, Thersites hits the bull's-eye. Agamemnon
proclaims the filthy railing wretch "hath with contumely wrongd a better
man than hee— / Achilles, from whose armes, in spight that all the world
might see, / He tooke a prise wun with his sword." If Achilles weren't so
effeminate, Agamemnon's foolishness would have proved his "last injurious
deede." Thersites's speech provokes an immediate reaction from no less a
figure than "wise Ulysses," who repudiates, threatens, and strikes "prophane" Thersites. The hero's intervention, humiliating Thersites, amuses
the soldiers and quells the incipient mutiny. So much, it would seem, for
"prating Thersites" and his "barbarous tauntes": "A baser wretch came not
to Troy to take the Grecians' part."

Despite the efforts of Ulysses to discredit Thersites as a jester, "vaine foole," and railing madman, the soldier compels our attention. His trenchant mockery challenges the heroic ideal. No wonder Ulysses responds quickly and decisively to suppress it. Thersites raises substantive issues and asks questions that are tellingly ignored by Ulysses and essentially unanswerable. Even the indignant Ulysses recognizes that Thersites "canst raile so cunninglie." Thersites ventilates issues Ulysses would rather not contemplate and cannot abide. The public quarrel between Agamemnon and Achilles must have astounded and dismayed the Greek host. The king's outrageous presumption, eventually acknowledged by Agamemnon himself as madness (*até*), collided with the implacable, preposterous pride of the hero. Thersites's tirade, however impolitic and intemperate, is credible. In several ways, Thersites's diatribe recalls the (more dignified) disquisition of the affronted Achilles; he almost seems to speak on behalf of the "dishonoured" Achilles. Of course, Thersites only momentarily pretends to laud Achilles; mordantly sarcastic in his mock-praise, he locates (one might say) the Achilles heel of each noble antagonist. Thersites characterizes and evaluates the quarrel sharply. Cunningly, he recognizes the seriousness of the king's transgression, and he intuits how close Agamemnon was to being killed by the outraged Achilles.

Thersites is a cawing chorus delivering a crippling critique: such ravaging mockery is seditious, bad for morale, and potentially disastrous. Thersites scorches the earth and annihilates the Greek army, "commanded by General Ineptitude, backed by Major Disaster, Corporal Punishment, and Private Interest."[30] Again the comparison between Thersites and Achilles is telling: both Greeks are publicly humiliated. Thersites strikes a nerve and threatens the power structure enough to provoke instant reprisals. Ulysses may be humorless, but he can't afford to suffer fools gladly. In the inauspicious person of Thersites is the vital voice of dissent and the antithesis of the heroic ideal. It makes good Greek sense that their scourge is scourged with Agamemnon's scepter and cast out. Though myriad-minded Homer lets us see that, he also subtly distinguishes the perspective Ulysses denigrates. And motley Shakespeare perceives the inestimable value of such a potent scourge—far more clearly than most critics and commentators of *The Iliad*, who, like the Greek troops, applaud the swift judgment of Ulysses visited upon this bilious slanderer.[31] In *The Iliad*, Shakespeare could appreciate the dialogic and polyphonic techniques that we call "Shakespearean." The Thersites sequence is a midnight foray from the epic fields of glory to the shifting terrain of satiric humor, neither a smooth passage nor a comfortable place to stand but a vantage point Homer insists we visit.

The humiliation of Thersites also anticipates Shakespearean comedy of abjection in *Twelfth Night*, in *All's Well That Ends Well*, and (as we will see) in *Othello*. Like Parolles and Malvolio, Thersites is enabled and disabled. Primarily, though, Homer's Thersites is a lightning bolt, a flash of illumination, flaring, ephemeral, and potentially destructive. Shakespeare envisions characters who might be both lightning bolt and lightning rod, both source and object of mockery. It is here that Shakespeare plants his flag and builds his Troy, the site of a daringly original tragic farce. Within four years of *Chapman's Homer*, Shakespeare's *Troilus and Cressida* was in production.

Homer's Thersites—frankly repellant yet insidious and insinuating, weirdly charismatic, and strangely compelling—inspires the much more prominent Thersites in *Troilus and Cressida*.[32] Played by the estimable Robert Armin, Shakespeare's Thersites is a licensed fool or "a privileg'd man" (2.3.57) and an implacable foe of folly. In his first appearance, Thersites tells Ajax, "Thou art proclaim'd fool, I think" (2.1.25). It is as if Thersites were the playwright sounding his theme and summonsing all the prodigious fools to the pageant of folly; spot on cue, Agamemnon enters. Incessantly railing, proclaiming everyone fool, Thersites scorns the "valiant ignorance" (3.3.312) of Achilles, dubs Diomede "a false-hearted rogue" (5.1.88), mocks Menelaus and Paris as "the cuckold and the cuckold-maker" (5.7.9), and depicts Ajax as a preening peacock: "If Hector break not his neck i' th'combat he'll break't himself in vainglory" (3.3.258–59).

One by one, the heroes fall beneath his withering invective. No folly is spared; no ideal—not love or valor, romance or nobility—survives his onslaught. Like a surgeon dissecting a diseased organ, Thersites exposes the soft flanks of Homer's epic figures, from larger-than-life heroes to stupid clods, besotted lechers, corrupt authorities, and vile brutes. Besides formulating pithy insults, Thersites makes resounding generalizations: "Here is such patchery, such juggling and such knavery! All the argument is a whore and a cuckold" (2.3.71–73). In these astringent, embittered tirades, he sounds like Hamlet without the prince's flashes of joy or glory.

To Thersites, the Trojan War is a panorama of depravity. Whatever comes into his ken, Thersites instantly reduces; everything is ground to powder: "I'll see some issue of my spiteful execrations" (2.3.6–7). This iota of candid self-knowledge is intriguing: he knows he is good for nothing but railing. For this reason, Thersites is denied any ultimate opportunity to carry on and hold forth; Pandar, not Thersites, delivers the final speech. Thersites has been ignominiously dispatched, forced to proclaim not the folly of his betters but his own bastardy and cowardice. He disappears, like Lear's Fool unnoticed and unregretted. This is rough justice, Aristotle might say, for

Thersites is (in Aristotelian terms) a boor, who "contributes nothing, and takes offence at everything."[33]

How reliable, how creditable, is his perspective? As in *The Iliad*, a "plague of opinion" obscures the origins, status, and standing of this scathing, scurrilous cynic. Nestor insultingly calls him a "slave" (1.3.193), though Thersites is bound to no man. Detached and disinterested, he is a Greek serving "voluntary" (2.1.94); his identity and status appear unclear even to his comrades. Ulysses thinks Thersites is or was Ajax's "fool" (2.3.91), now attached loosely to Achilles. Evidently Thersites offends everybody. No Shakespearean character—not Iago, Edmund, or Richard III—is more uniformly maligned. To many viewers and readers, as well as to the objects of his vituperation, Thersites is reprehensible and disgusting. Thersites is regularly berated as salacious, vicious, pitiless, prurient, venomous, and contemptible: a railing detractor or vile slanderer, "beyond faith, beyond hope, beyond the charity of the imagination, and beneath humanity."[34]

Resented and roundly condemned, Thersites is also cogent and enabled. A dynamic figure, virtually a one-man chorus, Shakespeare's Thersites comments pertinently and frequently in direct addresses to the audience. Who can ignore his pungent opinion that Agamemnon "has not so much brain as earwax" (5.1.52–53)? He is irresistibly outrageous, as when he presumes equality with Priam's illegitimate son—a fellow bastard!—and impudently professes indignation at being mistaken for King Agamemnon: "A plague of opinion!" (3.3.264). With ruthless zeal, reveling in the ubiquity of fools, Thersites conducts a probing anatomy of folly.

Thersites sees a world upside-down with knaves and fools on top. He thus parodies the hierarchies constructed by Troilus, vainly seeking "rule in unity" (5.2.141); figured by Agamemnon, orating about providence; and elaborated by Ulysses, expounding upon "degree" (1.3.86). Thersites's chain of fools (2.3.52–68) imitates and sabotages such specious affirmations of order. Reflected and reversed in the fool's mirror, the degree of folly is the folly of degree. To Thersites, fools are everywhere and life is a "fool's play" (5.3.42), as tragic Troilus eventually realizes. Onstage strut and fret a host of asinine characters: a silly, deluded youth who loves a frivolous, calculating coquette; a lecherous, voyeuristic pander; pompous elders; benighted leaders; buffoonish and bragging warriors; "fools on both sides" (1.1.90). Thersites echoes Erasmus's Moria: "But after all, what is the whole subject matter of that revered poem the Iliad but 'the broils of foolish kings and the foolish populace?'" (118).

Hence, we had best heed Thersites. Unlike the pariah and scapegoat in *The Iliad*, Shakespeare's Thersites, however despised, commands grudging respect from his betters. Agamemnon pointedly evokes the lowly figure utterly ignored by Homer's Agamemnon: "When rank Thersites opes his mastic jaws, / We shall hear music, wit, and oracle" (1.3.73–74). Agamemnon's sarcasm recognizes qualities of wise fools: clever banter, germane observations. For these attributes, the Greeks suffer fools gladly! When Achilles calls for Thersites to serve as "my ambassador" (3.3.266) to the obstreperous Ajax, he must know that jeering and not diplomacy is the fool's forte. Like the overzealous clowns Hamlet describes and also like rambunctious Mercutio, Thersites is too busy by half. But he upstages everyone and leaves Achilles in the shade. Evidently appreciated if not esteemed, his views are often reinforced by other characters. In his "lost in the labyrinth" speech (2.3.1–22), Thersites reiterates Ulysses's skeptical remarks about Troy, Achilles, and Ajax and anticipates the responses of Pandarus. Troilus in his "madness of discourse" speech (5.2.142–60) justifies Thersites's pessimism.[35] His mantras—"war and lechery confound all!" (2.3.75) and "all the argument is a whore, and a cuckold" (2.3.72–73)—resonate here. Shakespeare endows Thersites, empowering him to frame and summarize several scenes and to end two successive scenes in act 5. His persistence and volubility make him redoubtable. Ultimately Thersites is left standing, the resilient fool surviving disastrous follies. The final hectic scene of chaos and despair reflects Thersites's vision, painful and awful as it is. His objectionable attitudes and repugnant style appear to be validated despite considerable resistance.[36]

If to heed Thersites is crucial, to regard him uncritically is foolish. The play, I believe, tempts us to either overestimate or discount Thersites by attributing to him a particularly foolish kind of wisdom and authority. Frequently in error, he is never in doubt; invariably memorable, he is not always relevant. His slings and arrows may be bull's-eyes or in the range or wide of the mark. *Troilus and Cressida* certainly dramatizes what Thersites calls the "common curse of mankind, folly" (2.3.27–28). But the play also deploys folly shrewdly, selectively justifying the fool's views. Neither simply nor wholly a "fool's play," *Troilus and Cressida* is more capacious and complicated than Thersites perceives; much is undreamt of in his philosophy. *Troilus and Cressida* is neither tragedy nor comedy but more like "tragic farce," as Ionesco subtitles his play *The Chairs*. Shakespeare's alternations of prose and verse, high and low, inflation and deflation convey the play's mixed mode, to which Thersites contributes substantially but only to a degree. Partial and hyperbolic like Jaques, he never changes his mind or his tune, never revises or qualifies any utterance. Thersites is overly determined to be unsurprised. He uniformly and unceasingly sees folly because he brings it as much as perceives it. To the cynical, everything is suspicious.

I disagree that Thersites remains "beyond the charity of the imagination, and beneath humanity." He is a particularly fertile and provocative fool who threatens values we ardently wish to maintain: he is "false to human nature as *we hope we may* finally describe it" (my emphasis).[37] More pertinent, I believe, is whether Thersites belies human nature as Shakespeare renders it in *Troilus and Cressida*. Like Erasmus's Moria, Thersites is a canny critic of folly; like Erasmus, Shakespeare provides more complex ways of comprehending folly than any single character recognizes. To see everything as folly and to exempt oneself are traditional forms of folly Thersites vividly demonstrates.

Holding up his mirror to the world, he sees only himself. Projecting onto everyone, his vision is subjective and self-reflecting, as when he asks nastily of Troilus, "Will 'a swagger himself out on's own eyes?" (5.2.136). At such moments, we do well to remember another question posed by Troilus: "What's aught but as 'tis valued?" (2.2.52). He gives apt, partly correct, but limited or distorted pictures because he cannot imagine possibilities beyond his scope. Like all fools, Thersites is full of words, incessantly talking, always with utter assurance and confident bravado: "Nothing but lechery! all incontinent varlots!" (5.1.97–98). Thus he defines Diomed's motives, of which he knows nothing. He is right to see Achilles and Patroclus as "too much blood and too little brain" (5.1.48).

But Thersites sees through a glass darkly, never face to face. Like so many fools we have considered, he has no conception of the feelings, interiority, or otherness, not of Ajax or Achilles or of anyone. It is Thersites, not Shakespeare, who reduces Helen and Cressida to trollops. His antipathy to women and sex is more pathological than privileged. With gleeful malice and dubious accuracy, he outs Achilles.[38] Like Malvolio, Thersites resents festivity, decries holiday; part of his own foolishness is stubborn hostility to pleasure, play, and sex. (On the stage, his denunciations may be more obviously hyperbolic and amusing than on the page.) To Thersites, Troilus is a "scurvy doting foolish young knave" (5.4.3–4). Troilus is love's fool— beyond which Thersites cannot know and does not care. When a pickpocket looks at a saint, he sees a pocket; so Thersites easily pockets Cressida: "She's noted" (5.2.11). Similarly, Helen is not simply a "whore." Troilus regards her very differently, as a "spur to valiant and magnanimous deeds" (2.2.200). Belying Thersites's caustic mockery, Paris and Helen appear to be true lovers and compelling characters.

The world Thersites envisions is *always* repulsive, fatally diseased, and hopelessly corrupt. He judges his comrades as harshly as his adversaries because he has no connections to the human community. His ugliness, it was believed, reflects his moral monstrosity. Brower argues that Thersites, "as diseased as his victims, will not do as 'the heav'n-directed' voice of satire" like Pope or Juvenal.[39] Whereas Thersites remains doggedly monologic,

Figure 5.2 Albrecht Durer, Fool and Death, woodcut engraving originally published in Sebastian Brandt's *The Ship of Fools*.

Troilus and Cressida is wildly polyphonic. Thersites is one of many powerful, competing voices, none triumphing or obliterating others. In this disturbing play, the multiplicity of incompatible viewpoints is striking even by Shakespearean standards; every perspective is subjected to harsh scrutiny and substantially undermined. *Troilus and Cressida* anatomizes folly clinically and thoroughly. Prismatic and kaleidoscopic, it enables many characters to speak persuasively, including Thersites, whose contentions are foolishly compelling, particularly objectionable, and foolishly inadequate. When the worlds of Shakespearean theater become more like Thersites's world, we enter tragedies. To the tragic motley of *Hamlet*, *King Lear*, and *Othello* we now turn.

CHAPTER 6

There the Antic Sits

How often motley Shakespeare runs with the hares and hunts with the hounds! Sir Philip Sidney's *Defense of Poesy* (1595) deplores "mongrel" plays that "thrust in the clown by head and shoulders to play a part in majestical matters, with neither decency nor discretion."[1] Though the 1623 Folio crisply distinguishes comedy, tragedy, and history, Shakespeare's unruly hybrids (flagrantly violating neoclassical decorum) are more like Polonius's Foolio: "tragical-comical-historical-pastoral...or poem unlimited" (*Ham.* 2.2.398–400). Barriers between genres appear as permeable as the wall separating Pyramus and Thisby. Shakespeare's theater accommodates all manner of "strange bedfellows" (*Tmp.* 2.2.40) and mixes royalty and revelry, high tragedy and low farce. Mingling kings and clowns produces a kind of tragic motley and constitutes another chapter in Shakespeare's anatomy of folly. Most remarkable are the numerous affinities between Shakespeare's tragic heroes and fools. Romeo is "fortune's fool" (3.1.136); Hamlet plays the fool; Lear abides and cherishes his jester; Othello is gulled and grotesque. In Shakespearean tragedy, fooling matters seriously and fools take center stage.

Like Richard II, these tragic figures discover where the antic sits and see themselves "monarchizing" on a great stage of fools. To his astonishment and dismay, King Richard learns that "within the hollow crown / That rounds the mortal temples of a king / Keeps Death his court, and there the antic sits, / Scoffing his state and grinning at his pomp" (*R2* 3.2.160–63). Richard envisions the monarch's sacred state upstaged by "the antic" Death. Though the grotesque mocker is *within*, he is distinct, a usurper rather than a second self: "Allowing him a breath, a little scene, / To monarchize, be fear'd, and kill with looks, / Infusing him with self and vain conceit." Richard recognizes that fool's dreadful sovereign power, "As if this flesh which walls about our life, / Were brass impregnable; and humor'd thus, / Comes at the last and with a little pin / Bores through his castle wall, and farewell king!" (3.2.164–70). Richard well knows that "to monarchize" is to play a role. Hearing the jester's jibe that monarchs are mortal and that only a fool would think otherwise, he asks, "How can you say to me I am a king?" (3.2.177). Though he discerns the antic "within the hollow crown," Richard cannot yet identify king and clown. Nor does Richard "humour'd thus" attain the foolosophy divined, as we shall see, by Hamlet or Lear. In the fool's mirror, the Clown Prince of Denmark and the Crazed King on the Heath glean "the thing itself" (*Lr* 3.4.106), "this thing of darkness I / Acknowledge mine" (*Tmp.* 5.1.275–76).

Fortune's Fool

Many-minded Shakespeare especially loves the "mongrel tragic-comedy" Sidney derogates. *A Midsummer Night's Dream* contains an incipient tragedy and *The Tragedy of Romeo and Juliet* a truncated romantic comedy. Tragic protagonists like Romeo are conspicuously foolish. Like the young lovers who amuse Puck, Romeo is a fool for love—but he doesn't need any love-juice to play the part. Before encountering Juliet, he is melancholy and extravagant, recycling onerous oxymorons and hackneyed images: "Alas that love, whose view is muffled still, / Should, without eyes, see pathways to his will! /...O any thing, of nothing first create! / O heavy lightness, serious vanity, / Misshapen chaos of well-seeming forms, / Feather of lead, bright smoke, cold fire, sick health," and so on (1.1.171–80). Romeo utters hand-me-down Petrarch because his feelings are fabricated. In love with love, Romeo hardly mentions Rosaline; his beloved remains a phantom. Probably Romeo would be disappointed if she, dear she, acquiesced! He would rather moon or make "himself an artificial night" (1.1.140). Solely interested in himself ("O me!"), he is more foolish than interesting, self-dramatizing without being self-aware. Though he thinks he feels profoundly, he lacks interiority, introspection, or complexity. When Romeo's intervention between Tybalt and Mercutio backfires disastrously and he is reproached by the dying Mercutio, Romeo can only mumble feebly, "I thought all for the best" (3.1.104). Inarticulate and bewildered, Romeo reverts to Mercutio-like machismo, bashing love as unmanly: "O sweet Juliet, / Thy beauty hath made me effeminate" (3.1.113–14). After killing Tybalt, Romeo defines himself forlornly: "O, I am fortune's fool!" (3.1.136). Fleeing to refuge, Romeo is self-pitying and hysterical, a "fond mad man" (3.3.52) as the friar says. Prostrate and bawling "like a mishaved [misbehaved] and sullen wench"

(3.3.143), Romeo tries to kill himself. Though Romeo revives, matures, and attains a measure of tragic dignity, he remains indeed "fortune's fool." Romeo's uneven and incomplete development is the work of an apprentice tragedian content to rely on accident, coincidence, bad luck, and ill timing. Later tragic heroes such as Othello and Hamlet certainly display much more depth and stature than "young Romeo." But they are also more profoundly foolish—not merely flawed or all-too-human, nor fooled in the general sense of misperception or self-delusion.

Antic Disposition

In a court without a jester, Hamlet leaps into the breach: no jester performs more flamboyantly or charismatically than the Clown Prince of Denmark. Cracking wise and witty, heedless of protocol, Hamlet mocks authority and wreaks havoc; he deliberately stages several fool scenes. Hamlet is at once a scourge mercilessly excoriating fools and a deft trickster cozening the court and baffling everybody. Because he contemplates the stratagems of fooling—tergiversation, illusion, acting, mirth making, and dissembling—Hamlet is a shrewd connoisseur of folly as well as a sly practitioner of foolery. To everyone at Elsinore, of course, he seems crazy.[2] But why does Hamlet maintain an "antic disposition" (1.5.172) when he no longer needs protective camouflage? With breathtaking bravado worthy of Falstaff, Hamlet seesaws between divinity and degradation, the numinous and the ludicrous. Like a god "kissing carrion" (2.1.182), to invoke his own enigmatic image, Hamlet bridges the sublime and the ridiculous. However confounding his oscillations between mirth and metaphysics, circus and seminar, Hamlet's gaudy jumble is "pregnant sometimes," as even Polonius gleans: "Though this be madness, yet there is method in 't" (2.2.205–6). Fooling and folly in all their many guises are so vital to Hamlet that his tragic motley epitomizes the significance, variety, and complexity of Shakespearean foolosophy.

Hamlet talks like a jester whether or not he is playing the fool. He can hardly speak without equivocation.[3] Fooling by definition is ironic—not only in the binary sense of saying one thing and meaning another but also in the capacious sense of conflating two (or more) simultaneous references. Foolish equivocation is verbal fission and fusion, what a biologist might see as mitosis and meiosis. For Hamlet, "quips" and "quiddities" (*1H4* 1.2.45) are second nature. Like Feste, that corrupter of words, Hamlet relentlessly fractures and disperses meanings. He is a word-juggler *nonpareil*, from his very first line, a complicated pun that implies more than disdain for his uncle Claudius: "A little more than kin, and less than kind" (1.2.65). To this "pregnant" wordplay we will have reason to return.

As in a jester's mirror, Hamlet's discourse highlights doubles, reflections, and reiterations.[4] If puns and quibbles are Hamlet's forte, equivocation is his default mode. Excited or under stress, Hamlet compounds his repetitions: he tells the king that the dead Polonius is at supper, "Not where he eats but where 'a is eaten." (4.3.17–19). Then he addresses Claudius as "my mother" because "father and mother is man and wife, man and wife is one flesh" (4.3.51–52). Much of Hamlet's jesting is war by other means, a scorched-earth strategy: fools are everywhere and his mission is to scourge them. Hamlet humiliates Polonius mercilessly at every opportunity. He tells Ophelia that her father should "play the fool nowhere but in 's own house" (3.1.132). Like the scourges discussed in the previous chapter—Thersites, Mercutio, and Jaques, all preternaturally alert to folly and keen to entrap unwitting adversaries—Hamlet stages tiny fool's plays, such as *The Clown Prince and Foolonius*:

> *FOOLONIUS*: My lord, the Queen would speak with you, and presently.
> *SHAMLET*: Do you see yonder cloud that's almost in shape of a camel?
> *FOOLONIUS*: By th' mass and 'tis, like a camel indeed.
> *SHAMLET*: Methinks it is like a weasel.
> *FOOLONIUS*: It is back'd like a weasel
> *SHAMLET*: Or like a whale.
> *FOOLONIUS*: Very like a whale.
>
> (3.2.375–82)

Hamlet's antics would grace Beckett's *Waiting for Godot* or Stoppard's *Rosencrantz and Guildenstern Are Dead*.[5] With a jester's zest, he exploits ambiguities and changes the subject, figured and refigured like that protean cloud. Hamlet's bamboozling of Polonius recalls Feste's catechism of Olivia or Jaques's rendition of "*Ducdame.*" The difference is that Hamlet's flapdoodle viciously lashes folly. He can be ferocious when flailing Ophelia or base when flaunting "country matters." Though he says he is "your only jigmaker" (3.2.116, 3.2.125)—that is, your only song-and-dance man—such joking is more appalling than amusing.

The hero's righteous wrath erupts in every encounter with Polonius. Accosted while reading, Hamlet gleefully, maliciously catalogs the infirmities of old men: "For if the sun breed maggots in a dead dog," Hamlet intones, "being a good kissing carrion." To mock Polonius's paternal authority, Hamlet feigns solicitude: "Have you a daughter?" he asks and continues sanctimoniously, "Let her not walk i' th' sun. Conception [understanding] is a blessing, but as your daughter may conceive, friend, look to't"

(2.2.181–86). The homonym, sun/son, echoes Hamlet's first quibble with Claudius and bolsters the implicit associations among this son and two false fathers whom he loathes. Prone to pontifical judgments, Hamlet is initially self-deceived and somewhat deluded. He flaunts his own singularity, exceptional honesty, and implicit authenticity: "Seems madam? nay, it is. I know not 'seems'" (1.2.76). Not for Hamlet are the mere "shapes of grief," the "actions that a man might play" (1.2.82–84). He sees himself as the single wise man in a world of fools, the one who knows, or thinks he knows, who's who and what's what. No less than Polonius he is sure and certain, the quality in Polonius he deplores and mocks. Hamlet learns better, beginning when he confronts the ghost.[6] Though unsure how to address that highly "questionable shape" (1.4.43)—Hamlet, King, Father, Royal Dane?—the prince nevertheless presumes that the shape, whatever it is, has access to truth: "O, answer me!... tell why... What may this mean?... Say why is this? wherefore? What should we do?" (1.4.44–57). But Hamlet's desperate questions go unanswered; instead, the shape undermines the misguided certainty of the man who knows not seems.[7] Construing that "questionable shape" more skeptically and mindful of "such ambiguous giving out" (1.5.178), Hamlet speculates that the devil "hath power / T' assume a pleasing shape" (2.2.599–600). Hamlet acknowledges the deceivable nature of shapes.[8] After the shock of the ghost's visitation, for the first time, Hamlet associates himself with folly: "We fools of nature" (1.4.54), he says, cannot be so sure of anything. Thus the hero begins his tortured, wayward course toward foolosophical enlightenment.

Professional fools make hay of identity by mirroring and duplicating the subject, to show that no one is singular and nothing is simple: all is flux, like that metamorphosing cloud. After seeing the ghost, Hamlet announces he will *put on* an antic disposition and insists that he can tell a hawk from a handsaw. Thinking that he is playing the fool to expose folly, Hamlet gazes into the jester's mirror and spies everyone but himself—through a glass darkly, not face to face. Only gradually does Hamlet discover that he is both perceiver and source of folly, inside and outside. To be is to be a fool. Hence, extraordinary "complementarity with other characters"[9] is a trait often found in fools. Perhaps fools connect promiscuously because, as Wallace Stevens writes, "Life's nonsense pierces us with strange relation."[10] A joker's puns *create* strange relations by associating far-fetched words and making likeness of difference. Another sign of "complementarity" is that Hamlet uncannily mirrors so many characters. Some of his doubles Hamlet highlights sardonically: "I'll be your foil, Laertes" (5.2.255). Other correspondences discernible to us Hamlet neglects.

After killing Polonius, the prince remorselessly dismisses the "wretched, rash, intruding fool" (3.4.31), who "was in life a foolish prating knave" (3.4.215)—as if such fools deserve retribution! What most infuriates Hamlet are the sententious old man's glib aphorisms. To Polonius, things are what they seem: "For the apparel oft proclaims the man" (1.3.72). Such a sage has no difficulty identifying himself or any hesitation assessing reality: "This above all: to thine own self be true" (1.3.78). Polonius is hobgoblinly consistent, true to his fatuity, when he assures Claudius and Gertrude he will plumb the mysterious Hamlet, to "find / Where truth is hid, though it were hid indeed" (2.2.157–58). If only truth were so accessible and apprehensible! Hamlet is right that Polonius is "a rash intruding fool," brazenly reducing complexity to simplicity. Still, the hero's hostility to specious confidence is telling.

Perhaps Hamlet's animosity toward Polonius is stoked by his disturbing intuition of their shared follies. Both fabricate gratuitous, disconcerting wordplay; both vaunt their wit, flaunt verbal grandiosity, and critique the arts of theater and oratory. Entreating the players to "suit the action to the word, the word to the action" (3.2.17–18), Hamlet echoes Polonius badgering Laertes. Like Polonius, Hamlet would "by indirections find directions out" (2.1.63). It's Polonius who notices his own "foolish figure" (2.2.98), and it is Polonius, not altogether foolishly, who remarks their correspondence: he recognizes the "very cause of Hamlet's lunacy" (2.2.49) because "truly in my youth I suffer'd much extremity for love—very near this" (2.2.189–90).[11] They too are *a little more than kin*: Polonius might have been Hamlet's father-in-law.

Such disconcerting connections suggest another link that Hamlet vehemently repudiates, his kinship with "kin" Claudius. Hamlet's opening pun lays open a stranger relation than the prince recognizes or can stomach.[12] In soliloquy, struggling to pray, Claudius sounds very like Hamlet: the king speculates imaginatively, interrogates himself unsparingly, and remains agonized, baffled, and paralyzed. When Claudius characterizes himself as "a man to double business bound" (3.3.41), his ambivalence mirrors that of Hamlet, "obsessed with doubles of all kinds."[13] Initially blind to this particularly discomfiting image of himself, Hamlet eventually infers that he and Claudius are secret sharers, trapped in a hall of mirrors, a fatal *folie à deux*. Finally glimpsing affinities with the fools he originally excoriates, Hamlet says that the king and he are "mighty opposites" (5.2.62). When Hamlet, using his father's signet ring, forges the king's writ for the death of Rosencrantz and Guildenstern, he "emblematically becomes" both king and "Hamlet the Dane" (5.1.258).[14] His last words to the "incestuous, murd'rous, damned Dane" reflect upon himself with one last, savagely apposite pun: "Drink off this potion! Is thy union here?" (5.2.325–26). Literally, that "union" is the pearl ceremoniously dropped into the drink by Claudius: "The King shall drink to Hamlet's better breath, / And in the cup an union shall he throw" (5.2.270–71). Hamlet transforms the "union" of triangulation among father, mother, and son into the ultimate sundering of Claudius from Gertrude, from kinship, from life. Like Richard's antic death, the prince, "scoffing his state and grinning at his pomp," very effectively bids "Farewell, King!" (*R2* 3.2.162–70).[15]

Hamlet's frenzied word juggling becomes more reflective, increasingly receptive to strange relations and implicit connections. By observing the players, Hamlet sees that show and matter are indistinct, for one might enact a feeling that expresses or becomes something real.[16] The player "in a fiction, in a dream of passion," imitates passion to produce feelings in the audience—"And all for nothing" (2.2.552–57). Yet something may come of nothing, as Lear's Fool says. In the fool's vision and in Hamlet's burgeoning foolosophy, dichotomies such as illusion/reality, madness/sanity, and self/other break down, become more fungible.[17] By playing the fool and watching the players, Hamlet discovers the proximity of folly and wisdom—and thus, like Polonius, "by indirections find[s] directions out" (2.1.63).

Once returned from his sea voyage, Hamlet finds firmer footing at the burial ground, where he meets the gravediggers, who are bantering foolishly and joking shrewdly. Fortuitously situated to mark a threshold for the prince, the clowns seem to have been watching a play called *Hamlet*: "An act hath three branches," says one, "it is to act, to do, to perform" (5.1.11–12). It's as if the gravedigger heard the prince directing the visiting players not to clown gratuitously but to address "some necessary question of the play" (3.2.42–43). The graveyard scene begins (as does *Hamlet*) with a question. In 55 lines, the two clowns ask 11 questions, reinforcing the interrogative mood of the play. Their mock-logic and spoofing caricature the Prince of Riddles, "sicklied o'er with the pale cast of thought" (3.1.84) or "thinking too precisely on th' event" (4.4.41). "Cudgel thy brains no more about it" (5.1.56), says the clown, as if counseling Hamlet; the gravediggers' banter expresses their distrust of answers, explanations, and resolutions: "Marry, now I can tell" gives way to "Mass, I cannot tell." (5.1.52–55).

Spot on cue enters our hero who cannot go "to't," who talks and talks and cannot tell, who ruminates endlessly about acting and performing. Freshly home from sea, apparently invigorated by his escapade with pirates and his triumphant escape from death, Hamlet evidently revives: even his verbs stir. His characteristically striking formulations now include more active verbs. Observing the gravedigger casually tossing skulls here and there, he remarks, "How the knave *jowls* it to the ground... This might be the pate of a politician, which this ass now *o'erreaches*, one that would *circumvent* God, might it not" (5.1.76–80; my emphasis).

Like Shakespeare's great fool, the marvelously resilient Falstaff, *Hamlet riseth up*. In the cemetery where he too will soon rest, Hamlet continues his long dialogue with himself. Now, though, his tone shifts from acerbic rancor and self-lacerating egocentricity to bemused equanimity or whimsy, more like the detachment of Moria or a sage fool. In the graveyard, Hamlet appears contained within himself, less distraught, perhaps calmer with his own bewilderment. Summoning "imperious Caesar" (5.1.213) in a nursery rhyme that Lear's Fool might sing, Hamlet cavorts with death. When the gravedigger (who is designated "Clown") refers to the prince, "he that is mad, and sent into England" (5.1.148), Hamlet reacts casually and curiously: "Ay, marry, why was he sent into England?" (5.1.149). Hamlet also unearths, at least briefly, the consolations of foolosophy. Joshing and musing, Hamlet permits himself to be fooled and schooled by the Clown. Holding Yorick's skull, Hamlet indicates that mortality and corruption are not the be-all and end-all: "That skull had a tongue in it, and could sing once" (5.1.75–76). Returning to the matter of bodies, Hamlet seems less obsessed, more clinical: "How long will a man lie i' th' earth ere he rot?" (5.1.163–64). Realizing his distant connection with the skull he holds, Hamlet fondly raises Yorick: "Alas, poor Yorick! I knew him, Horatio, a fellow of infinite jest, of most excellent fancy. He hath bore me on his back a thousand times" (5.1.184–86). Affectionate and appreciative, Hamlet recalls being entertained and sustained, physically supported by the fool.

Prompted by clowns to acknowledge his kinship with fools, Hamlet attains an antic recognition of himself, crystallized in his old jester's skull. Like Richard II, Hamlet discerns his "weav'd-up follies" (*R2* 4.1.229) and sees where Death "the antic sits, / Scoffing his state and grinning at his pomp" (*R2* 3.2.162–63). For a moment, Hamlet plays peek-a-boo with that ancient jester death. After killing Polonius, Hamlet justified himself as heaven's "scourge and minister" (3.4.175). Now, instead of the scourge's single-minded rectitude, Hamlet seems myriad-minded and polyphonic. His new tones and attitudes are more measured and contingent. That Hamlet henceforth abandons soliloquy shows his altered disposition: rather than a uniquely privileged, singularly suffering soul, he situates himself more substantially in the world. Recognizing his relatedness, he senses that to be is to be implicated. Part of foolish wisdom is that death always has the last joke: "Make her laugh at that" (5.1.194–95). This is not the good cheer of salvation nor the life-affirming humor of comedy. It is grim laughter. Here there is no comfort to be found, no still point or safe place. Hamlet remains appalled by mortality: "And now how abhorr'd in my imagination it is! my

Figure 6.1 Hamlet and the skull of Yorick, original woodcarving by Robert H. Bell, 1963. Photographed by Eileen Foley; reproduced with kind permission of Beverly Coughlin, Belmont Hill School, Belmont, Massachusetts.

gorge rises at it" (5.1.186–88). When Hamlet concludes, "But it is no matter" (5.1.290), does he mean that nothing matters? Is this heroic equanimity or bitter resignation?

Whipsawed between contradictions, unable to resolve the tension or reconcile the paradox, Hamlet has glimmerings of a foolosophy that recognizes his liminality, "being *both* this *and* that."[18] "How absolute the knave is!" remarks the prince, expressing his distance from the clown's simpler truths. How peripatetic the hero has become. He revels in folly as he plays the fool. He intuits that fooling can be galvanizing and mysteriously illuminating. In the graveyard, on the threshold of death, he glimpses the union of everything and nothing. He raises the most serious of questions—only to shift styles and alter attitudes, to interrogate and inter seriousness itself.[19]

The relative calm of this "grave man"[20] does not last, any more than his revelations illuminate life's mysteries or affirm redemption. Hamlet's state is never either/or. At Ophelia's grave, when he asks her brother's forgiveness, the prince specifically divides himself into Mad Hamlet and Honorable Hamlet. He flatly proclaims, it "was madness" (5.1.232). He acknowledges publically that inside him is "something dangerous" (5.1.262). Yet there is no still point for this hero, as his frantic strutting, fierce threats, and lunatic cries dramatize: "'Swounds, show me what thou't do. / Woo't weep, woo't fight, woo't fast, woo't tear thyself? / Woo't drunk up eisel, eat a crocodile?" (5.1.274–76). Hamlet's ravings stage the paradoxes of foolosophy, the entanglement of wisdom and folly, and his own tragic motley. Thus he leaps into the grave, in a gesture that both enacts and parodies his heroic identity: "This is I, / Hamlet the Dane!" (5.1.257–58). Hamlet mingles clowns and kings by embodying what cannot be reconciled.

Thus Credulous Fools Are Caught

Shakespeare's mélange of theatrical genres, I've contended, flaunts "motley to the view." From *Romeo and Juliet* through *Troilus and Cressida*, one finds "How Tragedy and Comedy embrace; / How Farce and Epic get a jumbled race."[21] In no Shakespearean tragedy are clowning and fooling, burlesque and commedia dell'arte more prominent and unsettling than in *Othello*: an abandoned father vainly upholds patriarchal privilege and accuses the hero of bewitching his daughter; a besotted suitor is gulled and bamboozled; a "profane wretch" (*Oth.* 1.1.114) alarms the sleeping father and spews vile invective. *Othello* begins where romantic comedies culminate—with the triumphant hero and heroine joyously wedded. Overcoming social barriers, the lovers are publically authorized by the senate and apparently validated by nature when the storm that destroys the Turkish fleet grants the lovers safe passage to Cyprus.[22] Othello and Desdemona seem to reach a romantic haven or green world, a time and place for holiday celebration and festive revelry.

Of the several comic elements, the most conspicuous and problematic is the "bestial comic agony" of the hero.[23] Othello is Shakespeare's most egregiously foolish tragic protagonist. Long ago, Thomas Rymer compared the "Monstrous" antics of this "Bloody Farce" to the "Mops and the Mows [tricks or jests], Grimace, Grins and Gesticulation" of "Harlequin and Scarramuccio," clown and braggart in popular Italian comedies.[24] The noble hero is sublimely ridiculous, inclined to grandiosity and naively presuming that he is regarded at his monumental self-image. Despite or even because of his gorgeous, resounding timbre, Othello might have been regarded by Elizabethan audiences as a misfit and fool even *before* he is tricked and debased. Othello brandishes emblems of folly, including exotic apparel reminiscent of jester's attire, and his cherished handkerchief is a standard fool's prop known as the *muckender*.[25] To his fellow Venetians as well as to Renaissance Londoners, Othello might well seem an "extravagant and wheeling stranger" (1.1.136), "bragging and telling...fanastical lies" (2.1.223–24). Hardly ever addressed or referred to by name, Othello is invariably "the Moor." Most likely played by a white actor in blackface (accentuating his weirdness), the hero is fooled, gulled, and deluded until he becomes a veritable buffoon. As in *opera buffe* or commedia dell'arte, the old, ludicrous husband is outwitted, though not by a younger, more appropriate lover seeking the favors of the foxy wife. The positioning of Othello to misconstrue Cassio's remarks about his courtesan Bianca is pure farce. In this gruesome comedy of abjection, the noble Moor degenerates into a "madly deluded and murderous clown."[26]

To Iago and perhaps to the audience, Othello becomes a figure of fun, a farcical fool, and finally a kind of comic monster. The extraordinary power of the trickster and foolish susceptibility of the hero make this disturbing comedy grotesque. Iago is not an unfamiliar type: an abusive trickster, juggler of words, punster, riddler, and scourge, shrewd, vulgar, and cogent. Though he sometimes sounds like Hamlet in his misanthropic fury or like Thersites in his cynical disgust, Iago seems to have more fun; he enjoys pranks and flaunts his prowess. Initially, Iago cavorts like a frat boy on spring break, playing the wise guy to Roderigo's straight man and mark. Several of Iago's high jinks seem right out of farce. One zany instance takes place at Cyprus as Desdemona anxiously awaits the separate arrival of Othello. For a full hundred lines, Iago vilifies Emilia and apparently entertains Desdemona, who encourages him, she says, to "beguile / The thing I am by seeming otherwise" (2.1.123). Oddly beguiled by Iago's demeaning jests, Desdemona becomes entangled in a fool's routine, "old fond paradoxes to make fools laugh i' th' alehouse" (2.1.138–39).

Though often excised in productions, Iago's clowning and jesting are deliberate and consequential. He doesn't just make wisecracks. He delivers apothegms about folly: "She never yet was foolish that was fair, / For even her folly help'd her to an heir" and "There's none so foul and foolish thereunto, / But does foul pranks which fair and wise ones do" (2.1.136–42). Like countless fools, Iago emphasizes the ubiquity of folly, the unreliability of women, and the foolishness of deceived husbands. Misogyny and nastiness come with the cap and bells.[27] Women exist "to suckle fools and chronicle small beer" (2.1.160). Finally, Iago's vulgar "lame and most impotent conclusion!" (2.1.161) provokes Desdemona's indignant termination of his "profane" misogyny. Iago's foolery is "superfluous folly" (*AWW* 1.1.105) in its gratuitous redundancy—the extravagant excess of a "profane wretch" enjoying himself immensely. It is self-generating and self-delighting, "to provoke degrading laughter at the follies of others rather than enjoy the social experience of laughter *with* others."[28]

The trickster truly makes his world. To Iago, reality is always only constructed and words are merely signifiers. A demon of deconstruction, Iago flaunts his wit-craft and deploys his acute intelligence for "sport and profit." As he stresses, "Thou know'st we work by wit, and not by witchcraft" (2.3.372). Brilliantly, like Falstaff, he adopts values and ideas without any vested interest to assert "prepost'rous conclusions" (1.3.329). He does to Virtue what Falstaff does to Honor. Iago's "Virtue? A fig!" (1.3.319) is very nearly an orthodox Christian sermon with shades of Augustine, 40 lines derogating "the blood and baseness of our natures" (1.3.328). Sounding very much like Shakespeare's scourges of folly, Iago also has the fool's knack for equivocal self-characterizations. He pretends to define himself in gnomic utterances of paradoxical profundity that cannily conceal himself: "Were I the Moor, I would not be Iago…I am not what I am…I am nothing if not critical…Men should be what they seem, / Or those that be not, would they might seem none!…And knowing what I am, I know what she shall be" (1.1.57, 1.1.65, 2.1.118, 3.3.127–28, 4.1.73). How often Iago says "I am" and how rarely he reveals anything.

The contagion of folly can be virulent. In addition to deceiving Cassio, Roderigo, and Othello, Iago also tricks the audience: "Thus credulous fools are caught" (4.1.44–45). The "pander who opens the door to the listener's pornographic imagination,"[29] Iago offers access to taboo pleasures. Most of the action occurs in darkness, like dreams and nightmares.[30] Desdemona's bed was the first on an English stage to be more than a deathbed. Like Thersites, Iago is situated on the border between the stage and the audience; he addresses us frequently, directly, and at length. He speaks some 40 percent of the play's lines, dominates the first two acts, and frames our viewpoint. Intimately and insinuatingly, Iago confides his thoughts and solicits our complicity "in double knavery" (1.3.394). "Led by th' nose / As asses are" (1.3.401–2), we are prodded not with a stick but a carrot. This play, it has been well said, "mercilessly exposes the complicity of the audience's spectatorship."[31] Audiences are horrified to be entertained by desecration and degradation, mortified by their tacit acquiescence, and ashamed of their perverse delectation.

All the more unnerving is our seduction by a villain who takes such pleasure in his machinations while announcing so boldly what he is doing! Repeatedly he says that he feasts on anything "that folly and green minds look after" (2.1.246–47). He excoriates fools everywhere and plays them for profit and "sport" (1.3.368), as he tells Roderigo, while conning him. In soliloquy he boasts, "Thus do I ever make my fool my purse" (1.3.383), and reiterates his credo: "For my sport and profit" (1.3.386). Why do we neglect signs of clear and present danger? One reason might be that Iago is the only one in this play who *enjoys* himself. Even in newly wedded bliss, Othello seems wary or apprehensive: "It is *too much* of joy" (2.1.197; my emphasis). Iago is a breath of fetid air. Weirdly ebullient, utterly cynical, but undismayed, Iago toots his horn and trumpets his mastery to manipulate fools. With voyeuristic glee and unfeigned enjoyment, Iago invites us to *look, watch, see!* How zealously he revels in the illicit scenes he conjures! "Even now, now, very now, an old black ram / Is tupping your white ewe" (1.1.88–89). When Othello demands proof of Desdemona's perfidy, Iago asks, "But how? How satisfied, my lord? / Would you, the supervisor, grossly gape on? / Behold her topp'd?" (3.3.394–96). Iago's astonishing question provokes the "supervisors" in the audience whose fascinated revulsion and prurient curiosity are stoked, *now, even now, very now.*

Iago is the maestro who creates a *show,* a triumph of artifice or compelling illusion. "Show" is one of his favorite words. Playing roles, inventing dialogue, improvising deftly, he conceives, stage-manages, and directs the whole enterprise. Conning Roderigo, he is also a producer, funding his production! Enforcing his interpretation, he is drama critic. Infinitely resourceful, creating something out of nothing, Iago sounds like a playwright exulting in his artistry or the capacity to trick.

> Cassio's a proper man. Let me see now:
> To get his place and to plume up my will
> In double knavery—How? how? Let's see—...
> The Moor is of a free and open nature,
> That thinks men honest that but seem to be so,
> And will as tenderly be led by th' nose
> As asses are.
> I have't. It is engend'red. Hell and night
> Must bring this monstrous birth to the world's light.
>
> (1.3.392–404)

Iago's "double knavery" beguiles us with topsy-turvy, confounding birth and death, night and light, humanity and bestiality: the "monstrous birth" of evil. Like the scourges of folly examined in the previous chapter, wildly reductive and outrageously unfair, Iago can also be disconcertingly accurate, taking measure of his victim maliciously but not inaptly. Iago woos us by reading Othello like an open book. He anticipates that Othello can be tricked. So *easily* fooled, strangely receptive to Iago's demonic ministrations, Othello seems half-willing to be deceived.

In this tragedy, trickster and fool are intimately, terribly connected—dreadfully, fatally linked. "Exchange me for a goat" (3.3.180), Othello says, ominously echoing Iago. The hero is quick to invent his own vile toads and noxious vapors. Othello's sordid fantasy of Desdemona violated by the camp, pioneers and all, seems to spring from the Iago within Othello. At the dead center of the play, these "strange bedfellows" merge uncannily and creepily in a ritual resembling marriage—or a black mass confounding sacred and profane. Othello's "bloody thoughts" become "the due reverence of a sacred vow" (3.3.457–60); kneeling as if in prayer, he swears by "marble heaven." When Iago commands, "Do not rise yet" (3.3.462), general and ensign reverse roles. Iago's acquiescent "I am your own for ever" (3.3.480) seals their contract, parodies the wedding rite, and means the opposite of what it says.[32]

No wonder that *Othello* so profoundly disturbs audiences. Instead of precipitating tragic catharsis and enabling affirmation, this play produces sickening recognitions. Samuel Johnson could not endure reading it, not because it treats taboo subjects (race, sex, violence) but because it exposes our terrified fascination; and there are still people who cannot bear to watch it. Hence the play's reception history is full of "attempts to articulate ideologically correct, that is, palatable interpretations" to evade the "morally disquieting" sense of our participation.[33] Many performances and interpretations of *Othello* strive to cushion the hero's humiliation and to succor our intolerable discomfort. To compensate for the degradation of the hero, and to protect ourselves, we might stress the magnificent nobility of Othello and the disgusting wickedness of Iago. The triangulation—joining audience, fool, and trickster—is horrific, Othello's "bestial comic agony." Although we might prefer to see Noble Othello undone by Demonic Iago in order to cleanse ourselves of the whole dirty business, the play forces us to realize where that antic sits, scoffing at our state. The last thing Othello says before his suicide speech resounds: "O, fool, fool, fool!" (5.2.323).

Lear's Shadow

An actor about to play King Lear asked his director for advice: "Mind your Fool," he was urged. Though fool and king are intimately associated, Lear is initially, instinctively, loath to identify with his jester: "Dost thou call me fool, boy?" To which the Fool replies, "All thy other titles thou hast given away, that thou wast born with" (*Lr* 1.4.148–50). Sharing a "title," like Othello and Iago, the two outcasts are linked in ways the hero only painfully, grudgingly realizes. Thundering imprecations, disclaiming paternity, banishing Kent, Lear presumes godlike prerogatives and flaunts his ridiculous, terrible follies. Willfully blind to his basic humanity, Lear loses power, pride, and "all." The fool is there to mock majestic pretense and to lay bare regal folly. Like Hamlet, this "sweet and bitter fool" (1.4.144) is tender and ruthless, amusing and disturbing.

Sometimes diverting, sometimes mocking, Lear's Fool harps on his royal master's folly: "Thou hadst little wit in thy bald crown when thou gav'st thy golden one away.... Thou shouldst not have been old till thou hadst been wise" (1.4.162–63, 1.5.44–45). He can be quite ruthless.[34] Telling truth to power is the jester's job: deflation brings "down" the high and mighty, stresses the low and ridiculous. Yet this fool's lèse majesté spares neither Lear's pathos nor agony. To the king's cry, "O me, my heart! my rising heart! But down!" the Fool replies, "Cry to it, nuncle, as the cockney did to the eels when she put 'em i' th' paste alive" (2.4.120–23). Presuming privileged authority with the king as well as the audience, the Fool remarks himself teaching or preaching: "We'll set thee to school to an ant, to teach thee" (2.4.67–68). Despite such weird outbursts as the cockney's eels, there are dazzling flashes of insight, strangely cogent hey nonny-nonny. He recites riddles, paradoxes, and conundrums and Biblical travesties, inverted parables, and surrealistic images. His wit is intermittently quick and germane. In the hovel, when Lear arraigns Goneril, the Fool pretends to apologize for neglecting her august presence: "Cry you mercy, I took you for a join-stool" (3.6.52). His jest is idiomatic, with a metaphysical dimension, for this "Goneril" *is* a join stool, such a one as Snug the Joiner might make. Like his question, "Can you make no use of nothing, nuncle?" (1.4.130–31), this joke dissolves the ordinary distinction between nothing/everything or between imaginary/real.[35]

Though such fooling seems grounded in common sense or conventional wisdom, a second kind of fooling is nonsense, stock banter or folderol, often cryptic. Lear's Fool seems to have a private agenda: "Yet I can tell what I can tell" (1.5.16). Perplexing and perplexed, he flaunts his bewilderment: "So out went the candle, and we were left darkling" (1.4.217). But something quite peculiar to Lear's Fool illuminates this dark world. Perhaps the rub is not so much *what* Lear's Fool means as *how* he means, or refuses to mean; whatever his enigmatic motives, the effects of his fooling produce debasement, uncrowning, desecration, the break up rather than the idealizing unification of feeling and effect.

Constantly yoking "wise man" and "fool" reinforces the Fool's incessant point—that Lear has foolishly yielded power and made himself a fool. The fool addresses the mighty king in his diminished capacity not as "your majesty" but as *nuncle*: "O nuncle, court holy-water in a dry house is better than this rain-water out o' door. Good nuncle, in, ask thy daughters blessing. Here's a night pities neither wise men nor fool" (3.2.10–13). This is usually understood to mean, "Flattery at court is better than this miserable storm. Ask forgiveness of Regan and Goneril, and get us inside."

I read this exchange two-sidedly, as both uncrowning and crowning, abasement and exaltation. Though the phrase "court holy-water" might signify "flattery," it also conjures Cordelia, whose tears of commiseration are "the holy water from her heavenly eyes" (4.3.30). A second meaning is similarly available in "thy daughters blessing," referring not to Regan and Goneril but to Cordelia. Though an auditor hears no difference between *daughters'* plural and *daughter's* singular and because we do not have Shakespeare's original punctuation, the latter makes more sense, for Lear eventually does implore Cordelia's forgiveness. We've been told that the Fool is pining for Cordelia, and Lear's lament, "And my poor fool is hang'd" (5.3.306) conflates them.

This dual possibility suggests that the Fool is less expedient and self-interested than commonly regarded and more deeply implicated with the promise of redemption. Pathetically vulnerable, frantic and debased, the Fool has resources beyond this wretched mortal state: the Fool's duality reflects the king's dividedness. Sometimes the Fool's language wafts like seeds and germinates elsewhere; flashes of illumination and intimations of foolosophy double as jests and quibbles. Here in the hovel on the heath, Kent's simple question, "Who's there?" prompts the Fool's Delphic utterance: "Marry, here's grace and a cod-piece—that's a wise man and a fool" (3.2.39–41). Lear struggles to preserve body and soul by vainly vowing patience; he will learn much more about "nothing," its depths and uses. The Fool's cryptic response suggests several associated but distinct senses: literal, ironical, "foolish," and "foolosophical."

1. Here are the king and his fool—his grace, a wise and good monarch, and a fool, sporting a codpiece to signify "that selie part," as Moria calls the penis.
2. Here is the king, appropriately near the fool because he has been acting quite foolishly.
3. Here am I who represent "grace" and "wisdom," fool though I be. This other guy who used to be king is now truly the fool.
4. Here we are, king and fool, "graced" and foolish.

The last possibility—figuring king and fool as doubled doubles, each reflecting the other's twinned state—is appealing. Kent, for instance, is moved to generalize, to look up as well as down, from "here" to "the wrathful skies" (3.2.42–43), and to contemplate "man's nature" (3.2.48) more speculatively than usual. Lear, never reluctant to invoke the gods, again does so but begins to sense the duality of "man's nature," perhaps including his own. Those darker impulses "that under covert and convenient seeming" and "close pent-up guilts" (3.2.56–57) represent humanity as irreparably split—indeed, Christian—striving spirits and fallen bodies. Though Lear does not yet see himself fully and truly, he begins the process: "I am a man / More sinn'd against than sinning" (3.2.59–60) has a telling line break: "I am a man…" As Lear's Fool flirts with chaos, his proximity to peril (skirting the abyss) gives him an eerie aura of sanctity, a hint of divine impunity, like a saint touching lepers.

If clowns confuse, this Fool baffles. Though much of his fooling counsels common sense, some of it is nonsense, with dollops of vulgarity, misogyny, and misanthropy. He makes hay of heartbreak and voices the unutterable, like a fury harassing and harrying the king. Like Hamlet, Lear's Fool also illuminates this dark world with mysterious flashes, opaque riddles, and reverberating paradoxes. The Fool's language also has a haunting, magical quality that recalls *A Midsummer Night's Dream* and foreshadows *The Tempest*. That may be the point of another much-disputed soliloquy that troubled Samuel Johnson and has been rejected by many editors as interpolated.[36] For an anatomist of folly, or maybe just because fools *will* rush in, the problematic source of this speech makes it all the more enticing:

This is a brave night to cool a courtezan.
I'll speak a prophecy ere I go:
When priests are more in word than matter;
When brewers mar their malt with water;
When nobles are their tailors' tutors;
No heretics burn'd, but wenches' suitors;
Then shall the realm of Albion
Come to great confusion.
When every case in law is right;
No squire in debt, nor no poor knight;
When slanders do not live in tongues;
Nor cutpurses come not to throngs;
When usurers tell their gold i' th' field,
And bawds and whores do churches build;
Then comes the time, who lives to see't,
That going shall be us'd with feet.
This prophecy Merlin shall make, for I live before his time.
(3.2.79–94)

Lear's Fool is a partly reliable guide and generally beneficent force but not entirely so. This soliloquy displays the Fool's characteristic duality by exaggerating the incongruity between higher wisdom and lower imperatives. Full of irrelevant nonsense widely regarded as spurious, this little ditty is eminently foolish. Burlesquing affectation or mocking aspiration, it begins with lewd sarcasm and leaps from the vile to the precious: "I'll speak a prophecy." Nothing typifies the Fool more than to juxtapose ridiculous and sublime or to oscillate between high and low matter. Satiric allusions to venereal disease jostle with biblical idiom. Determined to obfuscate, the Fool has several tricks up his sleeve. There is the convincing impersonation of Jeremiah's prophetic timbre: "Then shall the realm of Albion / Come to great confusion." Predicting confusion, it makes sense that his vision is topsy-turvy, turning upside down ordinary social exchanges: "When priests...When brewers..." These four lines issue in a bawdy pun, slipping from numinous to profane with the joke about venereal heat and disease: "No heretics burn'd, but wenches' suitors." The next four lines are a utopian vision, the opposite of corrupt inversion, representing the handy-dandy motion of time itself from satiric to idyllic. Nothing rests in folly, so the third phase ("When usurers...And bawds and whore") is indeterminate both in chronology and quality: When *is* this, and is this good, bad, or indifferent?

Now the Fool rises to his apex. "Then shall the realm of Albion" parodies Lear's majestic strutting and godlike declamations. The heroic, high idiom collapses bathetically into a truism, that one goes on *feet*, rhymed doggerel-like with "see't." What goes up must come down, says the Fool; deflation is his mission. So too he flaunts his own outrageous presence with the self-regarding anachronism, "This prophecy Merlin shall make, for I live before his time." Initially depicting a Christian society of priests and heretics, he loops back to the mythic pagan past of Albion and ends with Arthur's magus—yet to come! Whether or not this speech is genuine, it is genuinely fake and befits the fool. If not written by Shakespeare, as some editors suggest, it was forged by a skillful counterfeiter, heeding and impersonating the fool. The speech, addressing us directly, breaks the barrier between audience and performer. In a meta-theatrical gesture, the Fool transcends time and confounds present and future; he is on the edge, ignoring boundaries, testing the limits. Conspicuously, he is double, an actor exposing the artifice yet "really" a fool, a creature of two bodies. What the right hand giveth, the left hand taketh—handy-dandy all the way, dizzying and discombobulating.

Lear's Fool is a far more complicated figure than Feste or Touchstone. One might say that, like Hamlet, his antic disposition appears less than madness, more than feigned. Initially a sane man playing the jester's role, Lear's Fool later seems unhinged, hysterically terrified. Is he *loony*, a "natural fool," deranged or disturbed? Like most jesters, this Fool contradicts everything and anything: "Change places, and handy-dandy" (4.6.153).[37] Up and down, down and up, everything and nothing: the Fool sees and makes topsy-turvy. Such an avatar of arsy-versy, this geyser of gallimaufry—source of significance, contrary tendencies, and competing attitudes—tempts us to simplify and reassure ourselves. Wisdom and folly, folly and wisdom. Does Lear's Fool identify wisdom with folly? Is every jest, snatch of song, and random remark encoded prophecy? Moments when Lear would disregard his Fool—"This is nothing," says Lear—provoke uncanny replies: "Can you make no use of nothing, nuncle?" (1.4.128–31). Their exchange echoes the fatal encounter when the king rebuffs Cordelia's offer of "nothing," with a telling echo: "Nothing will come of nothing, speak again" (1.1.90). Lear's tragic experience is implicit in that inversion of everything and nothing. Touting the uses of nothing, the Fool anticipates Lear's progress, from the deluded assumption that he is everything, all in all, to the naked truth that he is nothing, to the discovery that nothing might be something after all.

Melvin Seiden poses a riddle in the manner of Lear's Fool: "What is it that is what it is and no other thing and yet is also nothing," that "both transcends the best that humanity is capable of yet also is inferior to, has less dignity and worth than what is merely human?"[38] The solution to the riddle is the Fool—or Death. Contrary to what Lear initially tells Cordelia, something comes of nothing, and *nothing* accrues meaning and value. "Between the positive and negative poles of a battery," says Seiden, "a powerful current, one that will destroy" Lear and others. And the Fool, "who is the voice of Nothing, the affirmer of the potency of negation, has as his first role the task of reminding Lear that there is something immanent in these nothings"—a vain and futile effort it may be. The Fool says the unsayable, affirms contradiction, and represents everything and nothing. In *King Lear*, nothing is something, even everything.

King and Fool are polar opposites, first and last, yoked by violence together. The Fool intuits their intricate affiliation when he answers the king's question, "Who is it can tell me who I am?" Fool says, "Lear's shadow" (1.4.230–31).[39] Such pregnant replies indicate the scope of this Fool's pertinent impertinence. This man or "boy" in motley is emblematic: he appears just after Lear behaves "like a fool" and disappears before Lear's madness abates. This Fool affects Lear more profoundly than Touchstone influences Rosalind or Feste moves Viola. Arguably, the Fool catalyzes Lear's progress, or what Bradley termed "redemption." In a fool's-eye view, Lear absorbs perceptions suggested by his Fool: "Change places, and handy-dandy" (4.6.153). In this reading, some follies can and may be corrected: Lear discovers that his reality is an illusion, a shadow show on the wall of a cave; disabused of delusions, he sees himself more truly and comprehends "this great stage of fools" (4.6.183) more clearly.[40]

Shakespeare's early comedies deploy fools to confound perceptions and generate laughter. Gradually, Shakespearean fooling conducts seriocomic investigations of identity and relationship. The degree of correspondence between king and fool is unmistakable in Lear's great speech, "My wits begin to turn" (3.2.67). Fearing loss of sanity, his expression underscores the "turn" of events linking two separate and distant beings. The Fool is now "*my* boy," whose condition Lear feels and shares: "I am cold myself" (3.2.69). The extension of empathy through suffering suggests the foundational paradoxes of Christian faith: "The art of our necessities is strange / And can make vild [vile] things precious" (3.2.70–71). That "one part" of Lear's heart feels sorry for the "poor fool and knave" suggests the bifurcation of body natural and body sacred and implies that recognizing the first might be the condition of realizing the second. Their mysterious bond is evident in the storm, especially when Lear tenderly addresses the Fool as "*my* boy." Rather than expect the Fool to share his extremity, Lear now notices and pities the Fool's plight. Lear's intuition of himself as one with the untouchables and scapegoats foreshadows his direct identification of himself as a fool. His "poor fool" he now addresses in the hovel as "sapient sir" (3.6.22). Empson is helpful here: "The royal prerogative has become the power of the outcast to deal directly on behalf of mankind with the Devil," [41] which is remarkably close to Paul's conception of "fools for Christ."

Lear's Fool is persistently both shadow and substance. When Lear begins to lose his bearings and asks rhetorically, who am I, the Fool responds, as we heard, cruelly and truly, "Lear's shadow" (1.4.231). The mirroring and doubling of earlier fooling—such as Jaques's encounter with Touchstone or Parolles's meeting with Lavatch—gain intimacy, urgency, and resonance. As Lear's Fool merges with the king and the power of monarchy, Lear begins to share the Fool's state. When fool urges king to come in from the storm, Lear ignores him and confronts his harrowing. The Fool takes Lear *only* so far—partway. If more comprehensive possibilities lie ahead for Lear, they are beyond the Fool's ken. Accordingly, he dwindles; in 3.4, as Poor Tom takes over the discourse, Fool utters just four single lines and one short speech. Suddenly, mysteriously, he disappears: "And I'll go to bed at noon" (3.6.85).[42] Unlike the casual disappearance of Launce the Clown from *Two Gentlemen of Verona*, this Fool's absence is conspicuous.

Inexplicably gone, the Fool is not forgotten. Effectively, he is replaced by Edgar playing Poor Tom. During his agonizing meeting with blinded Gloucester on the heath, the king uses the Fool's idiom, mixing nonsense and wisdom. Ultimately, in lunatic clarity, Lear seems to confuse Cordelia with the Fool himself. Stripped of delusions, Lear discovers that reality is an illusion, a shadow show. He comes to see everyone, especially himself, performing upon "this great stage of fools" (4.6.183). Perhaps the Fool disappears when Lear recognizes that he is truly a fool. Like Hamlet, Lear sees and accepts his antic role; like Hamlet, the king participates in folly to glean

Figure 6.2 Albrecht Durer, Ship of Fools fly the flag, woodcut engraving originally published in Sebastian Brandt's *The Ship of Fools*.

fragments of foolosophy. Having attended "the school of fools," Lear internalizes Foolosophy 101.

When Lear encounters Gloucester in 4.6, the king is "fantastically dressed with wild flowers" and babbling like a lunatic or natural fool; he misperceives Gloucester, forgets or misunderstands his own state, and is distracted by a random mouse, with whom he sports at length. This situation Gloucester understandably regards as Lear's nadir: "O ruin'd piece of nature!" (4.6.134). But the ruin of monarchy is the revival of nature. Attired like a May Day or Carnival King, crowned with flowers or perhaps wearing his Fool's cap, Lear holds court in a meadow and, like a Lord of Misrule, derogates the authority of government and "enables" the liberation of "nature." He embodies man's "natural state," not culture or civilization, for "Nature's above art in that respect" (4.6.86). As usual, Gloucester is a well-meaning but unreliable commentator, whose "ruined piece of nature" remark is prompted by this extraordinary exchange: "O, let me kiss that hand!" Lear responds, "Let me wipe it first, it smells of mortality" (4.6.132–33). To speak thus would be inconceivable for the mighty king of yore. Lear plays the fool's part, but Gloucester is too distraught to gaze into the abyss and plumb the depths.

That way madness lies. Lear's lunacy is inseparable from his perception in the tangle of illusions and recognitions, delusions and illuminations. As always, folly lures us into a counterfeit distinction between apparently antithetical opposites. It is hard to say if or when Lear is foolishly asserting his majestic prerogatives, or pretending to display monarchy, or mocking his former illusions of power and delusions of majesty: "When I do stare, see how the subject quakes" (4.6.108). To proclaim "Let copulation thrive" (4.6.114) sanctions natural instinct—or condones debauchery. What does the riot of carnality portend? Lear's recognitions, ambiguous in themselves, are mixed with blindness and no little cruelty, like the barbs of the Fool. Pathetically, Gloucester asks, "Dost thou know me?" Lear responds, "I remember thine eyes well enough. Dost thou squiny at me? No, do thy worst, blind Cupid. I'll not love" (4.6.135–38). Sometimes it seems that Gloucester is closer than Lear to the light. When Gloucester says he cannot see, Lear replies jovially, "O ho, are you there with me? No eyes in your head, nor no money in your purse? Your eyes are in a heavy case, your purse in a light; yet you see how this world goes" (4.6.145–48). It is the blind Gloucester who delivers the heartbreaking, beautiful line, "I see it feelingly" (4.6.149).

Yet out of this grotesque "ruin" emerges a mysterious lucidity reminiscent of Lear's Fool: "What, art mad?" asks the king. "A man may see how this world goes with no eyes. Look with thine ears." Lear echoes the least of our brethren, Bottom, confounding seeing and hearing in the clown's most rare vision. Lear now sees feelingly: "See how yond justice rails upon yond simple thief. Hark in thine ear: change places and handy-dandy, which is the justice, which is the thief? Thou hast seen a farmer's dog bark at a beggar?" (4.6.150–55). Like a veritable Lord of Misrule, or a rude and blessed mechanical, or a Falstaffian foolosopher, the desolated king declares, "There thou might behold the great image of authority" (4.6.157–58).

As we should not sentimentalize the Fool, we must not romanticize Lear's vision of misrule; it teems with grotesque horrors: "There's hell, there's darkness" (4.6.127).[43] In this carnival of carnality, Lear expresses furious disgust toward sexuality and violent terror of women, depicted as loathsome beasts. Hatred and the desire for revenge persist: "And when I have stol'n upon these sons-in-law, / Then, kill, kill, kill, kill, kill, kill!" (4.6.186–87). Only intermittently does he indicate gentle solicitude for Gloucester. He ends the scene blithering mindlessly, foolishly, madly: "I will die bravely, like a smug bridegroom...I will be jovial" (4.6.198–99) (shades of Malvolio in that last bit). Running away from Cordelia's soldiers, he eludes help and precludes any simple formulations such as Redeemed Hero and Holy Fool.

But Lear's scene with Gloucester also has the piercing clarity of revelation, beyond pretense and beneath roles: "Robes and furr'd gowns hide all" (4.6.164). Some of Lear's realizations are pellucid: "I know thee well enough, thy name is Gloucester" (4.6.177). Lear senses that he now sees better—further, beyond himself, more like the Fool: "Yet you see how this world goes...A man may see" (4.6.147–50). That "man" is telling. Now Lear recovers the perspective of the least of our brethren, a "simple thief" or "beggar." This vivid, topsy-turvy vision is summarized cogently by the Fool's term "handy-dandy."

The Fool affects Lear profoundly. In this fool's-eye view of the play, Lear absorbs his Fool: "*Change places...*" (4.6.153; my emphasis). If we maintain the principle of handy-dandy, including the possibility that the last might be first, Lear's hectic vision comes into focus as an apotheosis of folly or the gospel of a holy fool. Of course, fools like Falstaff and Feste have always played the role of preachers and saints for various untoward ends. Still, it takes a pretty stubborn skepticism not to notice in Lear's discourse intimations of spirituality: "To say 'ay' and 'no' to every thing that I said! 'Ay' and 'no' too, was no good divinity" (4.6.98–100). Here, *divinity* means theology, and Lear may be recalling scripture: "Let your yea be yea and your nay, nay" (James 5:12). Indisputably, Lear's raving madness touches some good divinity. He acknowledges his heart of darkness and our state of sin, associated with fallen nature: "It smells of mortality." He repudiates the foolish delusion that a king is godlike. As the Fool urged, Lear reverses his assessments of *everything* and *nothing* to affirm the uses and value of nothing. He observes the extent of rampant injustice and corruption: "Plate sin with gold, / And the strong lance of justice hurtless breaks" (4.6.165–66). Instead of authority and judgment thundered on high by Lear-as-Jehovah, we hear the tender mercies of forgiveness: "None does offend, none, I say, none, I'll able 'em" (4.6.168).[44] I love this line, moving from a triple negative to a strong positive. The word *able* signifies "to empower, strengthen, fortify. To warrant, vouch for; to aver, confirm"—as opposed to *counterfeit*, that term prominent in the foolery of both Falstaff and Rosalind and also implicit in Lear's parodic self-mockery: "No, they cannot touch me for coining, I am the King himself" (4.6.83–84). This counterfeit self Lear rejects: "They told me I was everything. 'Tis a lie, I am not ague-proof" (4.6.105).

Far from the bogus identity of omnipotent monarch is the fool-self Lear becomes. Out of the mouths of babes and fools, with whom Lear identifies: "We came crying hither. / Thou know'st, the first time that we smell the air, / We wawl and cry" (4.6.178–80). Explicitly Lear decides, "I will preach to thee: Mark"—and maybe some Luke, Matthew, and John—in Lear's sermon: "When we are born, we cry that we are come / To this great stage of fools" (4.6.182–83). Lear's "we," signifying not the royal we, the commanding king, but everyman—all of us—is not merely rhetorical as he reiterates: "I am even / The natural fool of fortune" (4.6.190–91). How very different Lear sounds reiterating Romeo's formulation! The sense of redefined identity—fool's person singular?—is underscored by the repeated first-person singular and the verb *to be*: "I am...Come, come, I am a King" (4.6.190–99). We have already observed the germination of the Fool's words, soaring and settling. Now Lear's modest, honest "I am" anticipates his awakening to the face of Cordelia. He asks his daughter not to "mock" him, for "I am a very foolish fond old man" (4.7.59). His recognition is heavily underscored by reiterations:

> I fear *I am* not in my perfect mind.
> Methinks I should know you, and know this man,
> *Yet I am* doubtful: for *I am* mainly ignorant
> What place this is, and all the skill I have
> Remembers not these garments; nor I know not
> Where I did lodge last night. Do not laugh at me,
> For (*as I am a man*) I think this lady
> To be my child Cordelia.
>
> (4.7.62–69; my emphasis)

And naturally, beautifully, she echoes her father to verify his recognitions: "And so I am, I am" (4.7.68). Further than this, and further from Lear's original foolishness, foolosophy cannot go.

CHAPTER 7

No Epilogue, I Pray You

Conventionally, the highest-ranking personage onstage retains the privilege of the final word; in Shakespeare, the custom is honored more in the breach than the observance. In defiance of decorum and without rhyme or reason, the unruly likes of Puck, Feste, and Falstaff return to make the denouement all the more discombobulating. Shakespeare's epilogues tend to overflow the boundaries rather than draw the line, a phenomenon compounded when the epilogue is delegated to the fool.

Shakespeare's ongoing reliance upon such irresponsible spokesmen also represents the cyclical reappearance of fools. Ubiquitous and ostentatious, they are prone to disappear, such as Lear's Fool to who-knows-where or Falstaff into banishment. The prologue to *Henry VIII* actually apologizes for the missing "motley" (Prologue 16), lest indignant audiences demand their money back. Where's Will Somers? Everyone knew the king's jester and remembered Cardinal Wolsey's fool Patch.[1] Fools are conspicuous even in their absence, what Lear's Fool calls an "O without a figure" (*Lr* 1.4.192–93). Though marginal and borderline, potential outcasts or scapegoats, Shakespeare's fools defy oblivion and persevere by hook or crook, magic or providence, tricks and bravado. Elastic and resilient, fools fall and revive: "Falstaff riseth up" (5.4.110 s.d.). On their account, everything toggles to and fro, "up and down, up and down" (*MND* 3.1.396), as Puck chants gleefully. The unending zig-zaggery of foolery evokes everything and nothing, the sublime and the ridiculous, the first and the last. Always in play, the fool is never finished. Lo and behold: here he is again.

Our study of fools began in earnest with Bottom, whose topsy-turvy "upsomdowns"[2] reveal how indeed the last is first. And vice versa, for there appears to be a competition for the distinction of speaking last. *A*

Midsummer Night's Dream is Shakespeare's first play that resists closure through the naughty offices of the fools. Though its plot is resolved in act 4 and the fifth act is a coda, nobody seems ready to call it a wrap. Flushed with triumph, Bottom wants to perform Will Kemp's specialty—a jig. Duke Theseus politely refuses: "No epilogue, I pray you" (5.1.355). To whom does the honor of the epilogue pass? Putatively to Puck, whose twenty-line speech ceremoniously sweeps the dust behind the door. But then Oberon and Titania each deliver lovely yet gratuitously protracted benedictions. Surely this must be the end. But no, Puck riseth up, trying once more to finish, in effect offering his second epilogue: "If we shadows have offended, / Think but this, and all is mended" (5.1.423–24). Puck's reiterated *Ifs* and conditionals raise the dust he had brushed away. Another inconclusive conclusion! Never good at setting things straight, like the Cheshire Cat, Puck points in opposite directions. Flouting the illusion of verisimilitude, Puck reveals himself to be an actor situated between the dream world of the play and the real world of the theater—hence, a "shadow" or counterfeit. Stranger still, Puck no longer sounds like that "merry wanderer of the night" proudly proclaiming his vocation, to "jest to Oberon and make him smile" (2.1.43–44). Now the merry jester is a suffering sinner begging forgiveness, anxious to "scape the serpent's tongue" (5.1.433). Doubtful "we will mend," he repeats, "If you pardon, we will mend" (5.1.430). Exhorting the audience to validate the players with applause, Puck underscores the deliquescence of dreams already disappearing.

The ending of *A Midsummer Night's Dream* holds—provisionally. In 1599 the visitation of Queen Elizabeth called for another epilogue—spoken this time by the playwright himself: "As the dial hand tells o'er / The same hours it had before, / Still beginning in the ending, / Circular account lending."[3] Standing in Puck's stead, "still beginning in the ending," Shakespeare recycles a fool's trope elaborated that same year (1599) by Touchstone: "And so from hour to hour" (*AYL* 2.7.26). Too true, all things must pass—except our "most mighty Queen," whose glorious reign transcends the generations. So the dial hand moves like the fool's wand in "circular account," and the ending is an echo of an echo: "Once I wish again, / Heaven subscribe it with 'Amen.'" Bowing low to his queen, Shakespeare leaves no room for any other fool to "wish again . . . 'Amen.'"

The epilogue to *Henry IV, Part 2* is another story. It takes place, it will be recalled, right after the newly crowned King Henry V banishes the old "fool and jester" (5.5.48). Traditionally ascribed to an anonymous "Dancer," this final speech includes conventional elements that might be spoken by anyone: deference to the audience, request for "pardons," topical allusions and in-jokes, and another prayer "for the Queen" (Epilogue 3, 17). Someone speaking for "our humble author" promises to continue the saga "with Sir John in it" (Epilogue 28). I don't think this speaker is some anonymous Dancer. The disclaimer that distinguishes Falstaff from the historical Oldcastle, "this is not the man,"[4] hints that the speaker is in fact Falstaff continuing to play "now you see it, now you don't" and "peek-a-boo, I see you"—his old tricks of comic self-denial and glorious self-aggrandizement.

Banished Falstaff thus makes another miraculous getaway: "you undo me, for what I have to say is of mine own making, and what indeed (I should say) will (I doubt) prove mine own marring" (Epilogue 4–6). Falstaff feasts on this sort of hocus-pocus proliferation and disavowal of identity. In true Falstaffian fashion, he exposes his own pretense: unmasking the unmasking. Also characteristic of Falstaff are the mock-humility, sham deference to authority, and financial idiom: "mine own making," "pay you with this," "an ill venture," "creditors," "as most debtors do," "promise you infinitely." Falstaff, we've just heard, is massively in debt: "Master Shallow, I owe you a thousand pound" (5.5.73). Anyone who knows the old counterfeiter knows enough to suspect his voucher.

References to the body and appetite also point to Falstaff as the "real" speaker: "If you be not too much cloy'd with fat meat... My tongue is weary, when my legs are too, I will bid you good night" (Epilogue 26–34). Falstaff reprises his favorite joke about his own "fat meat." Alertly turning defect into opportunity, Falstaff makes a Delphic prophecy or another specious guarantee that the story will continue, "with Sir John in it." Though "for any thing I know," he adds, Falstaff might "die of a sweat"—the mysterious, often fatal epidemic periodically sweeping Shakespeare's London—"unless already 'a be kill'd" by "your hard opinions" (29–31). If the speaker is Falstaff, as I would stake a thousand pound, these lines very likely belong to Will Kemp, about to leave the company to jig from London to Norwich. Hence the promise to recall Falstaff in *Henry V* is conditional: "unless already 'a be killed." This epilogue might indeed be the "last...speech" (Epilogue 1) for both Shakespeare's "great fool" Falstaff and for Will Kemp, the celebrated clown and "Dancer." Deftly the playwright hedges his bets and blazons *Henry V*—with or without Will Kemp. A weak pun on the Christian name shared by Kemp and Shakespeare reinforces this web of foolery connecting playwright, character, and actor. The epilogue displays Falstaff playing *fort/da* (gone/there!), the game of disappearance and return, a game he would if he could play without end.

Feste's epilogue to *Twelfth Night* is another oddly discombobulating finale, expressing the fool's power to distrust closure, dissolve meanings, and contest feelings. No one more carelessly or cruelly dismisses Malvolio's mortification than Feste. Like Puck with his broom, Feste whisks away care and mocks Malvolio's pain. Yet here at last is Feste singing a frankly plaintive song, punctuating the desperate revelry of *Twelfth Night* with melancholy blues in a minor key. Autumnal and haunting, Feste surveys the stages of life, mournfully ending every stanza, "for the rain it raineth every day" (*TN* 5.1.392). Far from the sun-drenched Arden of *As You Like It*, we seem closer to Lear's blasted heath where Lear's Fool literally repeats Feste's song. Eerily, Feste's "I will awake it anon" (5.1.48–49) also anticipates the enigmatic final line of Lear's Fool: "And I'll go to bed at noon" (*Lr* 3.6.85). Thus *Twelfth Night* concludes more in sorrow than in celebration: "A great while ago the world begun, / With hey, ho, the wind and the rain. / But that's all one, our play is done, / And we'll strive to please you every day" (5.1.405–8).

Feste's *striving* seems calculated or determined. So too is his emphatic reiteration of singularity: "I was *one*, sir, in this enterlude—*one* Sir Topas, sir, but that's all *one*" (5.2.372–73; my emphasis), as if unity itself doubles and splits again, reiterated in his final lines: "But that's all one, our play is done, / And we'll strive to please you every day." How the fool giveth and taketh away! No sooner does he finish, "our play is done," than he acknowledges that the show goes on tomorrow and tomorrow. Instead of providing comfort and joy or concluding with the satisfying click of closure, Feste evokes the strain of resolution, the artifice of production, and the onerous effort to please. In this sense, Feste's song appropriately ends the play's laborious endeavors to be amusing and amused, felicitous and fulfilled. In the spirit of Elizabeth's jester, Dick Tarlton (said to "undump-ish" the queen with his "*happy unhappy* answers"[5]), Feste's elegiac valediction accommodates the bleak facts without rancor or resentment. Such is life, suggests Feste, resigned to folly everywhere.

The epilogue to *As You Like It* is delivered by Shakespeare's foolosopher queen Rosalind, fooling with such charming gusto that we might believe after all that fooling and feeling are "all one." Rosalind's epilogue is a spectacular demonstration of counterfeit, role-playing, and make-believe in a play in which the oscillation between artifice and reality is both the subject and the method. Where Falstaff sacrifices himself—"If you be not too much cloy'd with fat meat"—Rosalind serves a miraculous cuisine, that we may have our cake and eat it too. Now the basic distinctions between acting and being and between fooling and feeling waver and topple as the actor playing the actress unmasks and offers to kiss anyone, if only he were a woman. Who *is* this figure before us—Rosalind dressed as Ganymede? Rosalind arrayed as the bride? A boy actor half-costumed, toggling between himself and his role? Like uncanny Hymen at the wedding, and like many Shakespearean fools, Rosalind of the epilogue is splendidly liminal. The performance completed, on the threshold of the tiring house, the actor asks the audience poised to exit on the streets of Stratford or London to join with him, whoever he is and wherever he is, partly "obscured in the circle of this forest" (5.4.34).

Rosalind remains abundantly present yet coyly elusive. Coming out, speaking directly, Rosalind remains willfully "obscured," as if "prolonging the duplicity of self-discovery and self-concealment, the enchanting game of both/and."[6] Why would anyone want to end this play? Rather than awaken the audience from the dream world of make-believe, "Rosalind of many parts" (3.2.149) makes us all actors and spectators, synthesizing feeling and fooling. The epilogue "reminds us of reserve—the actor behind the character—and crosses a boundary that only the speaker can cross," Jonathan Goldberg explains, as he "speaks and unspeaks himself at once."[7] In *As You Like It*, Rosalind's coup de grâce affirms the triumph of artifice and the efficacy of fooling, very much in the entrancing spirit of Moria's beguiling performance, overflowing with gaiety, enthusiasm, and mirth. This is Rosalind's Erasmian moment. Like Moria and like Shakespeare's greatest fools, Rosalind has the rare power to enchant and disenchant. She exposes, debunks, and mocks the pretenses and illusions of romance while she conjures and creates a visionary realm. She radiates that aura of magic associated with fools, powerfully evident in Falstaff's double-dealing and in Shakespeare's feigning and fooling.

Like *Praise of Folly*, Shakespearean drama stresses that we are all actors and spectators. Rosalind is neither detached nor trapped in a double bind: she does not require us to distinguish illusion and reality nor prefer one to the other. On the contrary—and like the queen of contradiction, Moria—Rosalind compels us to believe "both/and," representing the saving delusion of foolery. Rosalind reminds us what Moria preaches, that we find joy and love in spite of or because of the pervasiveness of folly. Irreverent and naughty, laughing and teasing, coaxing and flirting, Rosalind cajoles audiences into self-indulgence, pleasure, and irresponsibility—folly in the highest degree! Like Moria, Rosalind is poised between game and earnest, play and seriousness, fooling and feeling. Revealing herself as a fool for love and trickster extraordinaire, she is a foolosopher one wishes to believe in.

The Folly of This Island

How lovely it would be if Rosalind were Shakespeare's ultimate foolosopher and her epilogue our fare-thee-well. The reality is less congenial and less tidy, to the evident chagrin of Prospero, delivering Shakespeare's final epilogue.[8] Among many uncanny splits and mystical mergers in *The Tempest*, the most remarkable mirroring juxtaposes Prospero and

Caliban—Shakespeare's final variation on mingled clowns and kings. As in *King Lear*, *Hamlet*, and *Othello*, the protagonist has an intimate, disturbing relationship with his mirror opposite and foil, a fool who defies definition. Nobody knows who or what Caliban is. To Prospero, Caliban is the *slave* "who never / Yields us kind answer" (1.2.309–10). He is subhuman—"not honor'd with / A human shape" (1.2.283–84)—fundamental, and common as dirt; Caliban is earth as Ariel is air.[9] Like earth, he is elemental but unformed; whereas Ariel can take various shapes, Caliban is shapeless; he is nothing—or anything. One of those colonial "subjects" (1.2.341), he is usurped and exploited, forcibly suppressed, defined by his oppressors. Prospero strives bootlessly to master Caliban: not to understand but to command him. Caliban is rarely addressed by name. Who christened him we can't say. Perhaps it suggests "cannibal." He himself breaks his name into syllables—"'Ban, 'Ban, Ca-Caliban!" (2.2.184)—suggesting the fragmentation and dispersal of self. Like Prospero and like the island itself, Caliban is never clearly known but variously constructed, identified differently by disparate observers. Not only is Caliban a hodgepodge of identities, but the valences of these identities are helter-skelter. A "most delicate monster" (2.2.89–90), Caliban is an amphibious creature, divided (like so many fools) between innocence and malevolence. Responding to Prospero's abuse, Caliban voices crude resentment and gorgeous lyricism.[10] Despite years of oppression and vituperation, he preserves surprising tenderness, remembering and articulating that "then I lov'd thee" (1.2.336). He still relishes "all the qualities o' th' isle" (1.2.337) and wants to share the best springs, berries, and fish. When Caliban describes his isle "full of noises" that "give delight and hurt not" (3.2.135–36), he seems a most delicate monster indeed. Caliban's alert sensibility—he loves "every fertile inch" (2.2.148) of his island home—contrasts Prospero's severe austerity: to Prospero "this island" is simply a barren place of exile.

Caliban's nature flummoxes Stephano and Trinculo. Is he man or fish? Monster? Devil? Savage? A moon-calf?[11] A prize for his captors, a nine days' wonder to every "holiday fool" (2.2.29)? All these possibilities occur to the befuddled castaways. Manically *designating* Caliban, Stephano and Trinculo think they have the measure of this strange beast: he is "some monster of the isle" (2.2.65), as they repeatedly say: "a most delicate monster!" (2.2.89–90), "a very shallow monster!" (2.2.144–45), a "very weak monster!" (2.2.145). Monstrous Caliban is "perfidious" (2.2.150), "most scurvy" (2.2.155), "abominable" (2.2.159), and "most ridiculous" (2.2.165). Stephano and Trinculo bumblingly notice Caliban's duality, a doubleness embodied in the great clown scene depicting the "strange bedfellows": literally, two fools' bodies; figuratively, the fool's bifurcation.

It is a very funny scene that still provokes kids and lovers of buffoonery to bounce and squeal with delight. First spying Caliban playing possum to escape danger, Trinculo murmurs, "Were I in England now...would this monster make a man; any strange beast there makes a man" (2.2.27–31). Though he simply means that he could "make" a fortune displaying such a strange beast to the paying public, he stumbles on a foolosophical issue in *The Tempest*: to what extent is any strange beast a man or every man a monster? Trinculo seeks refuge under Caliban's garment. Enter Stephano pickled on port. Stephano notices the double styles and incongruity of the four-legged beast: "His forward voice now is to speak well of his friend," observes Stephano, "his backward voice is to utter foul speeches and to detract" (2.2.90–92). Let the fun begin, as the strange bedfellows become an unholy trinity, trade vulgar insults, sing "very scurvy" songs, and get royally drunk. Pulling Trinculo from under the cloak, Stephano asks, "How cam'st thou to be the siege [excrement] of this mooncalf? Can he vent [shit] Trinculos?" (2.2.105–7). Stupidity and cupidity, inebriation and dissipation, and follies tried and true abound. Why not "be jocund" and make "merry" (3.2.116–17), as Caliban says?

Amid such frivolous frolics, the "pied ninny" (3.2.63) Trinculo occasionally hits the target: "that a monster should be such a natural!" (3.2.32–33). A "pied ninny" signifies a motley fool, and of course a "natural" means a fool by nature: fools of a feather flock together, or it takes one to know one. Defined in the dramatis personae as a jester, the sole character in all Shakespeare to be so distinguished, Trinculo probably wears motley. Caliban regards him as a "scurvy patch" (3.2.63) or clown, and Stephano calls Trinculo a "jesting monkey" (3.2.46). Therefore, it's not entirely surprising that some pertinence pops from Trinculo: "The folly of this island! They say there's but five upon this isle: we are three of them; if th' other two be brain'd like us, the state totters" (3.2.4–7).

Their foolish shenanigans mirror larger themes. Consider Caliban's daft conversion from Prospero's sullen slave to Stephano's obsequious "footlicker" (4.1.219). Kneeling and pledging faithful service, Caliban beseeches "Lord" Stephano, "I prithee be my god" (2.2.149). His servile worship of a drunken rascal ludicrously exaggerates the mutual adoration of Miranda and Ferdinand; at first sight, she calls him "a thing divine" (1.2.419), and he designates her "the goddess" (1.2.422). When Caliban dubs Stephano "thou wondrous man" (2.2.164), he all but spells Miranda's name. In Shakespeare's hall of mirrors, these "strange bedfellows" parody (proleptically) the romantic lovers and mock (clownishly) the sacred. Stephano's repeated invocation, "kiss the book" (2.2.130), inflates drunkenness into holiness; the booze that fuels unruliness is the fun house reflection of Prospero's white magic and spiritual powers. Stephano reports that he was literally saved by sack: "I escap'd upon a butt of sack" (2.2.121) from the shipwreck. Their foolish drunkenness is self-medication and self-intoxication.

This inspired clown scene stages a burlesque regeneration. As Caliban and Trinculo lie hidden under a cover, two pairs of legs extended from opposite ends, Stephano impersonates the Savior calling Lazarus: "If thou beest Trinculo, come forth" (2.2.103). The legs-first extraction of Trinculo resembles a breached birth. To the "two Neapolitans scap'd" (2.2.113) and saved from drowning, it is certainly a joyous reunion and revival—humorously ballasted, of course: "Prithee do not turn me about," says Stephano to his jubilant companion, "my stomach is not constant" (2.2.114–15). Stephano envisions a carnival kingdom: "Wit shall not go unrewarded while I am king of this country" (4.1.242–43). Ah, to be king of Cockayne! Addled to incapacity, Stephano overlooks the lack of subjects in his domain.

But their harebrained revelry turns ominous when these jokers plan murder and rape. "Batter his skull, or paunch him with a stake" (3.2.90), Caliban gleefully urges Stephano—"brain" (3.2.88) Prospero with a vengeance. Once they kill the old man, his daughter "will become thy bed" (3.2.104). The farcical delivery thus enacts the birth of evil. It is troubling how closely the clowns' gambols ape their betters and how much tomfoolery looks like sin. In *Twelfth Night*, only Malvolio really pays the price of folly. Here, Trinculo's buffoonery, Caliban's idiocy, and Stephano's pipe dreams metamorphose into a genuinely disquieting plot. "The folly of this island" does not simply dissolve or change fortuitously, as in *A Midsummer Night's Dream*; rather, more like the tragedies, "what's past is prologue" (2.1.253). Antonio's usurpation, Sebastian's projected regicide, and Caliban's revenge are eerily similar ruthless reenactments of the primal curse, Cain's murder of Abel. Caliban promises Stephano to be "thine own forever" (4.1.218). Reinforcing the allusion to *Othello* is a second verbatim echo, when Stephano tells Caliban "thou shalt be my lieutenant" (3.2.15): wickedness takes root. Like Sebastian and Antonio contemplating the murder of their king, the fools speak in euphemisms to cloak their vile designs; Caliban actually calls the scheme to kill Prospero "that good mischief" (4.1.217).

Delicate and lyrical Caliban is also base and vicious: "And yet I *needs must* curse" (2.2.4; my emphasis).[12] He has another role associated with the fool: the jeering gargoyle or face of death. Caliban becomes a memento mori, like the antic mocking Richard II. That jest is a curse, haunting Richard in prison, Hamlet in the graveyard, and Prospero in his glory.[13] "Curs'd" (1.2.339) Caliban comes back to plague Prospero.[14] In the King James translations of the Hebrew Bible, *fool* and *folly* are invariably curses, characterizing incredibly stupid attitudes or deliberately wicked conduct; in effect, folly is a sin and fools are evil. *The Tempest*, like the Book of Ecclesiastes or Proverbs, bristles with curses. These fools are no mere laughing matter nor easily ignored, though eventually foiled.[15] The clowns land in the "filthy-mantled pool…dancing up to th' chins, that the foul lake / O'erstunk their feet" (4.1.182–84). A noisome bit of equine offal is Trinculo's lament, "Monster, I do smell all horse-piss, at which my nose is in great indignation" (4.1.199–200).

But the fools' humiliation humorously reminds us that almost everyone in this play is mired in muck. No Shakespeare play, except possibly *Othello*, includes more virulence, vilification, pestilence, and infection than *The Tempest*. The word *foul* recurs several times, as in "that foul conspiracy / Of the beast Caliban" (4.1.139–40). Prospero regards Caliban with the outraged contempt of a scourge: "Filth as thou art" (1.2.346). Prospero regularly berates Caliban and heaps maledictions upon him: "Thou poisonous slave, got by the devil himself" (1.2.319). Prospero's Thersitic revulsion is not abating, at moments very like that of Hamlet: "And is't not to be damn'd, / To let this canker of our nature come / In further evil?" (*Ham.* 5.2.68–70). Prospero finds filth, corruption, and disease everywhere—and it contaminates his language. "Do not infest your mind" (5.1.246), he exhorts Alonso in an odd formulation he favors; an earlier iteration is "infect his reason" (1.2.208). Most puzzling is the father's comment on his daughter's love: "Poor worm, thou art infected!" (3.1.31).[16] Prospero cannot imagine love or beauty without disease and "canker" (1.2.416).[17]

Like Shakespeare's scourges of folly who "needs must curse" (2.2.4), Prospero vows, "I will plague them all" (4.1.192). One must wonder whether Prospero is remedy or source of the plague. To Prince Ferdinand, Prospero seems "compos'd of harshness" (3.1.8–9). Ferdinand better wait for the wedding night, Prospero warns, lest

> barren hate,
> Sour-ey'd disdain, and discord shall bestrew
> The union of your bed with weeds so loathly
> That you shall hate it both.
>
> (4.1.19–22)

What provokes Prospero's outburst and his catalog of tortures threatening Ferdinand? Embarrassed by her father's "anger, so distemper'd" (4.1.145), Miranda wonders, "Why speaks my father so ungently?" (1.2.445). Prospero's fury erupts at slight pretext. Even loyal and tender Ariel incurs Prospero's wrath: "Thou liest, malignant thing!" (1.2.257).[18]

The special object of Prospero's fury is Caliban. Understandably, in part: fathers don't like monsters who imperil their daughters. But Prospero treats

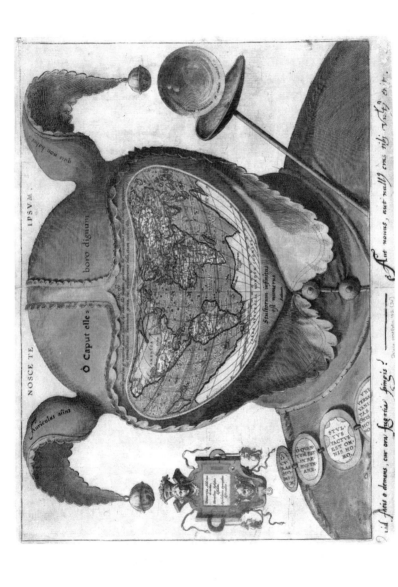

Figure 7.1 The Fool's Cap World Map, ca. 1620. Photograph reproduced with permission of Bodleian Libraries Imaging Services.

Caliban with extraordinary contempt and enthusiastic persecution. For minor offenses such as surliness, Prospero punishes Caliban with cramps and pinches "as thick as honeycomb, each pinch more stinging / Than bees that made 'em" (1.2.329–30). Caliban's afflictions arouse the *poetry* in Prospero! A connoisseur of torture, his modus operandi is a show of force. His attack dog, named Fury, is loosed upon Caliban, Stephano, and Trinculo (4.1.257).

Prospero scourges folly with the righteousness of the Hebrew prophets and the mercilessness of Jehovah. Though *sin* is a word Shakespeare uses very sparingly, in *The Tempest* it resounds from Ariel's prophetic denunciation of "three men of sin" (3.3.53) through Prospero's epilogue.[19] Prospero judges Caliban indelibly wicked: "A devil, a born devil, on whose nature / Nurture can never stick; on whom my pains, / Humanely taken, all, all lost, quite lost" (4.1.188–90).[20] Prospero's obsession with evil Caliban causes him to disrupt the wedding masque staged for Miranda and Ferdinand. His only explanation for interrupting and terminating the performance is that he suddenly remembers Caliban's "foul conspiracy" (4.1.139).

Time was when Prospero's "so potent art" (5.1.50) seemed more powerful and promising: when he freed Ariel from the "torment" of "the damn'd" (1.2.89, 1.2.90), Prospero specifies, "It was mine art" that "let thee out" (1.2.291–293). Now, redemption seems beyond the "vanity of mine art" (4.1.41), and Caliban shadows Prospero. In the mirror of cursed Caliban, Prospero sees his mortal, unredeemable defectiveness: like Lear and his Fool, like Hamlet and Claudius, and Othello and Iago, Caliban and Prospero are kin and kind. Either could say "curs'd be I" (1.2.339). Like Lear, Hamlet, and Richard, Prospero perceives the antic within, the skull beneath the skin: *ego in Arcadia*. Ruefully acknowledging Caliban, Prospero recognizes their kinship: "this thing of darkness I / Acknowledge mine" (5.1.275–76).

Prospero's elegiac lament for "this insubstantial pageant faded" (4.1.155) directly follows. Gorgeously, plangently, Prospero measures the *limits* of his powers: his art is deception, illusory, mortal, and passing.[21] "Yea, all which it inherit, shall dissolve" (4.1.154). In Prospero's vision, life is an insubstantial pageant played upon "this great stage of fools" (*Lr* 4.6.183): "We are such stuff / As dreams are made on; and our little life / Is rounded with a sleep" (4.1.156–58). Both Lear and Prospero resemble the prisoner in Plato's parable (cited near the climax of *Praise of Folly*) "who escaped but returned to the cave to tell them he had seen things as they truly are and that they were very much deceived in thinking that nothing else exists except those wretched shadows" (133). Unlike Moria, Prospero lacks faith that anything else exists except those wretched shadows. Moria stresses that the body will undergo a "transformation" (136) and the redeemed soul "will receive unspeakable joy from that Highest Good which gathers all things to Himself" (137). Without such faith, Prospero foresees only a little life and long sleep. When Prospero abjures his magic, it is an uncrowning like that of Richard or Lear.[22] Prospero's renunciations of power are not regenerative revivals but painful intimations of mortality: "my weakness, my old brain…my infirmity" (4.1.159–60). Divested and disrobed, he is Lear's "thing itself" (3.4.106), truly "mortal in folly" (*AYL* 2.4.56).

After such knowledge, what forgiveness? In struggle, still isolated, Prospero's conversations continue to seem like the soliloquies of a "dismayed," "vexed," "troubled" old man (4.1.147, 4.1.158, 4.1.159). Inexplicably, Prospero delays the good news of Ferdinand's recovery and prolongs Alonso's grieving. The word *loss* is echoed seven times in seventeen lines.[23] And how stubbornly Prospero clings to his resentments: "Behold…the wronged Duke of Milan" (5.1.106–8). When he forgives his brother, it is hardly mercy that falleth like the gentle rains from heaven: "most wicked sir, whom to call brother / Would even infect my mouth" (5.1.130–31). Forgiveness—with a vengeance!

When the villains are contained, the lost found, and festive celebrations in order, Gonzalo proclaims, "O, rejoice / Beyond a common joy, and set it down / With gold on lasting pillars" (5.1.206–8). But Gonzalo, foolishly optimistic and fondly exuberant, never gets it quite right. Prospero refrains this time from dispelling the illusion and exposing the delusion. To say the unsayable: 'tis new to thee, and nothing gold can stay—not love or life nor gilded monuments nor these revels, nor the baseless fabric of this vision, these our actors, the great Globe itself, not this rough magic or airy charm, nor our little life. The best is past, old Gonzalo, and every third thought should be your grave. Wisely and kindly, to spare the newlyweds his abridgement of hope, Prospero keeps such knowledge to himself and feigns otherwise. It is better, as Moria preaches, to fool oneself, to live as if life were beautiful and forever.

Prospero appears ultimately as a man "most faint" (Epilogue 3), lacking "spirits to enforce, art to enchant" (14). He makes a very difficult passage and does not go gentle into that good night; his strain shows in a valediction that resembles a deathbed confession and a last-ditch Hail Mary: "And my ending is despair, / Unless I be reliev'd by prayer" (15–16). He feels mortified: "Which pierces so that it assaults / Mercy itself, and frees all faults" (17–18). Like Moria, at the last, Prospero addresses fellow sinners in peril: "As you from crimes would pardon'd be, / Let your indulgence set me free" (19–20). But when Prospero says that he has provided the model and "pardon'd the deceiver" (7), one must wonder: Who is fooling whom? As Fats Waller would say, "one never knows, do one?"

Figure 7.2 A court fool, reproduction of a miniature from a fifteenth-century manuscript, from *Le Moyen Age et La Renaissance* by Paul Lacroix (1806–84) published 1847 (color litho) by the French School (nineteenth century). Private Collection/Ken Welsh. Reproduced with permission of the Bridgeman Art Library International.v

Motley to the View

A fool never knows when to shut up. Indeed, that is one foolproof sign of a fool: "A fool also is full of words...who can tell him?" saith the Preacher (Eccles. 10:14). My daughters occasionally mention that sometimes professors talk too much, explaining that there is no end to wisdom and that folly hath no bottom, et cetera.[24] Is there not always another question to be asked?[25] Erasmus explains *Praise of Folly* in a long appendix.[26] The quest of folly is never finished, only abandoned. In another book or another life, I would explore such feasts of folly as *Love's Labor's Lost*, *Merchant of Venice*, and *Antony and Cleopatra*. And how could one neglect great clowns such as Macbeth's Porter and Juliet's Nurse, tricksters such as Autolycus, deceivers such as Richard III and Edmund the Bastard, vital rebels such as Jack Cade, seriocomic commentators including Enobarbus, wise fools such as Edgar's Poor Tom, madmen such as Leontes? One never knows, do one?

If defining folly is futile, exploring or evaluating Shakespearean folly is never ending. The student of fooling, poor freak of nature, resembles Rabelais's mouse: "The more it tries to get free of the pitch, the more it gets stuck. You likewise, straining to get yourself out of the nets of perplexity, remain stuck in them more than ever."[27] Beguiled into believing we are in on the trick, we are taken in and fooled. If I realize I am being fooled, am I not a fool? And if I am a fool, how do I know when I am being fooled by my attempts to fool others? Sometimes the effects seem positive, sometimes negative, often both. The Fool's Uncertainty Principle might be: to observe folly is to participate in it.

Though it may or may not be inspiriting, it is instructive to remember that Shakespeare represents himself as a fool: "Alas, 'tis true I have gone here and there, / And made myself a *motley to the view*" (*Son.* 110). Never reluctant to play the fool, Shakespeare bestows his own name on William, the country bumpkin and clown overawed by the wordsmith Touchstone in *As You Like It*. ("Will" also alludes to Shakespeare's estranged colleague Kemp.) I like to imagine as coat of arms for Motley Shakespeare that figure from Gestalt therapy. Is it a duck or a rabbit? Like Shakespeare, the fool is everyone and no one, essential yet without essence. Like the playwright, fools contrive and cultivate illusions, suggesting without guaranteeing something real, valuable, and vital. Life in play may be life in earnest, as Falstaff and Rosalind attest. Shadow-like, evidently not all there, the fool sometimes seems to be all we have. We *need* folly and want to believe in illusions, counterfeit, and dreams. "Wishers were ever fools" (*Ant.* 4.15.37), says Cleopatra, succumbing to a delusion more substantial and compelling than meager reality. Wishers were ever fools, and a good thing, too, says Moria. That's as may be. "No more, the text is foolish" (*Lr* 4.2.37).

Glossary; or, A Rhetoric of Fooling

amphibology: "the ambiguous, or figure of sence incertaine" (Puttenham 1589).

anatomy: a subject for minute dissection or analysis. Hence, to *anatomize* folly.

aporia: "make doubt of things when by a plaine manner of speech wee might affirme or deny him" (Puttenham 1589).

commedia dell'arte: Italian drama, often improvised, featuring stock characters such as Pantaloon and Harlequin.

counterfeit: Pretended, disguised, feigned, false, sham; to imitate with intent to deceive. To make pretence, practice deceit; to represent, portray, depict.

dulce et utile: Latin, meaning sweet and useful; referring to the purpose of art, to entertain and instruct.

fain: To be delighted or glad, rejoice. To pretend kindness.

feign: To fashion fictitiously or deceptively. To invent, to forge, to contrive. To allege falsely against. To make fictitious statements; to indulge in fiction. To disguise, dissemble, conceal, practice dissimulation. To make a show of, put on an appearance of, put on, pretend.

flyting: To contend, strive; chide, wrangle; debate or dispute. Abusive speech.

fol or *folie*: French for madness.

foolosophy: A coinage by Sir Thomas Chaloner in his 1549 translation of Erasmus; used by Shakespeare in *Timon of Athens*: "my fooleosophers" (5.5.94).

geck: A fool, simpleton; one who is tricked or derided, a dupe.

gull: A credulous person; one easily imposed upon; a dupe, simpleton, fool. A trick, deception, fraud; a false report. A trickster, cheat, impostor (*OED*).

handy-dandy: "A children's game in which a small object is shaken between the hands by one of the players, and, the hands being suddenly closed, the other player is required to guess in which hand the object remains. With change of places; alternately, in rapid alternation. Offering a choice, or when it is indifferent which of two things is chosen" (*OED*).

hendiadys: A figure of speech in which a single idea is expressed by two words connected by a conjunction.

hobby-horse: Ridiculous antics, foolish obsession.

hocos-pocos: "Trickster, conjurer, or juggler" (*OED*), supposedly satirizing the Catholic priest conducting mass: *hoc est corpus*.

misprision: Misunderstanding; a mistake.

moon-calf: "A born fool; a congenital idiot; a simpleton"; "A deformed animal; a monster." Also, a malformed fetus (*OED*).

mountebank: Itinerant charlatan who sold supposed medicines and remedies.

natural fool: A disturbed or deranged person, lunatic or insane.

oxymoron: Self-contradicting term; combines *oxus*, "sharp," and *moros*, "fool."

preposterous: Inverted in position or order. Unnatural, irrational, perverse, absurd.

prestidigitation: Sleight of hand, legerdemain; conjuring.

real names of artificial fools: Bubble, Baubel, Bob Bell, Patch, Sexton, Will Somer, Simplicity, Ambidexter, Richard Tarlton, Will Kemp, Merry Andrew, Jack Pudding, Changeling.

sotie: Foolishness, folly. A species of broad satirical farce in early modern France.

sot: Fool. *OED* cites Heywood's *Witty and Witless*: "I would now rather be / Sage Solomon than sot Somer."

Zanna: The zany figure in *commedia dell'arte*.

Notes

1 In Quest of Folly

1. All Shakespeare citations are from *The Riverside Shakespeare*, ed. G. Blakemore Evans et al. (Boston: Houghton Mifflin, 1974) and specified by parenthetical references to play, act, scene, and line numbers. This one is (*TN* 3.1.38–39).
2. James Joyce once agreed with a critic that he was trivial. "Also quadrivial," he added.
3. For "Ruinous Folly" see Homer, *The Iliad*, tr. Robert Fitzgerald (Garden City, NY: Anchor, 1975), 460. Richmond Lattimore's translation dubs this goddess "Delusion," whereas Alexander Pope sticks with an anglicized "Ate." Erasmus cites Até in *Praise of Folly*, ed. and tr. Clarence H. Miller (New Haven, CT: Yale University Press, 1979), 26.
4. All biblical citations are from *The Holy Bible, Containing the Old and New Testaments, in the Common Version. With Amendments of the Language*, ed. Noah Webster (New Haven, CT: Durrie and Peck, 1833).
5. All definitions in this book unless otherwise specified are from the *Oxford English Dictionary*.
6. A popular English translation of Erasmus illustrated by Hans Holbein appeared in 1515–16. Shakespeare very likely read the 1549 translation by Sir Thomas Chaloner.
7. The term *hocos-pocos* signified a trickster, conjurer, or juggler, supposedly satirizing the Catholic mass: *hoc est corpus*.
8. When the high-end call girl Christine Keeler was cross-examined by John Profumo's lawyers, she was asked if she realized that the distinguished Secretary of State for War denied all charges of impropriety. She replied, "Well, he *would*, wouldn't he?"
9. Though this sounds like good news for fools, Paul is neither an apostle of folly nor a member of folly's party without knowing it. The key text for the student of folly is 1 Corinthians 1:20–28: "Hath not God made foolish the wisdom of this world? ... Because the foolishness of God is wiser than men; and the weakness of God is stronger than men. ... But God hath chosen the foolish things of the world to confound the wise; and God hath chosen the weak things of the

world to confound the things which are mighty; And base things of the world, and things which are despised, hath God chosen." In Paul's revaluation, it is truly wise to ignore or reject the foolish things of this world. Paul's reversal of meanings comes clear: "If any man among you seemeth to be wise in this world, let him become a fool, that he may be wise" (1 Cor. 3:18). Of course, any fool or devil "can cite Scripture for his purpose" (*MV* 1.3.98). One such textual deviate is Moria, moving heaven and earth in *Praise of Folly*.

10. Thomas Chaloner, tr. and ed., *The Praise of Folie*, ed. Clarence H. Miller (London: Oxford University Press, 1965). Clarence Miller also did his own translation of Erasmus. Henceforth, unless otherwise specified, my quotations of Erasmus are from *Praise of Folly*, ed. and tr. Clarence H. Miller (New Haven, CT, and London: Yale University Press, 1979).

11. George Santayana, *Soliloquies in England and Later Soliloquies, The Works of George Santayana*, IX (New York: Scribner's, 1937), 142.

12. Jonathan Bate stresses this point in his exceptional book *The Genius of Shakespeare* (New York: Oxford University Press, 1998), 307. Bate's "Quantum Shakespeare" adumbrates the principles of complementarity and uncertainty in twentieth-century physics. Bate also notes that Keats's "Negative capability," an almost oxymoronic fusion of a negative and positive term, anticipates Heisenberg's uncertainty principle.

13. William Empson, *Seven Types of Ambiguity* (London: Chatto & Windus, 1930), 192.

14. In *Merchant of Venice*, the clown maintains "intimate contact" through direct address, as in the imperative, "Mark me now." See David Wiles, *Shakespeare's Clown: Actor and Text in the Elizabethan Playhouse* (Cambridge: Cambridge University Press, 1987), 102.

2 This Great Stage of Fools

1. Archie Armstrong, an ornery little fool, despised the diminutive, prickly Archbishop Laud. Once at a banquet he offered grace: "give great praise to the Lord, and little Laud to the devil." By this rather good pun, Laud was not amused.

2. Kemp's title was thus proclaimed by Shakespeare's contemporary Thomas Nash in 1590. Cited in Edward I. Berry, *Shakespeare's Comic Rites* (Cambridge: Cambridge University Press, 1984), 110.

3. A "wafer" is an orb-shaped disk; a marotte is a stick often adorned with a replica of the jester's head. Scholars disagree on whether an English fool would sport a marotte before 1611. Marottes were certainly deployed in sixteenth-century France, depicted in many medieval images, and mentioned in John Gower's *Confessio Amantis* (ca. 1390) and John Skelton's *Magnyfycence* (ca. 1515).

4. In Kemp's book about his jigging exploit, *Nine Days Wonder*, he bids "Farewell Congruity"!

5. "Folly" turns up eighty times. In addition, of course, are scores of synonyms and cognates for *fool* and *folly*, such as jest, cozen, trick. See the glossary for examples and definitions.

6. In *Jocoserious Joyce: The Fate of Folly in* Ulysses (Ithaca, NY: Cornell University Press, 1991), I described a belle époque Parisian performer who could fart musical notes. In extending my research, I learn that this skill was hardly unique and harkens back at least to the early modern era. I am happy to correct my early misconception of musical effluvia.

7. Robert Payne, *Charlie Chaplin (Orig. Title: The Great God Pan)* (New York: Ace Books, 1952), 25–26.

8. "Jester" as defined by *OED*.

9. The "rude mechanicals" are, of course, workmen or artisans. *Mechanical* also means automatic, as in Henri Bergson's conception of humor as a mechanical or inorganic encrustation upon the living, a default mode rather than a vital response.

10. In both Middle English and Russian, the word *blessed* is itself paradoxical. The English *sely* meant "blessed" and became the modern "silly." Similarly in Russian, *blazzhennyi* signifies "blessed" as well as "silly, foolish."

11. See Jan Kott, *The Bottom Translation: Marlowe and Shakespeare and the Carnival Tradition*, tr. Daniela Miedzyrzeka and Lillian Vallee (Evanston, IL: Northwestern University Press, 1987).

12. Paul, 1 Corinthians 2:9. This is the Geneva translation known to Shakespeare.

13. Jonathan Bate notes this wonderful detail. See Bate, *Soul of the Age: A Biography of the Mind of William Shakespeare* (New York: Random House, 2009), 57. Emphasis mine.

14. As Edward Berry cogently remarks in *Comic Rites*, 136.

15. In the 1935 Reinhardt/Dieterle film *Midsummer Night's Dream*, Mickey Rooney makes Puck a snorting, grunting Huck Finn; Moshinsky's 1982 version produces a punk Puck baring fangs and sniffing bestially whenever humans approach.

16. Puck also traces his lineage to the tricky slave of Roman comedy and to Cupid, another unreliable marksman. Another source for Puck is Reginald Scot's catalog of demons, *The Discoverie of Witchcraft* (1584), including Robin Goodfellowe and hobgoblin.

17. See George Puttenham, *The Arte of English Poesie* (Kent, OH: Kent State University Press, 1970), 180–81, originally published in London in 1588. Shakespeare immediately scooped this new word: Hortensio in *Taming of the Shrew* is termed a "preposterous ass" (3.1.9).

18. His emphasis upon "sight" stresses the subjectivity of perspective and the accuracy of his own view. Another hint of Puck's enhanced role as "master of the discourse" might be suggested by Puck's pun on tale/teller/tailor: "The wisest aunt, telling the saddest tale, / Sometime for three-foot stool mistaketh me; / Then slip I from her bum, down topples she, / And 'tailor!' cries, and falls into a cough" (2.1.51–54). Puck playing the stool for the old aunt's bum also associates this trickster with that other agent of folly, Bottom.

19. *Presence* maintains its old meaning, "high bearing."

20. James L. Calderwood, *A Midsummer Night's Dream* (Hempel Hempstead: Harvester Wheatsheaf, 1992), 94.

21. It is very likely but not certain that Will Kemp played Falstaff. Possibly the role was played by Thomas Pope.
22. Robert Frost, "Education by Poetry," in *Frost: Collected Poems, Prose, and Plays*, ed. Richard Poirier (New York, NY: Library of America, 1995), 723–24.
23. One indication that Will Kemp played both characters is the in-joke, "O, that I had been writ down an ass!" (4.2.88–89).
24. James Shapiro speculates intriguingly about the discord between Shakespeare and Kemp in *A Year in the Life of William Shakespeare: 1599* (New York: HarperCollins, 2005).
25. Robert Armin, *Fools and Jesters: With a Reprint of Robert Armin's Nest of Ninnies: 1608* (London: Shakespeare Society, 1842).
26. In that Bible of Folly, *The Marriage of Heaven and Hell*, Blake's Devil proclaims, "The road of excess leads to the palace of wisdom." William Blake, *The Marriage of Heaven and Hell* (London and New York: Oxford University Press, 1975).
27. According to Puttenham, *Arte of English Poesie*, 267, 234.
28. Thus Samuel Johnson glosses "mortal."
29. In this instance, I cite Richard Knowles, ed., *A New Variorum Edition of Shakespeare's As You Like It* (New York: Modern Language Association of America, 1977), 190–91, based on the folio edition. As Empson puzzled, editors since Johnson almost uniformly amend *faining* to *feigning*. See William Empson, *Some Versions of Pastoral* (New York: Penguin, 1966), 113.
30. *Jocoserious* is a Joycean neologism in the Ithaca episode of *Ulysses*.
31. Robert Frost, interview by Richard Poirier, *Paris Review* 24 (Summer–Fall 1960), 892.
32. E-mail correspondence with Lawrence Raab, April 2009. Some critics consider Touchstone less complex, shallower than Feste, who is a wit unlike Touchstone, a raconteur who recites stock bits.
33. Cf. Groucho Marx: "These are my principles. If you don't like them I have others."
34. Cf. Prospero's rueful remark about Caliban, "this thing of darkness I / Acknowledge mine" (*Tmp.* 5.1.275–76).
35. Jaques bestows this dubious title, meaning *substantial* but also *dull, shallow-witted*.
36. C. L. Barber, *Shakespeare's Festive Comedy: A Study of Dramatic Form and Its Relation to Social Custom* (Princeton, NJ: Princeton University Press, 1959), 232.
37. Feste is "discomforting, an outsider, almost malevolently saturnine, defying the sentimental response." See Ralph Berry, "The Season of *Twelfth Night*," in *Changing Styles in Shakespeare* (London: Routledge, 2005), 116.
38. Lavatch alludes to the recently staged *Troilus and Cressida* and parodies Marlowe's mighty line: "Was this fair face the cause" (1.3.70).
39. Richard Hillman observes, "Like the other late clowns, Lavatch serves as an index of the progressive displacement and enervation of the subversive.... Even the impotent disruptions of an 'allow'd fool,' it seems, belong to the past." See

Hillman, *Shakespearean Subversions: The Trickster and the Play-Text* (London and New York: Routledge, 1992), 166. Price agrees that Lavatch is "only a shadow of the former Shakespearian clown." See Joseph G. Price, *The Unfortunate Comedy: A Study of All's Well That Ends Well and Its Critics* (Toronto: University of Toronto Press, 1968), 126.

40. Still called "innocents" in Elizabethan England, natural fools were associated with children: "out of the mouths of babes and fools."

41. Perhaps his name evokes *cow* or *beef* in French. Jokes, Freud thought, are textbook illustrations of displacement: "Such a shift from the consequent to the inconsequent that allows the unsayable to be said, in some distorted form, is the very basis of the displacement process as expounded by Freud: the dream image of something trivial, the neurotic symptom centered in some 'innocent' bodily part, the joke that routes psychic intensity through a detour of absurdity, the screen memory that conceals another one more fraught with fear or guilt— all evade or placate the social or internalized censors by this same process of deviation and substitution." See Susan Snyder, *Shakespeare: A Wayward Journey* (Cranbury, London, and Ontario: Associated University Presses, 2002), 139.

42. Lavatch is designated "Clown" in the dramatis personae and stage directions.

43. David Garrick's 1756 production, for instance, featured "Capt. Parolles by Mr Woodward."

44. The term is reiterated three times: "This counterfeit lump of ore" (3.6.37), "this counterfeit" (4.3.34), and "this counterfeit module" (4.3.99).

45. It is "tempting to try to ameliorate, somewhat, the play's central difficulty by shifting the blame for Bertram's ignobility onto a figure who can be seen as his bad angel, as a version of the old Vice, who tempts Bertram and leads him astray. If Parolles could be so seen, could be found to function in the plays as a surrogate for the audience's dislike of his master, if we could legitimately allow Parolles to serve as a scapegoat for Bertram, [then] the difficulty of forgiving Bertram at the play's end would be considerably eased." See Bertrand Evans, *Shakespeare's Comedies* (Oxford: Clarendon Press, 1960), 119.

46. One of the rare critics to defend Parolles is G. Wilson Knight. "Indeed, he possesses a warm humanity causing Helena to prefer him with all his falsities," some "human ingredients which absolute virtue would seem to exclude." With rare candor "unfettered by principle," Parolles "knows precisely, *what he is*; what he can, and cannot, do." Perhaps, Parolles and Helena "alone of our people have this integrity; and that may be why she from the start recognizes in him a certain harmony." See G. Wilson Knight, *The Sovereign Flower: On Shakespeare as the Poet of Royalism Together with Related Essays and Indexes to Earlier Volumes* (London: Methuen & Co., 1958), 107, 121–22. For another "Vindication of Parolles," see Jules Rothman, "A Vindication of Parolles," *Shakespeare Quarterly* 23 (1972): 183–96.

47. See Robert Grams Hunter, *"All's Well That Ends Well* as a Comedy of Forgiveness," in *Shakespeare's Later Comedies: An Anthology of Modern Criticism*, ed. D. J. Palmer (Harmondsworth: Penguin, 1971), 32.

3   The History of Folly in the Henriad

1. David M. Bergeron, *"Richard II* and Carnival Politics," *Shakespeare Quarterly* 42 (Spring 1991): 36.

2. It might be *the* longest speech, not necessarily a distinction. Cf. the mock rockers Spinal Tap, renowned as "England's loudest band."

3. In an effort to give Henry IV his due, I once asked a student to recite the king's majestic speech, "I know not whether God will have it so ... To punish my mistreadings" (3.2.1–11). Unfortunately for the king's dignity, it came out, "To punish my missed readings."

4. A. C. Bradley, "The Rejection of Falstaff," in *Oxford Lectures on Poetry* (London: Macmillan, 1909), 273. In being metaphorically grounded yet aloft, Falstaff combines Caliban and Ariel.

5. Carrying the corpse of Hotspur, Falstaff probably means that he is neither a ghost nor a two-headed monster, as he might appear to be.

6. It is said that a distinguished philosopher lecturing at Columbia University stated that although in many languages a double negative constitutes an affirmative, "in no language does a double affirmative signify a negative." From the back row came a sarcastic, "Yeah, yeah."

7. A contemporary court jester was named Ambidexter.

8. *Reamalgamerge* is another Joycean coinage: "by a coincidence of their contraries reamalgamerge in that indentity of undiscernibles." See James Joyce, *Finnegans Wake* (New York: Viking, 1959), 49–50.

9. Traditionally wielded by Vice, the companion or double of Folly, in the old morality plays.

10. For a similar point, see David Wiles, *Shakespeare's Clown: Actor and Text in the Elizabethan Playhouse* (Cambridge: Cambridge University Press, 1987), 126–27.

11. See Bradley, "The Rejection of Falstaff," 261–62.

12. Roy Battenhouse, "Falstaff as Parodist and Perhaps Holy Fool," *PMLA* 90 (1975): 33.

13. Harold Bloom, *Shakespeare: The Invention of the Human* (New York: Riverhead Books, 1998), 275, 276, 279.

14. Samuel Johnson, *Samuel Johnson on Shakespeare*, ed. W. K. Wimsatt Jr. (New York: Hill and Wang, 1960), 315.

15. John Dover Wilson, *The Fortunes of Falstaff* (Cambridge: Cambridge University Press, 1943), 32, 95, 104.

16. J. W. Draper, "Falstaff, 'A Fool and A Jester,'" *Modern Language Quarterly* 7 (1946): 460.

17. Joyce, *Finnegans Wake*, 185.

18. Samuel Johnson, *A Dictionary of the English Language* (Longman, Hurst, Rees, and Orme, 1805).

19. Eric La Guardia, "Ceremony and History: The Problem of Symbol from *Richard II* to *Henry V*," *Pacific Coast Studies in Shakespeare*, ed. W. F. McNeir and T. N. Greenfield (Eugene: University of Oregon Books, 1966), 79. See also Jonas A.

Barish, "The Turning Away of Prince Hal," in *Twentieth Century Interpretations of Henry IV, Part One*, ed. R. J. Dorius (Englewood Cliffs, NJ: Prentice-Hall, 1970).

20. Michel Foucault suggests a latent link between punishment and folly itself: "In these executions ... there was a whole aspect of the carnival, in which rules were inverted, authority mocked and criminals transformed into heroes. ... It was evident that the great spectacle of punishment ran the risk of being rejected by the very people to whom it was addressed." See Michel Foucault, *Discipline and Punish: The Birth of the Prison*, tr. Alan Sheridan (London: Allen Lane, 1977), 61, 63.

21. The term "well farsed" adorns Chaloner's translation of Erasmus, 61, and (along with almost everything) surfaces in *Finnegans Wake* as Joyce's "farced epistol to the hibruws" (228).

4 Fools for Love: Fooling and Feeling

1. Dario Fo, *Tricks of the Trade*, ed. Stuart Clink Hood, tr. Joe Farrell (New York: Routledge, 1991), 176.

2. Desiderius Erasmus, *The Praise of Folie*, tr. Thomas Chaloner, ed. Clarence H. Miller (London: Oxford University Press, 1965), 38.

3. Erasmus also tells More that his encomium of folly is inspired by his friend's name, "so close to the Greek word for folly (Moria)" (2).

4. J. Huizinga, *Erasmus* (New York: Scribner's Sons, 1924), 95.

5. Falstaff calls Hal "the most comparative ... young prince" (*1H4* 1.2.80–81).

6. See William G. McCollom, "The Role of Wit in *Much Ado About Nothing*," *Shakespeare Quarterly* 19 (1968): 165–74. McCollom distinguishes four basic types of wit: verbal identifications and contrasts, quibbles, puns, etc.; conceptual wit including allusive understatement and sophistry; amusing flights of fancy; and short parodies, burlesque. McCollom conceives the play itself "is a kind of witticism in the tripartite form often taken by jests" and contends that the denouement celebrates "the triumph of true wit over false wisdom" (166, 173). This seems to me special pleading for wit and something of a shell game, replacing wit with something called "true wit," clearly distinguished from "false wisdom." The play is far more wary and critical of wit. See also Carl Dennis, "Wit and Wisdom in *Much Ado About Nothing*," *Studies in English Literature* 13, no. 2 (1973): 223–37.

7. Beatrice alludes to Benedick no fewer than twenty-six times in 1.1.

8. In this opening scene, Beatrice's exclamations, "O Lord" and "God help," are mildly intense and somewhat usual in Shakespeare. *Much Ado* mentions God fifty-six times, as opposed to sixteen iterations in *Twelfth Night* and nineteen in *Taming of the Shrew*.

9. The "Men's Club of Messina" is Harry Berger's deliciously apt phrase in "Against the Sink-a-Pace: Sexual and Family Politics in *Much Ado About Nothing*," *Shakespeare Quarterly* 33 (1982): 302–13. In fairness to Benedick,

everybody in Messina has cuckoldry on the brain; Beatrice also jests about the cuckold's horns with alarming frequency. Dr. Johnson worried that "neither [Shakespeare's] gentleman nor his ladies have much delicacy, nor are sufficiently distinguished from his clowns by any appearance of refined manners" ("Preface To Shakespeare" 363). Until quite recently, Beatrice's double entendres and bawdy jests were regularly sacrificed in production.

10. Samuel Johnson, "Preface to the Plays of William Shakespeare," 1765, *Selected Writings*, ed. Peter Martin (Cambridge, MA: Harvard University Press, 2009), 363.

11. Jean Paul, cited in Sigmund Freud, *Wit and Its Relation to the Unconscious*, tr. A. A. Brill (New York: Moffat, Yard, and Co., 1916), 6.

12. Her love of fun parallels that of Benedick, "merry" (2.1.206) and "all mirth" (3.2.9–10).

13. *Conveyance*, denoting removal and riddance, also means "furtive or light-fingered carrying off; stealing…associated with sleight of hand or jugglery," also "cunning management or contrivance."

14. Bamber argues that Beatrice, in rejecting the overture of the prince, "rejects the pressures of the extraordinary, here imagined in terms of the rank she would assume as a nobleman's wife." Linda Bamber, *Comic Women, Tragic Men: A Study of Gender and Genre in Shakespeare* (Palo Alto, CA: Stanford University Press, 1982), 40.

15. "Hobby-horse" is another newfangled word Shakespeare happily fetches.

16. Ralph Berry says that to "kill Claudio" is to kill "the force of distrust. It is to yield to the value of trust…and implicit faith." See Berry, *Shakespeare's Comedies: Explorations in Form* (Princeton, NJ: Princeton University Press, 1972), 162.

17. Benedick's reiteration recalls Prince Hal's emphatic assertions of "will" in *Henry IV, Part 1*.

18. *Buckler* is contemporary slang for vagina, though if we believe Partridge, virtually any word has a secondary sense of penis or vagina. See Eric Partridge, *Shakespeare's Bawdy* (London and New York: Routledge Classics, 2001).

19. One magnificent display of foolishness worthy of Malvolio is Benedick's determined parsing of Beatrice's simple notice of dinnertime: "There's a double meaning in that" (2.3.258–59). Now there is folly to entice any Shakespearean critic! Speaking of which, I discovered in the archives of Collegium Bufonis this report in the *Messina Aporia*, June 12, 1598, headlined "Mother of Fools Weds Prince's Jester in Messina": "Two celebrated wits exchanged wedding vows on June 12 when Beatrice, Lady Tongue, married Benedick Braggadocio. Beatrice kept her own name though she gives up her title. The ceremony took place at the villa of the bride's uncle Leonato, who gave away his niece and toasted the newlyweds. The bride, resplendently arrayed in a wreath of rosemary and daffydowndilly, wore a satin gown by Oscar de la Renta. Beatrice, the first woman to attend Padua University where she studied Anatomy and Rhetoric, is well known in Messina for jests and jibes and defense of undocumented immigrants. Benedick who served with distinction in the campaign against rebel insurgents is charter member of the Men's Club of Messina and performs standup comedy at the Palace. Best man

was Prince Don Pedro, lately victorious in the wars against Illyria. Proclaiming a match made in heaven, the Prince added that he didn't really want to marry Beatrice anyway. Also in attendance were Beatrice's uncle Antonio, numerous other Shakespearean Antonios, L. Boom late of Dublin, the maid of honor Hero, and her fiancé Claudio. Unable to attend owing to incarceration, Don John sent tortured congratulations. Sheriff Dogberry said although 'disinvited to the avuncular malapropism' he was 'in any eventuality on duty and off limits.' Guests enjoyed humorous roasts of the groom's former anti-feminism, several cuckold jokes, and the bride's recent mockeries of marriage. The couple will honeymoon in Ephesus, visit Bohemia, and live happily ever after in Messina."

20. C. L. Barber, *Shakespeare's Festive Comedy: A Study of Dramatic Form and Its Relation to Social Custom* (Princeton, NJ: Princeton University Press, 1959), 99, 236.

21. For a gloss on the archaic and local meaning of "mortal," see David-Everett Blythe, "Shakespeare's *As You Like It*," *Explicator* 42 (1984): 14–15.

22. Corin's description of Phebe and Silvius stresses the mixture of reality and artifice, the play's heightened conditionality:

    If you will see a pageant *truly* play'd
    Between the pale complexion of *true* love
    And the red glow of scorn ...
    If you will mark it. (3.4.52–56; my emphasis)

23. Ruth Nevo also notes the "interlocking and paradoxical partnership" of Rosalind and Touchstone. See Ruth Nevo, *Comic Transformations in Shakespeare* (London and New York: Methuen, 1980), 198. Another link between Shakespearean heroines and fools is that "both stand on the periphery of the serious world of men, assessing its wisdom from the perspective of not being of any account." See Juliet Dusinberre, *Shakespeare and the Nature of Women* (New York: Palgrave Macmillan, 1996), 114.

24. Shakespearean comedy—with its chicaneries, masquerades, and posings—highlights "counterfeit supposes" (*Shr.* 5.1.117).

25. A particularly pure expression of the comic credo is the song, "And therefore take the present time, / With a hey, and a ho, and a hey nonino" (5.3.30–31).

26. Frost, Interview, *Paris Review*, 893.

27. See Clara Claiborne Park, "As We Like It: How a Girl Can Be Smart and Still Popular," in *The Woman's Part: Feminist Criticism of Shakespeare*, eds. Carolyn Ruth Swift Lenz, Gayle Greene, and Carol Thomas Neely (Urbana: University of Illinois, 1980).

28. Marjorie Garber, "The Education of Orlando," in *Comedy from Shakespeare to Sheridan: Change and Continuity in the English and European Dramatic Tradition*, ed. A. R. Braunmuller and J. C. Bulman (Newark: University of Delaware Press, 1986), 104, 108.

29. Richard Knowles, ed., *A New Variorum Edition of Shakespeare: As You Like It* (New York: Modern Language Association of America, 1977) cites St. John and Evans, 614–15.

30. Edward I. Berry, *Shakespeare's Comic Rites* (Cambridge: Cambridge University Press, 1984), 81.

31. Like Groucho Marx wearing glasses without lenses and sporting an obviously fake moustache.

32. "In recognizing Rosalind and in participating in the playfulness of the disguise, he finds he can make conscious, witty love to her, repairing precisely the deficiency he earlier displayed in Act 1." See Neil Schaeffer, *The Art of Laughter* (New York: Columbia University Press, 1981), 150. Schaeffer is one of the rare critics who credits Orlando with enough awareness to participate in Rosalind's device.

33. Wolfgang Clemen, *Shakespeare's Dramatic Art* (New York: Methuen, 1972), 167.

34. Charles Cowden Clarke, *Shakespeare Characters, Chiefly Those Subordinate* (London: Smith, Elder, & Co., 1863), 46. I don't think Clarke means "subordinate" in the sense of *deferential*!

35. Barton's brilliant essay on comic closure, "*As You Like It* and *Twelfth Night*: Shakespeare's 'Sense of an Ending,'" *Essays, Mainly Shakespearean* (Cambridge: Cambridge University Press, 1994), inspired my consideration of the fate of foolery; my disagreement with Barton on this point is marginal. See Barton, 103.

36. Hymen wants "earthly things made even" (5.4.109), recalling Rosalind's last line before this reappearance: "And from hence I go / To make these doubts all even" (5.4.25–26). My wife insists that she showed me this connection and that I owe her at least a footnote. So there, or here.

37. For a bravura demonstration of the astonishing range of meanings and possibilities in this single line, see Malcolm Evans, "Truth's True Contents," in *Signifying Nothing: Truth's True Contents in Shakespeare's Text* (Athens: University of Georgia Press, 1986).

38. Similarly, Johnson's line notes on *As You Like It* gloss "if there be truth in sight" as "if a form may be trusted, if one cannot usurp the form of another." Johnson indicates no discomfort with the plain fact that in this play forms *cannot* be trusted and that appearances are deceptive.

39. M. Evans, "Truth's True Contents," 162.

40. Geoffrey Hartman suggests that *Illyria* is "compounded, to the sensitive ear, out of Ill and liar/lyre." See Geoffrey H. Hartman and Patricia A. Parker, eds., *Shakespeare and the Question of Theory*, (London: Routledge, 1985), 46. *The Land of Cokaygne* is a medieval poem depicting a make-believe place of carnival contraries and abundant luxuries; among many versions of Cockaigne or Cockayne, variously spelled, is a 1567 painting by Pieter Bruegel the Elder.

41. Maurice Charney, ed., *Comedy: New Perspectives* (New York: New York Literary Forum, 1978), 144.

42. In Trevor Nunn's film *Twelfth Night*, Ben Kingsley as Feste sees Viola putting on her male disguise.

43. A. Barton, *Essays*, 109.

44. Charney, *Comedy*, 161.

45. Catherine Belsey, "*Twelfth Night*: A Modern Perspective," in *Twelfth Night*, eds. Barbara A. Mowat and Paul Werstine (New York: Washington Square Press, 1993), 203.
46. See Barbara Hodgdon, "Sexual Disguise and the Theater of Gender," in *The Cambridge Companion to Shakespearean Comedy*, ed. Alexander Leggatt (Cambridge: Cambridge University Press, 2002), 187.

5 Folly Is Anatomiz'd

1. To such contumacious acquaintances, Alice Roosevelt would say, "If you can't say something nice, sit with me."
2. One might add the double twins from *The Comedy of Errors* and Costard and Armado in *Love's Labor's Lost*. Other matched fools in literature include Don Quixote and Sancho Panza, Panurge and Pantagruel, and Don Giovanni and Leporello. The clownish names of Beckett's Didi and Gogo are themselves stuttered or doubled syllables.
3. Harold Bloom wonderfully describes Mercutio in the Mab speech as "midwife to our erotic dreams." See Bloom, *Shakespeare: The Invention of the Human* (New York: Riverhead Books, 1998), 97.
4. James Calderwood, "*Romeo and Juliet*: A Formal Dwelling," *Shakespearean Metadrama: The Argument of the Play in Titus Andronicus, Love's Labor's Lost, Romeo and Juliet, A Midsummer Night's Dream, and Richard II* (Minneapolis: University of Minnesota Press, 1971), 106.
5. "Mercutio before his death manifests this liminality in his behavior, as when he turns aside from his companions as if rapt in his talk of dreams, fantasy, and the wind that, in Benvolio's words, 'blows us from ourselves' [(1.4.104)]." See Joseph A. Porter, *Shakespeare's Mercutio: His History and Drama* (Chapel Hill and London: University of North Carolina Press, 1988), 118.
6. Project Gutenberg e-book edition of John Dryden, "An Essay on the Dramatic Poetry of the Last Age," *The Works of John Dryden: Now First Collected in Eighteen Volumes* (Edinburgh: James Ballantyne and Co., 1808), 137.
7. Bloom, *Invention*, 89, 96–97.
8. An 1896 edition of *Romeo and Juliet* edited by the headmaster of Cambridge High and Latin "for school boys and girls" deletes most of Mercutio. The Bowdlerized Mercutio is a diminished figure, like the Knight in *Monty Python and the Holy Grail*, defiantly hurling abuse and challenges while losing all four limbs.
9. Coleridge notes, "By his loss it was contrived that the whole catastrophe of the tragedy should be brought about. ... Had not Mercutio been rendered so amiable and so interesting, we could not have felt so strongly the necessity for Romeo's interference." Samuel Taylor Coleridge, *Lectures 1808–1819 on Literature*, ed. R. A. Foakes, *Collected Works of Samuel Taylor Coleridge* (Princeton, NJ: Routledge Kegan Paul/Princeton University Press, 1987), II, 491.
10. As Berry argues, Mercutio's death does not refute him, it refutes the others: "The only man who could write sonnets of the first order prefers to parody

them; and he is dead at half-way, or perhaps at the parting of octave and sestet. ... The last words of the play's realist are a rejection of his society's preoccupation." See Ralph Berry, *Tragic Instance: The Sequence of Shakespeare's Tragedies* (London: Associated University Presses/University of Delaware Press, 1999), 69.

11. Calderwood, *"Romeo and Juliet,"* 106. Calderwood also asks whether the lyrical language of *Romeo and Juliet* is a style Shakespeare regards too pure and therefore needful of protection: "They simply have no public contact" and seem "insufficiently endowed with complexity, with the self-division that complexity makes possible" (104).

12. Sadly, only an English teacher could find humor in a subjunctive contrary to fact.

13. Willard Farnham says that Jaques lacks "the large capacity for acceptance of folly that leads Hamlet to enjoy the performance of even an unknowing fool. ... He does not go beyond satire in envisioning what he would offer as a fool. He is far from getting to any Erasmian praise of folly in the large. ... So much removed is Jaques from Hamlet, who as a knower and practiser of folly, is not shaped for comic defeat, not even in casual encounter." See Farnham, *The Shakespearean Grotesque: Its Genesis and Transformations* (Oxford: Clarendon Press, 1971), 122–23.

14. Nineteenth-century critics such as George Brandes regard Jaques as "a mouthpiece for the poet" and a "Hamlet avant la letter." See Brandes, *Shakespearean Criticism: Excerpts from the Criticism of William Shakespeare's Plays and Poetry, from the First Published Appraisals to Current Evaluations,* ed. Mark W. Scott (Detroit: Gale Research Company, 1999), 51.

15. We should remember that *libertine* did not necessarily mean anything more nefarious than "one who follows his own inclinations or goes his own way; one who is not restricted or confined" in 1599, according to *OED*. However, another intriguing etymology is the derivation of the word cynic from "doglike, currish" (Dictionary.com), which may account for the uniformly derogatory references to dogs in Shakespeare.

16. Michael Mangan, *A Preface to Shakespeare's Comedies, 1594–1603* (London and New York: Longman, 1996), 213.

17. *Zanna* is the zany figure in commedia dell'arte.

18. Terence Hawkes makes a similar point in "Comedy, Orality and Duplicity: *Twelfth Night,*" *Shakespeare's Comedies,* ed. Gary Waller (London and New York: Longman, 1991).

19. I follow the Riverside edition's "ayword," meaning byword or proverb, though the term is often emended to "nayword."

20. *Geck* is a fine old word for "a fool, simpleton; one who is befooled or derided, a dupe." "To get a geck" is "to be deceived or tricked." "To give one the geck" is "to mock, trick, deceive one" (*OED*).

21. Malvolio's fantasy almost seems to parody Prince Hal envisioning his newly crowned self in complete command and devoid of follies.

22. Still, it seems inapt to describe Malvolio as "terribly literal-minded and totally lacking in imagination." His dream of becoming Count Malvolio is marvelously inventive and imaginatively detailed. See Maurice Charney, ed. *Comedy: New Perspectives* (New York: New York Literary Forum, 1978), 159.

23. Does "M.O.A.I." suggest "AMO" plus "I"? The possibility is prompted by Moria in *Praise of Folly:* "Sometimes, like the old man in Plautus, he regresses to those three letters (a m o)—then, if he had any wisdom at all, he would be miserable beyond belief" (21).

24. Malvolio, static and rigid, is committed to "the single version of Puritanism," seen to "deny the fruitful duplicity that Carnival and playing enshrine.... In comedy, the double worlds of Carnival and everyday find themselves at first opposed, then fruitfully intertwined, and finally essentially twinned." See Hawkes, "Comedy, Orality and Duplicity," 173–74.

25. Feste echoes Fabian's bland observation, "Why, we shall make him mad indeed" (3.4.133).

26. Edward I. Berry, "Laughing at 'Others,'" in *The Cambridge Companion to Shakespearean Comedy,* ed. Alexander Leggatt (Cambridge: Cambridge University Press, 2002), 128.

27. *Chapman's Homer: The Iliad,* ed. Allardyce Nicoll (Princeton, NJ: Princeton University Press, 1998). This passage is from "The Second Booke," pages 531–32. All subsequent references to Chapman's translation signify this edition, pages 531–33, lines 205–73.

28. This is from "Erasmus' Letter to Martin Dorp," appended to Desiderius Erasmus, *Praise of Folly,* ed. and tr. Clarence H. Miller (New Haven, CT: Yale University Press, 1979), 141.

29. Chapman's Nireus is "the fairest man that to faire Ilion came" (63).

30. James Nohrnberg, "*The Iliad,*" in *Homer to Brecht: The European Epic and Dramatic Traditions,* ed. Michael Seidel and Edward Mendelson (New Haven, CT: Yale University Press, 1977), 17.

31. I survey critical commentary on Homer's Thersites in "Homer's Humor: Laughter in *The Iliad,*" *Humanitas* 20 (2007), 96–116.

32. I wonder if it is a coincidence that Ben Jonson invents another Thersitic descendant named Carlo Buffone in his 1599 play, *Every Man out His Humor.* Jonson's dramatis personae describes Carlo Buffone as an "impudent common jester, a violent rayler... he will sooner lose his soul than a jest, and prophane even the most holy things, to excite laughter."

33. Aristotle, *The Nicomachean Ethics,* ed. Hugh Tredennick, tr. J. A. K. Thomson (New York: Penguin, 2004), 109.

34. E. Talbot Donaldson, *The Swan at the Well: Shakespeare Reading Chaucer* (New Haven, CT: Yale University Press, 1985), 118.

35. Isaac Babel said anyone predicting doom all the time eventually becomes a prophet.

36. I. A. Richards notes, "It is like Shakespeare to give the summing-up to his almost monstrously detached and avid observer, the sick artist," in "*Troilus and*

Cressida and Plato." See *Troilus and Cressida,* ed. Daniel Seltzer (New York: Signet, 1963): 229–37.

37. R. A. Foakes, "The Owl and the Cuckoo: Voices of Maturity in Shakespeare's Comedies," in *Shakespearean Comedy,* Stratford-Upon-Avon Studies 14, ed. J. R. Brown and B. Harris, (London: Edward Arnold, 1972), 272.

38. Thersites makes what may be Shakespeare's only explicit reference to homosexuality in the plays (the sonnets are another matter). Kimbrough suggests that we may be "finding more decadence than the text warrants, scholars insisting, to give a small example, that Patroclus be called Achilles' 'brach' [bitch] instead of his 'brooch.'" See Robert Kimbrough, *Shakespeare's Troilus and Cressida and Its Setting* (Cambridge, MA: Harvard University Press, 1964), 139.

39. Reuben A. Brower, *Hero and Saint: Shakespeare and the Graeco-Roman Heroic Tradition* (New York and Oxford: Oxford University Press, 1971), 271.

6 There the Antic Sits

1. Sir Philip Sidney, *Sir Philip Sidney's Defense of Poesy,* ed. Dorothy M. Macardle (London: Macmillan, 1964), 46.

2. Shakespeare's probable source, Saxo Grammaticus, recounts the story of Prince Amleth, whose name in Norse means *insane.* See William F. Hansen, *Saxo Grammaticus and the Life of Hamlet: A History, Translation, and Commentary* (Lincoln: University of Nebraska Press, 1983). Also see H. R. Ellis Davidson, "Loki and Saxo's Amleth," in *The Fool and the Trickster: Studies in Honour of Enid Welsford,* ed. Paul V. A. Williams (Cambridge: D. S. Brewer, Rowan, and Littlefield, 1979).

3. In classical rhetoric, equivocation was termed *amphibology.* The two most prominent chapbooks of rhetoric available to Shakespeare were George Puttenham's *Art of English Poesie* and Thomas Wilson's *Art of Rhetoric* (1560), two treasure troves for clowns, fools, and jesters. Wilson elaborates "The Division of Pleasant Behavior," "Pleasant Sport Made by Rehearsing of an Old Matter," "Sport Moved by Telling of Old Tales," and other elements of "Witty Jesting." See Thomas Wilson, *The Art of Rhetoric,* ed. Peter E. Medine (University Park: Pennsylvania State University Press, 1994), 167–83, 206.

4. Elsinore is a chamber of echoes. "A double blessing is a double grace" (1.3.53), says Laertes to Polonius, who can't say anything less than twice.

5. Witty in himself, Hamlet is also the cause of wit that is other clowns. He has probably bequeathed more grist for the mill of comedians than any other tragic figure. One of my favorite parodies of *Hamlet* is in *The Terminator,* when Arnold Schwarzenegger muses, "to be or not to be," decides "not to be," and blows the place to smithereens.

6. The word *shape* has theatrical inflections, like so many terms in this play about action and acting: *OED* gives "assumed appearance, guise, disguise; a stage dress or suit of clothes; a part, a character impersonated; make-up and

costume suited to a particular part." Hamlet's language is shot through with theatrical tropes and allusions. After "The Mousetrap" apparently establishes the guilt of Claudius, Hamlet exults, "Get me a fellowship in a cry of players" (3.2.277–78). Hamlet would be very like Shakespeare, owning a partnership in an acting company!

7. Because the Ghost speaks from "Beneath," Hamlet calls it "ole mole" and says, "We'll shift our ground" (1.5.156–62).

8. When the king and Laertes devise the plot, Claudius anticipates what might "fit us to our shape" (4.7.150), that is, suit their scheme. Here *shape* means deception, feigned benevolence.

9. Ruth Nevo, "Shakespeare's Comic Remedies," in *Shakespearean Comedy*, ed. Maurice Charney (New York: New York Literary Forum, 1980), 12.

10 Wallace Stevens, "Notes toward a Supreme Fiction," in *The Collected Poems of Wallace Stevens* (Knopf: New York, 1965), 383. It's incidentally interesting that Shakespeare had twin boys, one named Hamleth.

11. Gertrude's horrified cry, "O, what a rash and bloody deed is this!" (3.4.27), connects Hamlet and the "rash, intruding fool." Another association is that, like Hamlet, Polonius has hyperbolic fear of "savageness in unreclaimed blood" (2.1.34).

12. Freudians stress the inherent rivalry and latent affinity between a son and his stepfather. See Ernest Jones, *Hamlet and Oedipus* (New York: Norton, 1976).

13. Another indication of his doubling is that Hamlet deploys more frequently than any Shakespearean character the rhetorical device known as hendiadys. See Frank Kermode, *Shakespeare's Language* (New York: Farrar Straus Giroux, 2000), 100; and George T. Wright, "Hendiadys and *Hamlet*," *PMLA* 96 (1981): 168–93. This rhetorical trope is featured in Puttenham's *Arte of English Poesy* (1589).

14. Marjorie Garber makes this point in her wonderful book, *Shakespeare After All* (New York: Anchor, 2005), 503.

15. When the king dies, Hamlet's "foil" Laertes reinforces the complementarities not only between Hamlet and Claudius—"It is a poison temper'd by himself"— but also between Hamlet and himself, "Exchange forgiveness with me, noble Hamlet" (5.2.328–29).

16. In *Principles of Psychology* (1890), William James speculates that we cry not because we feel sad; rather, we feel sad because we cry. Neuroscientists now report that feelings such as happiness precipitate hormones as well as the other way around.

17. Eliot cogently characterizes Hamlet's state as "less than madness, more than feigned." See T. S. Eliot, "Hamlet and His Problems," *Selected Essays 1917–1932* (London: Faber & Faber, 1932).

18. As Victor Turner characterizes the "most characteristic midliminal symbolism." Turner, "Variations on a Theme of Liminality," in *Secular Ritual*, ed. Sally Falk Moore and Barbara G. Myerhoff, 36–52 (Assen, Netherlands: Van Gorcum, 1977).

19. Samuel Beckett once remarked that he had no views to *inter*.
20. Readers will recall Mercutio's dying jest (*Rom.* 3.1.68).
21. Alexander Pope, *The Dunciad*, ed. John Butt, in *The Poems of Alexander Pope* (New Haven, CT: Yale University Press, 1963), 723. Pope pretends to deplore this mélange while producing his own potpourri.
22. Cassio seems florid but accurate when he remarks, "As having sense of beauty, do omit / Their mortal natures, letting go safely by / The divine Desdemona" (2.1.71–73).
23. Derek Walcott, "Goats and Monkeys," in *Collected Poems 1948–1984* (New York: Farrar Straus and Giroux, 1986).
24. See Thomas Rymer, *Short View of Tragedy*, reprinted in *A Casebook on Othello*, ed. Leonard F. Dean (New York: Crowell, 1961), 108–9. Rymer's casual racism and complacent chauvinism are pervasive. He finds it inconceivable that civilized Venetians would "set a Negro to be their General; or trust a Moor to defend them against the Turk" and insists that "should the Poet have provided such a Husband for an only Daughter of any noble Peer in England, the Blackamoor must have changed his skin, to look our House of Lords in the Face."
25. Robert Hornback, "Emblems of Folly in the First *Othello*: Renaissance Blackface, Moor's Coat, and 'Muckender,'" *Comparative Literature* 35:1 (2001): 69–99.
26. Michael D. Bristol, "Charivari and the Comedy of Abjection in *Othello*," in *Materialist Shakespeare: A History*, ed. Ivo Kamps (London: Verso, 1995), 152.
27. In fact, the word *folly* connotes lewdness, wantonness, as when Othello declares that Desdemona "turn'd to folly, and she was a whore" (5.2.132).
28. Bristol, "Charivari," 151. Though I disagree that Iago is a "Bakhtinian 'agelast,' that is, one who does not laugh," I am deeply indebted to Bristol's provocative reading in "Charivari and the Comedy of Abjection in *Othello*."
29. Lynda E. Boose, "'Let it be Hid': The Pornographic Aesthetic of Shakespeare's *Othello*," in *Othello: New Casebook*, ed. Lena Cowen Orlin (New York: Palgrave Macmillan, 2004), 27.
30. Hence the very opposite of *As You Like It*, soaked in sunshine and radiating Rosalind's luminescence.
31. As Boose formidably argues, "Let it be Hid," 25. Bristol makes a similar point: our "withdrawal of empathy" is remarkable because Shakespeare virtually invented "the pathos of individual subjectivity" (160).
32. In Verdi's opera *Otello*, the bond between the two at this moment is rendered musically by the joining of voices in duet.
33. Bristol, 161.
34. Grigori Kozintsev's glorious film *King Lear* (1971) depicts a "sweet fool," pathetic, terrified, affectionate, the king's comfort and darling. The Fool is played by a boy and given a flute whose plangent melodies pervade and conclude the film. Kozintsev's Fool never disappears; it is as if amid or just beyond the ruin there is some sliver of solace, a half-mad boy forlornly playing his pipe.
35. Not unlike the epistemological humor of Steve Reich: "I woke up one morning and somebody had stolen all my stuff, and replaced it with exact replicas. I said

to my roommate, wow, these are exact copies of everything. He said, 'do I know you? You look like my roommate.'"

36. In his annotations to the play, Samuel Johnson accepted Warburton's emendation and praised his predecessor's "sagacity" that "disentangled the confusion."

37. Cf. John Danby, "The Fool and Handy Dandy," in *Shakespeare's Doctrine of Nature: A Study of King Lear*, 102–13 (London: Faber & Faber, 1949).

38. Melvin Seiden, "The Fool and Edmund: Kin and Kind," *Studies in English Literature* 19, no. 2 (1979): 208–9.

39. Cavell's speculation as to how this phrase might be understood by Lear at the time is particularly astute. The king might think "Lear's shadow" simply means a shadow of his former glory. He might or might not sense the *shade* within *shadow*. Cavell supposes the Fool's reply indicates, "Lear's shadow can tell who you are," that he is "double and has a double." This confronts Lear with mankind's "lack of wholeness, their separation from themselves, by loss or denial or opposition ... the self is split from its past and from its own feeling, however intimately present both may be." Cavell concludes, "Either way, either by putting freedom or by putting integrity into question, doubling sets a task, of discovery, of acknowledgment. And both ways are supported in the moment" of Lear's "least ambiguous immersion in folly as madness, when Lear "faces Gloucester and confuses identities with him." See Stanley Cavell, "The Avoidance of Love: A Reading of *King Lear*," in *Shakespeare: An Anthology of Criticism and Theory 1945–2000*, ed. Russ McDonald (Oxford: Blackwell, 2004), 349–50.

40. Cavell contemplates the self-erasing force of folly. There is "no one to assert without asserting himself a fool. The world-accusing fool, like the world-accusing liar, suffers a paradox" (Ibid., 349).

41. William Empson, "Fool in Lear," *The Structure of Complex Words* (Ann Arbor: University of Michigan Press, 1967), 145.

42. Will Somers's penchant to fall asleep anytime, anywhere is perhaps reflected in the Fool's comment, "I'll to bed at noon." See John Southworth, *Fools and Jesters at the English Court* (London: Sutton, 1998).

43. I admire Seiden's formulation: "We should be able to agree about what the Fool is *not* saying; he is not saying, 'And ye shall know the truth, and the truth shall make you free' (John 8:32)." See Seiden, "Fool and Edmund," 211.

44. *Able*: "To empower legally. To endow with fitting or sufficient power or strength; to make capable; to capacitate, enable. To warrant, vouch for; to aver, confirm" (*OED*).

7   No Epilogue, I Pray You

1. A likely source for Shakespeare's *Henry VIII*, Samuel Rowley's *When You See Me, You Know Me* (ca. 1604) prominently features both jesters, Will Somers and Patch.

2. *Upsomdowns* is another Joycean neologism in *Finnegans Wake*.

3. As James Shapiro persuasively argues in his estimable book, *A Year in the Life of William Shakespeare: 1599* (New York: HarperCollins, 2005), 74. This epilogue, titled "to ye Q. by ye players 1598," was discovered and attributed to Shakespeare by Stephen W. May and William A. Ringler. See "An Epilogue Possibly by Shakespeare," *Modern Philology* 70 (1972): 138–39. I borrow Shapiro's modernized spelling and punctuation.

As the dial hand tells o'er
The same hours it had before,
Still beginning in the ending,
Circular account lending,
So, most mighty Queen, we pray,
Like the dial, day by day,
You may lead the seasons on,
Making new when old are gone.
That the babe which now is young,
And hath yet no use of tongue,
Many a Shrovetide here may bow,
To that empress I do now;
That the children of these lords,
Sitting at your council boards,
May be grave and aged seen,
Of her that was their father[s'] Queen.
Once I wish this wish again,
Heaven subscribe it with "Amen." (74–75)

4. The Falstaff figure in some of Shakespeare's source materials is named "Oldcastle" and possibly bore that name in earlier versions of Shakespeare's play, displeasing Oldcastle's prominent descendants. Traces of Oldcastle survive in Hal's throwaway jest, "my old lad of the castle" (*1H4* 1.2.41–42).

5. Thomas Fuller's *History of Worthies in England* says that when Queen Elizabeth was "out of good humor," her jester Tarlton "could un-dumpish her at his pleasure." Cited by Beatrice K. Otto, *Fools Are Everywhere: The Court Jester Around the World* (Chicago and London: University of Chicago Press, 2001), 90.

6. Ruth Nevo, *Comic Transformations in Shakespeare* (London and New York: Methuen, 1980), 196.

7. See Jonathan Goldberg, *James I and the Politics of Literature: Jonson, Shakespeare, Donne, and Their Contemporaries* (Baltimore and London: Johns Hopkins University Press, 1983), 153.

8. The jointly authored *Two Noble Kinsmen* and the still-disputed *Henry VIII* unsettle the hash a bit more.

9. The day after both Jackie Gleason and Fred Astaire died, some columnist described them as the Caliban and Ariel of entertainment.

10. For example, "As wicked dew as e'er my mother brush'd / With raven's feather from an unwholesome fen / Drop on you both!" (1.2.321–23). Caliban seems composed of dew as well as fen.

11. *Moon-calf:* "A born fool; a congenital idiot; a simpleton," "a deformed animal; a monster," also an aborted, malformed fetus. Apt for all three of these idiots is another definition: "An ill-conceived idea, enterprise, or undertaking" (*OED*).

12. His curses are vital and inventive: "All the infections that the sun sucks up / From bogs, fens, flats, on Prosper fall, and make him / By inch-meal a disease!" (2.2.1–3).

13. Triumphant generals and victorious emperors in Roman processions would ride next to a fool, reminding them that *sic transit gloria mundi.*

14. See Stephen J. Greenblatt, *Learning to Curse: Essays in Early Modern Culture* (London: Routledge, 1992).

15. I am overstating the evil of these clowns to make a point that is not widely appreciated. Of course Caliban, Trinculo, and Stephano are very funny and ridiculously futile. Once I sat with two adorable little girls at a production of *The Tempest* in which every appearance of the clowns provoked delirious squeals of delight.

16. Wouldn't this make a hell of a wedding toast?

17. Cankers proliferate on Miranda as on his ugly slave: "And as with age his body uglier grows, / So his mind cankers" (4.1.191–92).

18. Though some editions still attribute to Miranda the speech "Abhorred slave, / Which any print of goodness will not take, / Being capable of all ill!" (1.2.351–53), it seems indisputably Prospero's language: excessive, stressing a point to which he returns in the end, calling Caliban "slave" (as he does several times earlier in the scene), the speech has Prospero's prints all over it. Miranda is incapable of speaking with such indignation and unkindness.

19. The word *sinner* stands out in another cramped articulation: "Made such a sinner of his memory" (1.2.101).

20. Prospero ignores and probably discredits Caliban's belated pledge to "be wise hereafter, / And seek for grace" (5.1.295–96).

21. As a less than gracious host, Prospero displays "some subtleties o' th' isle, / That will not let you / Believe things certain" (5.1.124–25), where a "subtlety" suggests a "device," "trick," "cunning, especially of a treacherous kind," "guile," "artifice, frequently in an unfavorable sense, a wily stratagem or trick, something craftily invented" (*OED*). Prospero's illusions are a Pandora's box of follies; Prospero's affectionate term for Ariel, "my tricksy spirit!" (5.1.226), also associates artful tricks with deceptive practices.

22. Prospero invokes not the "poor naked wretches" (3.4.28) pitied by Lear but the spirits.

23. The chorus of despondency is joined by the clowns bemoaning the "infinite loss" (4.1.210) of their "bottles in the pool" (4.1.208).

24. I regret to report that at an MLA conference in New York City, I overheard a housemaid say, "I never heard so much talkin' and seen so little fuckin'!"

25. In Talmudic tradition, rabbinical commentary has the sacred value of scripture. In the *Book of Mishigas*, Rabbi Zanna is asked by the Yeshiva boy, "Why do you

answer all my questions with a question?" He replies, "Why shouldn't I answer questions with a question?"

26. In Miller's modern edition, it is "Erasmus' Letter to Martin Dorp (1514)," 139–74.

27. Francois Rabelais, *The Complete Works of Francois Rabelais*, III, tr. Donald M. Frame (Berkeley: University of California Press, 1991), 369.

Bibliography

Adelman, Janet. "Bed Tricks: On Marriage as the End of Comedy in *All's Well That Ends Well* and *Measure for Measure*." In *Shakespeare's Personality*, edited by Norman Holland, Sidney Homan, and Bernard J. Paris, 151–74. Berkeley: University of California Press, 1989.

————. *Suffocating Mothers: Fantasies of Maternal Origin in Shakespeare's Plays, Hamlet to The Tempest*. New York: Routledge, 1992.

Altman, Joel B. *The Improbability of Othello: Rhetorical Anthropology and Shakespearean Selfhood*. Chicago and London: University of Chicago Press, 2010.

Andrews, John F. *Romeo and Juliet: Critical Essays*. New York and London: Garland, 1993.

Aristotle. *The Nicomachean Ethics*. Edited by Hugh Tredennick. Translated by J. A. K. Thomson. New York: Penguin, 2004.

Armin, Robert. *Foole Upon Foole: Six Sorts of Sottes, Collected Works of Robert Armin*. Edited by I. J. Feather. London: Johnson Reprint, 1972.

————. *Fools and Jesters: With a Reprint of Robert Armin's Nest of Ninnies 1608*. London: Shakespeare Society, 1842.

Auden, W. H. *The Dyer's Hand and Other Essays*. New York: Random House, 1962.

Bakhtin, Michael. *Rabelais and His World*. Translated by Helene Iswolsky. Cambridge: Massachusetts Institute of Technology Press, 1968.

Bamber, Linda. *Comic Women, Tragic Men: A Study of Gender and Genre in Shakespeare*. Palo Alto, CA: Stanford University Press, 1982.

Barber, C. L. *Shakespeare's Festive Comedy: A Study of Dramatic Form and Its Relation to Social Custom*. Princeton, NJ: Princeton University Press, 1959.

Barber, C. L., and Richard P. Wheeler. *The Whole Journey: Shakespeare's Power of Development*. Berkeley: University of California Press, 1987.

Barish, Jonas A. "The Turning Away of Prince Hal." In *Twentieth Century Interpretations of Henry IV, Part One*, edited by R. J. Dorius. Englewood Cliffs, NJ: Prentice-Hall, 1970: 83–88.

Barker, Simon. *Shakespeare's Problem Plays: All's Well That Ends Well, Measure for Measure, Troilus and Cressida*. New York: Palgrave Macmillan, 2005.

Barton, Anne. *Essays, Mainly Shakespearean.* Cambridge: Cambridge University Press, 1994.

———. "Shakespeare in the Sun." *New York Review of Books*, May 27, 1993: 11.

Barton, Stuart. *Monumental Follies: An Exposition on the Eccentric Edifices of Britain.* Worthing, UK: Lyle Publications, 1972.

Barroll, J. Leeds III, ed. *Shakespeare Studies* XIII. New York: Burt Franklin, 1980.

Bate, Jonathan. *The Genius of Shakespeare.* New York: Oxford University Press, 1998.

———. *Soul of the Age: A Biography of the Mind of William Shakespeare.* New York: Random House, 2009.

Bates, Catherine. "Love and Courtship." In *The Cambridge Companion to Shakespearean Comedy*, edited by Alexander Leggatt. Cambridge: Cambridge University Press, 2002: 139–155.

———. *Play in a Godless World.* Trowbridge, UK: Cromwell Press, 1999.

Battenhouse, Roy. "Falstaff as Parodist and Perhaps Holy Fool." *PMLA* 90 (1975): 32–52.

Bell, Robert H. "Homer's Humor: Laughter in *The Iliad.*" *Humanitas* 20 (2007): 96–116.

———. *Jocoserious Joyce: The Fate of Folly in* Ulysses. Ithaca, NY: Cornell University Press, 1991.

Belsey, Catherine. "*Twelfth Night*: A Modern Perspective." In *Twelfth Night*, edited by Barbara A. Mowat and Paul Werstine. New York: Washington Square Press, 1993: 197–207.

Berger, Harry. "Against the Sink-a-Pace: Sexual and Family Politics in *Much Ado About Nothing.*" *Shakespeare Quarterly* 33 (1982): 302–13.

Bergeron, David M. "*Richard II* and Carnival Politics." *Shakespeare Quarterly* 42 (Spring 1991): 33–43.

Berry, Edward I. "Laughing at 'Others.'" In *The Cambridge Companion to Shakespearean Comedy*, edited by Alexander Leggatt. Cambridge: Cambridge University Press, 2002: 123–138.

———. *Shakespeare's Comic Rites.* Cambridge: Cambridge University Press, 1984.

Berry, Ralph. "The Season of *Twelfth Night.*" In *Changing Styles in Shakespeare.* Oxford: Routledge, 2005: 109–119.

———. *Shakespearean Structures.* Totowa, NJ: Barnes & Noble, 1981.

———. *Shakespeare's Comedies: Explorations in Form.* Princeton, NJ: Princeton University Press, 1972.

———. *Tragic Instance: The Sequence of Shakespeare's Tragedies.* London: Associated University Presses/University of Delaware Press, 1999.

Bethel, S. L. "*Troilus and Cressida.*" In *Shakespeare: Modern Essays in Criticism*, edited by Leonard F. Dean, 258–66. New York: Galaxy, 1961.

Bevington, David, ed. *Henry IV, Parts I and II: Critical Essays.* New York: Garland, 1986.

Bietenholz, Peter G. *Encounter with a Radical Erasmus: Erasmus' Work as a Source of Radical Thought in Early Modern Europe.* Toronto: University of Toronto Press, 2009.

Billington, Sandra. *Mock Kings in Medieval Society and Renaissance Drama*. Oxford: Clarendon Press, 1991.

———. *A Social History of the Fool*. New York: St. Martin's Press, 1984.

Blake, William. *The Marriage of Heaven and Hell*. London and New York: Oxford University Press, 1975.

Bleistein, E. M. "The Object of Scorn: An Aspect of the Comic Antagonist." *Western Humanities Review* 14 (1960): 209–22.

Bloom, Harold. *Shakespeare: The Invention of the Human*. New York: Riverhead Books, 1998.

Blythe, David-Everett. "Shakespeare's *As You Like It*." *Explicator* 42 (1984): 14–15.

Boose, Linda E. "'Let It Be Hid': The Pornographic Aesthetic of Shakespeare's *Othello*." In *Othello: New Casebook*, edited by Lena Cowen Orlin, 22–48. New York: Palgrave Macmillan, 2003.

Boose, Linda E., and Richard Burt, eds. *Shakespeare the Movie: Popularizing the Plays on Film, TV, and Video*. London and New York: Routledge, 1997.

Bradbrook, M. C. "The Theme of Honour in *All's Well That Ends Well*. In *Shakespeare's Later Comedies*, edited by D. J. Palmer, 15–24. New York: Penguin, 1971.

Bradbury, Malcolm, and David Palmer, eds. *Shakespearean Comedy*. Stratford-Upon-Avon Studies 14. London: Edward Arnold, 1972.

Bradley, A. C. *A Miscellany*. London: Macmillan, 1929.

———. *Oxford Lectures on Poetry*. London: Macmillan, 1909.

Brandes, George. *Shakespearean Criticism: Excerpts from the Criticism of William Shakespeare's Plays and Poetry, from the First Published Appraisals to Current Evaluations*. Edited by Mark W. Scott. Detroit: Gale Research Co., 1999.

Brant, Sebastian. *The Ship of Fools*. Edited by Edwin H. Zeydel. New York: Columbia University Press, 1944.

Braunmuller, A. R., and J. C. Bulman, eds. *Comedy from Shakespeare to Sheridan: Change and Continuity in the English and European Dramatic Tradition*. Newark: University of Delaware Press, 1986.

Bristol, Michael D. "Charivari and the Comedy of Abjection in *Othello*." In *Materialist Shakespeare: A History*, edited by Ivo Kamps, 142–156. London: Verso, 1995.

———. *Carnival and Theater: Plebian Structure and the Culture of Authority in Renaissance England*. New York: Methuen, 1985.

Brode, Douglas. *Shakespeare in the Movies from the Silent Era to Shakespeare in Love*. New York: Oxford University Press, 2000.

Brooke, Nicholas. *Horrid Laughter in Jacobean Tragedy*. New York: Barnes & Noble, 1979.

Brower, Reuben A. *Hero and Saint: Shakespeare and the Graeco-Roman Heroic Tradition*. New York and Oxford: Oxford University Press, 1971.

Brown, John Russell. "The Presentation of Comedy: The First Ten Plays." In *Shakespearean Comedy*, edited by Malcolm Bradbury and David Palmer, 9–30. Stratford-Upon-Avon Studies 14. London: Edward Arnold, 1972.

Burke, Kenneth. *A Rhetoric of Motives*. Berkeley: University of California Press, 1969.

Burton, Robert. *The Anatomy of Melancholy*. Philadelphia: J. W. Moore, 1850.

Busby, Olive Mary. *Studies in the Development of the Fool in the Elizabethan Drama*. London: Oxford University Press, 1923.

Calderwood, James L. *A Midsummer Night's Dream*. Hempel Hempstead: Harvester Wheatsheaf, 1992.

———. *Shakespearean Metadrama: The Argument of the Play in Titus Andronicus, Love's Labour's Lost, Romeo and Juliet, A Midsummer Night's Dream, and Richard II*. Minneapolis: University of Minnesota Press, 1971.

Callois, Roger. *Man, Play, and Games*. New York: Free Press of Glencoe, 1961.

Campbell, Oscar James. *Comicall Satyre and Shakespeare's Troilus and Cressida*. San Marino, CA: Huntington Library, 1938.

Carroll, William C. *The Metamorphoses of Shakespearean Comedy*. Princeton, NJ: Princeton University Press, 1985.

Castiglione, Baldesar. *The Book of the Courtier*. Translated by Charles S. Singleton. Garden City, NJ: Anchor, 1959.

Cavell, Stanley. "The Avoidance of Love: A Reading of *King Lear*." In *Shakespeare: An Anthology of Criticism and Theory 1945–2000*, edited by Russ McDonald, 338–352. Oxford: Blackwell, 2004.

———. *Disowning Knowledge in Six Plays of Shakespeare*. Cambridge: Cambridge University Press, 1987.

Chaloner, Thomas, tr. and ed. *The Praise of Folie*. Edited by Clarence H. Miller. London: Oxford University Press, 1965.

Chambers, E. K. *The Elizabethan Stage*. Oxford: Clarendon Press, 1923.

———. *The Medieval Stage*. London: Oxford University Press, 1925.

Champion, Larry S. *Evolution of Shakespeare's Comedy*. Cambridge, MA: Harvard University Press, 1970.

Charney, Maurice, ed. *Comedy: New Perspectives*. New York: New York Literary Forum, 1978.

———, ed. *Shakespearean Comedy*. New York: New York Literary Forum, 1980.

Chedgzoy, Kate, ed. *Shakespeare, Feminism, and Gender*. New York: Palgrave Macmillan, 2001.

Clarke, Charles Cowden. *Shakespeare Characters, Chiefly Those Subordinate*. London: Smith, Elder, & Co., 1863.

Clemen, Wolfgang. *Shakespeare's Dramatic Art*. New York: Methuen, 1972.

Cockrell, Dale. *Demons of Disorder: Early Blackface Minstrels and Their World*. Cambridge: Cambridge University Press, 1997.

Coetzee, J. M. *Giving Offense: Essays on Censorship*. Chicago and London: University of Chicago Press, 1996.

Coghill, Neville. "Wags, Clowns, and Jesters." In *More Talking of Shakespeare*, edited by John Garrett, 1–13. London: Longmans, Green, and Co., 1959.

Coleridge, Samuel Taylor. *Lectures 1808–1819 on Literature*. Ed. R. A. Foakes, *Collected Works of Samuel Taylor Coleridge*, II. Princeton, NJ: Routledge Kegan Paul/Princeton University Press, 1987.

Collins, Cecil. *The Vision of the Fool*. Chipping Norton, Oxfordshire: Kedros, 1981.

Cook, Carol. "The Sign and Semblance of Her Honour: Reading Gender Differences in *Much Ado About Nothing*." *PMLA* 101 (1989): 186–202.

Cordner, Michael, Peter Holland, and John Kerrigan, eds. *English Comedy*. Cambridge: Cambridge University Press, 1994.

Corrigan, Robert W., ed. *Comedy: Meaning and Form*. San Francisco: Chandler Publishing Company, 1965.

Cox, Harvey. *The Feast of Fools: A Theological Essay on Festivity and Fantasy*. Cambridge, MA: Harvard University Press, 1969.

Crane, William G. *Wit and Rhetoric in the Renaissance*. New York: Columbia University Press, 1937.

Creaser, John. "Forms of Confusion." In *The Cambridge Companion to Shakespearean Comedy*, edited by Alexander Leggatt, 81–101. Cambridge: Cambridge University Press, 2002.

Critchley, Simon. *On Humour*. London: Routledge, 2002.

Crowl, Samuel. "The Marriage of Shakespeare and Hollywood: Kenneth Branagh's *Much Ado About Nothing*." In *Spectacular Shakespeare: Critical Theory and Popular Cinema*, edited by Courtney Lehmann and Lisa S. Stark, 100–24. Madison, NJ: Fairleigh Dickinson University Press, 2002.

Culler, Jonathan, ed. *On Puns: The Foundation of Letters*. Oxford and New York: Blackwell, 1988.

Danby, John. *Shakespeare's Doctrine of Nature: A Study of King Lear*. London: Faber & Faber, 1949.

Dault, Gary Michael. "The Clowns." *BorderCrossings* 13, no. 4 (1994): 29–31.

Davidson, Carl, ed. *Fools and Folly*. Kalamazoo: Medieval Institute Publications, Western Michigan University, 1996.

Davies, Anthony and Stanley Wells, editors. *Shakespeare and the Moving Image*. Cambridge: Cambridge University Press, 1994.

Dean, Leonard F. *Shakespeare: Modern Essays in Criticism*. New York: Oxford University Press, 1961.

De Grazia, Margreta, Maureen Quilligan, and Peter Stallybrass, eds. *Subject and Object in Renaissance Culture*. Cambridge: Cambridge University Press, 1996.

Dennis, Carl. "Wit and Wisdom in *Much Ado About Nothing*." *Studies in English Literature* 13, no. 2 (1973): 223–37.

Desens, Marliss C. *The Bed-Trick in English Renaissance Drama: Explorations in Gender, Sexuality and Power*. Newark: University of Delaware Press, 1994.

Dessin, Alan C. *Shakespeare and the Late Moral Plays*. Lincoln and London: University of Nebraska Press, 1986.

Dickey, Franklin M. *Not Wisely But Too Well: Shakespeare's Love Tragedies*. San Marino, CA: Huntington Library, 1957.

Dollimore, Jonathan. *Radical Tragedy: Religion, Ideology and Power in the Drama of Shakespeare and His Contemporaries*. Chicago: University of Chicago Press, 1984.

Donaldson, E. Talbot. *The Swan at the Well: Shakespeare Reading Chaucer*. New Haven, CT: Yale University Press, 1985.

Donaldson, Ian. "Falstaff's Buff Jerkin." *Shakespeare Quarterly* 37 (1986): 100–1.

Drakakis, John, ed. *Alternative Shakespeares*. London and New York: Methuen, 1985.

Draper, J. W. "Falstaff, 'A Fool and A Jester.'" *Modern Language Quarterly* 7 (1946): 453–62.

Draper, R. F. *Shakespeare: The Comedies*. New York: St. Martin's Press, 2000.

Drayton, W. B. "Shakespeare's *Troilus and Cressida*." In *Essays in Dramatic Literature: The Parrot Presentation Volume*, edited by Hardin Craig, 127–56. Princeton, NJ: Princeton University Press, 1935.

Dryden, John. *The Works of John Dryden: Now First Collected in Eighteen Volumes*. Edinburgh: James Ballantyne and Co., 1808. Project Gutenberg e-book edition.

Duchartre, Pierre Louis. *The Italian Comedy*. New York: Dover, 1996.

Duncan-Jones, Katherine. "Shakespeare's Dancing Fool." *Times Literary Supplement*, August 11, 2010.

Dusinberre, Juliet. *Shakespeare and the Nature of Women*. New York: Palgrave Macmillan, 1996.

Dutton, Richard, and Jean E. Howard, eds. *A Companion to Shakespeare's Works*, vol. 3, *The Comedies*. Oxford: Blackwell, 2003.

Dyer, Geoff. *The Ongoing Moment*. New York: Pantheon, 2005.

Eliot, T. S. *Selected Essays 1917–1932*. London: Faber & Faber, 1932.

Ellis, David. *Shakespeare's Practical Jokes: An Introduction to the Comic in His Work*. Lewisburg, PA: Bucknell University Press, 2007.

Ellis, Roger. "The Fool in Shakespeare." *Critical Quarterly* 10, no. 3 (1968): 245–68.

Elton, W. R. *Shakespeare's Troilus & Cressida and the Inns of Court Revels*. Aldershot, Brookfield, Singapore, and Sydney: Ashgate, 2000.

Empson, William. *Seven Types of Ambiguity*. London: Chatto & Windus, 1930.

———. *Some Versions of Pastoral*. New York: Penguin, 1966.

———. *The Structure of Complex Words*. Ann Arbor: University of Michigan Press, 1967.

Erasmus, Desiderius. *Praise of Folly*. Edited and translated by Clarence H. Miller. New Haven, CT: Yale University Press, 1979.

Erasmus, Desiderius. *The Praise of Folie*. Translated by Thomas Chaloner, edited by Clarence H. Miller. London: Oxford University Press, 1965.

Erikson, Peter. *Patriarchal Structures in Shakespeare's Drama*. Berkeley: University of California Press, 1985.

Evans, Bertrand. *Shakespeare's Comedies*. Oxford: Clarendon Press, 1960.

Evans, Gareth Lloyd. "Shakespeare's Fools: The Shadow and Substance of Drama." In *Shakespearean Comedy*, edited by Malcolm Bradbury and David Palmer, 141–59. Stratford-Upon-Avon Studies 14. London: Edward Arnold, 1972.

Evans, Malcolm. "Deconstructing Shakespeare's Comedies." In *Alternative Shakespeares*, edited by John Krakakis, 67–94. London: Methuen, 1985.

———. *Signifying Nothing: Truth's True Contents in Shakespeare's Text*. Athens: University of Georgia Press, 1986.

Everett, Barbara. "Much Ado About Nothing." *Critical Quarterly* 3.4. 1961: 319–335.

Farnham, Willard. *The Shakespearean Grotesque: Its Genesis and Transformations.* Oxford: Clarendon Press, 1971.

Felver, Charles S. *Robert Armin, Shakespeare's Fool: A Biographical Essay. Kent State University Bulletin.* Kent, OH: Kent State University Press, 1961.

Fiedler, Leslie. *The Stranger in Shakespeare.* New York: Stein & Day, 1972.

Fisher, Seymour, and Rhoda L. Fisher. *Pretend the World Is Funny and Forever: A Psychological Analysis of Comedians, Clowns, and Actors.* Hillsdale, NJ: L. Erlbaum, 1981.

Fo, Dario. *Tricks of the Trade.* Edited by Stuart Clink Hood. Translated by Joe Farrell. New York: Routledge, 1991.

Foucault, Michel. *Discipline and Punish: The Birth of the Prison.* Translated by Alan Sheridan. London: Allen Lane, 1977.

———. *The Order of Things: An Archeology of the Human Sciences.* London: Tavistock, 1970.

Frail, David. "To the Point of Folly: Touchstone's Function in *As You Like It*." *Massachusetts Review* 22 (1981): 696–717.

Frankfurt, H. G. *On Bull Shit.* Princeton, NJ: Princeton University Press, 2009.

Fraser, Antonia. *The Six Wives of Henry VIII.* London: Weidenfeld & Nicolson, 2007.

Frost, Robert. *Frost: Collected Poems, Prose, and Plays*, edited by Richard Poirier. New York: Library of America, 1995.

Freud, Sigmund. *Wit and Its Relation to the Unconscious.* Translated by A. A. Brill. New York: Moffat, Yard, and Co., 1916.

Frye, Northrop. "The Argument of Comedy." In *Shakespeare's Comedies: An Anthology of Modern Criticism*, edited by Laurence Lerner, 315–25. Baltimore: Penguin Books, 1967.

———. *Fools of Time: Studies in Shakespearean Tragedy.* Toronto: University of Toronto Press, 1967.

———. *A Natural Perspective: The Development of Shakespearean Comedy and Romance.* New York: Columbia University Press, 1965.

———. *Northrop Frye on Shakespeare*, edited by Robert Dandler. New Haven, CT, and London: Yale University Press, 1986.

Fry, Paul H. *William Empson: Prophet Against Sacrifice.* London: Routledge, 1991.

Galligan, Edward L. *The Comic Vision in Literature.* Athens: University of Georgia Press, 1984.

Gantar, Jure. *The Pleasure of Fools: Essays in the Ethics of Laughter.* Montreal and Ithaca, NY: McGill-Queen's University Press, 2005.

Garber, Marjorie. "The Education of Orlando." In *Comedy from Shakespeare to Sheridan: Change and Continuity in the English and European Dramatic Tradition*, edited by A. R. Braunmuller and J. C. Bulman, 102–12. Newark: University of Delaware Press, 1986.

———. *Shakespeare After All.* New York: Anchor, 2005.

Gardner, Helen. "As You Like It." In *Shakespeare's Comedies: An Anthology of Modern Criticism*, edited by Laurence Lerner, 245–66. Baltimore: Penguin Books, 1967.

Gay, Penny. *The Cambridge Introduction to Shakespeare's Comedies*. Cambridge: Cambridge University Press, 2008.

Gill, R. B. "Why Comedy Laughs: The Shape of Laughter and Comedy." *Literary Imagination* 8, no. 2 (2006): 233–50.

Gladwell, Malcolm. *The Tipping Point: How Little Things Can Make a Big Difference*. New York: Little, Brown, 2000.

Goldberg, Jonathan. *James I and the Politics of Literature: Jonson, Shakespeare, Donne, and Their Contemporaries*. Baltimore and London: Johns Hopkins University Press, 1983.

Goldsmith, Robert Hillis. *Wise Fools in Shakespeare*. Liverpool: Liverpool University Press, 1974.

Grassi, Ernesto, and Maristella Lorch. *Folly and Insanity in Renaissance Literature*. Binghamton, NY: Medieval and Renaissance Texts and Studies, 1986.

Gray, J. C., ed. *Mirror Up to Shakespeare: Essays in Honour of G. R. Hibbard*. Toronto: University of Toronto Press, 1984.

Greenblatt, Stephen. *Learning to Curse: Essays in Early Modern Culture*. London: Routledge, 1992.

———. *Renaissance Self-Fashioning from More to Shakespeare*. Chicago: University of Chicago Press, 1980.

———. *Shakespearean Negotiations: The Circulation of Social Energy in Renaissance England*. Berkeley and Los Angeles: University of California Press, 1988.

———. *Will in the World: How Shakespeare Became Shakespeare*. New York: Norton, 2004.

Gutwirth, Marcel. *Laughing Matter: An Essay on the Comic*. Ithaca, NY: Cornell University Press, 1993.

Halio, Jay L. *All's Well That Ends Well*. *Shakespeare Quarterly* 15 (1964): 33–43.

Halpern, Richard. *Shakespeare Among the Moderns*. Ithaca, NY, and London: Cornell University Press, 1997.

Hansen, William F. *Saxo Grammaticus and the Life of Hamlet: A History, Translation, and Commentary*. Lincoln: University of Nebraska Press, 1983.

Hapgood, Robert. "The Life of Shame: Parolles and *All's Well That Ends Well*." *Essays in Criticism* 15 (1965): 269–78.

Hartman, Geoffrey, and Patricia Parker, eds. *Shakespeare and the Question of Theory*. London: Routledge, 1985.

Hassel, R. Chris. *Faith and Folly in Shakespeare's Romantic Comedies*. Athens: University of Georgia Press, 1980.

Hawkes, Terence. *That Shakespeherian Rag: Essays on a Critical Process*. London and New York: Methuen, 1986.

Hazlitt, William. *Lectures on the English Comic Writers*. New York: Everyman's Library, 1963.

Headley, Gwyn, and Wim Meulenkamp. *Follies: A National Trust Guide*. London: Jonathan Cape, 1986.

———. *Follies, Grottoes, and Garden Buildings*. London: Virgin Publishing, 1999.

Hillman, Richard. *Shakespearean Subversions: The Trickster and the Play-Text.* London and New York: Routledge, 1992.

———. *William Shakespeare: The Problem Plays.* New York: Maxwell Macmillan, 1993.

Hodgdon, Barbara. "Sexual Disguise and the Theater of Gender." In *The Cambridge Companion to Shakespearean Comedy,* edited by Alexander Leggatt, 179–97. Cambridge: Cambridge University Press, 2002.

Holcomb, Chris. *Mirth Making: The Rhetorical Discourse of Jesting in Early Modern England.* Columbia: University of South Carolina Press, 2001.

Holland, Norman, Sidney Homan, and Bernard J. Paris. *Shakespeare's Personality.* Berkeley: University of California Press, 1989.

Homer. *The Iliad.* Translated by Robert Fitzgerald. Garden City, NY: Anchor, 1975.

Hornback, Robert. "Blackfaced Fools, Black-Headed Birds, Fool Synonyms, and Shakespearean Allusions to Renaissance Blackface Folly." *Notes & Queries* 55 (2008): 215–19.

———. "Emblems of Folly in the First *Othello*: Renaissance Blackface, Moor's Coat, and 'Muckender.'" *Comparative Drama* 35.1 (2001): 69–99.

———. *The English Clown Tradition from the Middle Ages to Shakespeare.* Cambridge: D. S. Brewer, 2009.

Hosley, Richard, ed. *Essays on Shakespeare and Elizabethan Drama in Honor of Hardin Craig.* Columbia: University of Missouri Press, 1962.

Hopkins, Lisa. *Shakespeare on the Edge: Border-Crossing in the Tragedies and the Henriad.* Burlington, VT: Ashgate, 2005.

Hotson, Leslie. *The First Night of Twelfth Night.* New York: Macmillan, 1954.

———. *Shakespeare's Motley.* London: R. Hart-Davis, 1952.

Howard, Jean and M. F. O'Connor, editors, *Shakespeare Reproduced: The Text in History and Ideology.* London: Taylor and Francis, 2005.

Huizinga, Johan. *Erasmus.* New York: Scribner's Sons, 1924.

———. *Homo Ludens.* Boston: Beacon, 1971.

Huston, J. Dennis. "Some Stain of Soldier: The Functions of Parolles in *All's Well That Ends Well.*" *Shakespeare Quarterly* 21 (1970): 431–38.

Hutson, Lorna. "Not the King's Two Bodies: Reading the 'Body Politic' in Shakespeare's *Henry IV, Parts 1 and 2.*" In *Rhetoric and Law in Early Modern Europe,* edited by Victoria Kahn and Lorna Hutson, 166–198. New Haven, CT: Yale University Press, 2001.

Hutton, Henry. *Follie's anatomie, or, Satres & satirical epigrams: With a compendious history of Ixion's wheele.* London: Mathew Walbanke, 1619.

Hyde, Lewis. *Trickster Makes This World: Mischief, Myth, and Art.* New York: Farrar, Straus, and Giroux, 1998.

Hyers, M. Conrad, ed. *Holy Laughter: Essays on Religion in the Comic Perspective.* New York: Seabury Press, 1969.

Hyman, Timothy, and Roger Malbert. *Carnivalesque.* London: Hayward Gallery, 2000.

James, Russell. *Shakespeare's Troy: Drama, Politics, and the Translation of Empire.* Cambridge: Cambridge University Press, 1997.

Janik, Vicki K., ed. *Fools and Jesters in Literature, Art, and History: A Bio-Bibliographical Sourcebook.* Westport, CT: Greenwood Press, 1998.

Jensen, Ejner J. *Shakespeare and the Ends of Comedy.* Bloomington: Indiana University Press, 1991.

Johnson, Samuel. *A Dictionary of the English Language: In which the words are deduced from their originals, and illustrated in their different significations, by examples from the best writers, to which are prefixed a history of the language, and an English grammar, Vol. 3.* London: Longman, Hurst, Rees, and Orme, 1805.

———. *Samuel Johnson on Shakespeare*, edited by W. K. Wimsatt Jr. New York: Hill and Wang, 1960.

———. *Selected Writings*, edited by Peter Martin. Cambridge, MA: Harvard University Press, 2009.

Jones, Barbara. *Follies and Grottoes.* London: Constable, 1974.

Jones, Ernest. *Hamlet and Oedipus.* New York: Norton, 1976.

Joyce, James. *Finnegans Wake.* New York: Viking, 1959.

Jung, C. G. *Four Archetypes: Mother/Rebirth/Spirit/Trickster.* Translated by R. F. C. Hull. Princeton, NJ: Princeton University Press, 1970.

Kaiser, Walter. *Praisers of Folly: Erasmus, Rabelais, Shakespeare.* Cambridge, MA: Harvard University Press, 1963.

Kamps, Ivo, ed. *Materialist Shakespeare: A History.* London: Verso, 1995.

Kantorowicz, Ernst H. *The King's Two Bodies: A Study in Mediaeval Political Theology.* Princeton, NJ: Princeton University Press, 1957.

Kehler, Dorothy, ed. *A Midsummer Night's Dream: Critical Essays.* New York: Garland, 1998.

Kermode, Frank. *Shakespeare, Spenser, Donne: Renaissance Essays.* New York: Viking, 1971.

———. *Shakespeare's Language.* New York: Farrar Straus Giroux, 2000.

Kern, Edith. *The Absolute Comic.* New York: Columbia University Press, 1980.

Ketcham, Diana. *Le Désert de Retz: A Late Eighteenth-Century French Folly Garden: The Artful Landscape of Monsieur de Monville.* Cambridge, MA: MIT Press, 1994.

Kiernan, Pauline. *Filthy Shakespeare: Shakespeare's Most Outrageous Sexual Puns.* New York: Penguin, 2007.

Kimbrough, Robert. *Shakespeare's Troilus and Cressida and Its Setting.* Cambridge, MA: Harvard University Press, 1964.

Kinney, Arthur F., ed. *Comedy of Errors.* New York: Simon and Schuster, 2004.

———, ed. *English Literature 1500–1600.* Cambridge: Cambridge University Press, 2000.

———. *Humanist Poetics: Thought, Rhetoric, and Fiction in Sixteenth Century England.* Amherst: University of Massachusetts Press, 1986.

Kirsch, Arthur. *Shakespeare and the Experience of Love.* Cambridge: Cambridge University Press, 1981.

Knight, G. Wilson. *The Sovereign Flower: On Shakespeare as the Poet of Royalism Together with Related Essays and Indexes to Earlier Volumes.* London: Methuen & Co., 1958.

————. *The Wheel of Fire: Interpretation of Shakespeare's Somber Tragedies*. London: Oxford, 1930.

Knowles, Richard, ed. *A New Variorum Edition of Shakespeare: As You Like It*. New York: Modern Language Association of America, 1977.

Knowles, Ronald, ed. *Shakespeare and Carnival: After Bakhtin*. London: Macmillan, 1998.

Kott, Jan. *The Bottom Translation: Marlowe and Shakespeare and the Carnival Tradition*, tr. Daniela Miedzyrzeka and Lillian Vallee. Evanston, IL: Northwestern University Press, 1987.

————. *Shakespeare Our Contemporary*. New York: Norton, 1974.

Krapp, G. P. "Parolles." In *Shakespeare's Later Comedies*, edited by D. J. Palmer, 39–52. New York: Penguin, 1971.

Kuhn, Maura Slattery. "Much Virtue in *If.*" *Shakespeare Quarterly* 28 (1977): 40–50.

La Guardia, Eric. "Ceremony and History: The Problem of Symbol from *Richard II* to *Henry V*." In *Pacific Coast Studies in Shakespeare*, edited by W. F. McNeir and T. N. Greenfield, 68–88. Eugene: University of Oregon Books, 1966.

Langer, Susanne K. *Feeling and Form: A Theory of Art*. New York: Scribner, 1953.

Lanham, Richard. *A Handlist of Rhetorical Terms*. Berkeley: University of California Press, 1991.

————. *The Motives of Eloquence: Literary Rhetoric in the Renaissance*. New Haven, CT: Yale University Press, 1976.

Laroque, Francois. *Shakespeare's Festive World: Elizabethan Seasonal Entertainment and the Professional Stage*. Translated by Janet Lloyd. Cambridge: Cambridge University Press, 1991.

Lawrence, William Witherle. *Shakespeare's Problem Comedies*. New York: Macmillan, 1931.

Leggatt, Alexander, ed. *The Cambridge Companion to Shakespearean Comedy*. Cambridge: Cambridge University Press, 2002.

————, ed. *Shakespeare in Performance: King Lear*. Manchester and New York: Manchester University Press, 2004.

Leinwand, Theodore B. "Conservative Fools in James's Court and Shakespeare's Plays." *Shakespeare Studies* 19 (1987): 219–34.

Lerner, Lawrence, ed. *Shakespeare's Comedies*. New York: Penguin Books, 1967.

Lerner, Ralph. *Playing the Fool: Subversive Laughter in Troubled Times*. Chicago and London: University of Chicago Press, 2009.

Levin, Harry. *Playboys and Killjoys: An Essay on the Theory and Practice of Comedy*. New York: Oxford University Press, 1987.

Levin, Richard L. "*All's Well That Ends Well* and 'All Seems Well.'" *Shakespeare Studies* 13 (1980): 139–42.

————. *The Multiple Plot in English Renaissance Drama*. Chicago: University of Chicago Press, 1971.

Lewalski, Barbara K. "Love, Appearance, and Reality: Much Ado About Something." *Studies in English Literature* 8 (1968): 235–51.

Liddell, H. G., and Robert Scott. *Greek-English Lexicon*. Oxford: Oxford University Press, 1935.

Limon, John. *Stand-up Comedy in Theory, or, Abjection in America*. Durham, NC, and London: Duke University Press, 2000.

Mack, Maynard, Sr. *Everybody's Shakespeare: Reflections Chiefly on the Tragedies*. Lincoln and London: University of Nebraska Press, 1993.

Mack, Maynard, Jr. *Killing the King*. New Haven, CT: Yale University Press, 1973.

Mahood, M. M. *Shakespeare's Wordplay*. London: Methuen, 1957.

Mangan, Michael. *A Preface to Shakespeare's Comedies 1594–1603*. London and New York: Longman, 1996.

Mann, Thomas. *The Confessions of Felix Krull Confidence Man: The Early Years*. New York: Vintage, 1969.

Maslen, R. W. *Shakespeare and Comedy*. London: Arden, 2005.

Mast, Gerald. *The Comic Mind: Comedy and the Movies*. Indianapolis: Bobbs-Merrill, 1973.

May, Stephen W., and William A. Ringler. "An Epilogue Possibly by Shakespeare." *Modern Philology* 70 (1972): 138–39.

McCollom, William G. "The Role of Wit in *Much Ado About Nothing*." *Shakespeare Quarterly* 19 (1968): 165–74.

McDonald, Marcia. "Bottom's Space." In *Acting Funny: Comic Theory and Practice in Shakespeare's Plays*, edited Frances N. Teague, 85–109. Rutherford, NJ: Farleigh Dickinson University Press, 1994.

McDonald, Russ, ed. *Shakespeare: An Anthology of Criticism and Theory 1945–2000*. Oxford: Blackwell, 2004.

Michelson, Bruce. *Literary Wit*. Amherst: University of Massachusetts Press, 2000.

Miola, Robert S., ed. *The Comedy of Errors: Critical Essays*. New York and London. Garland, 1997.

Montrose, Louis. *The Purpose of Playing: Shakespeare and the Cultural Politics of the Elizabethan Theater*. Chicago: University of Chicago Press, 1996.

Mossner, Monique. "Paradox in the Garden: A Brief Account of *Fabriques*." In *The Architecture of Western Gardens: A Design History from the Renaissance to the Present Day*, edited by Monique Mossner and Georges Teyssot, 263–280. Cambridge, MA: MIT Press, 1991.

Muir, Kenneth, ed. *Shakespeare: The Comedies*. Englewood Cliffs, NJ: Prentice-Hall, 1965.

———, ed. *Shakespeare Survey* 25. Cambridge: Cambridge University Press, 1972.

———, ed. *Troilus and Cressida*. Oxford: Clarendon Press, 1982.

Nardo, Anna K. *The Ludic Self in Seventeenth-Century Literature*. Albany: State University of New York Press, 1991.

Neely, Carol Thomas. *Broken Nuptials in Shakespeare's Plays*. New Haven, CT: Yale University Press, 1985.

Nevo, Ruth. *Comic Transformations in Shakespeare*. London and New York: Methuen, 1980.

———. "Shakespeare's Comic Remedies," ed. Maurice Charney, 3–16. *Shakespearean Comedy*. New York: New York Literary Forum, 1980.

Newman, Karen. *Shakespeare's Rhetoric of Comic Character: Dramatic Convention in Classical and Renaissance Comedy*. New York: Methuen, 1985.

Nicoll, Allardyce, ed. *Chapman's Homer: The Iliad*. Princeton, NJ: Princeton University Press, 1998.

Nietzsche, Friedrich. *The Gay Science*. Edited by Walter Kaufman. New York: Vintage, 1974.

Nussbaum, Martha C. *Upheavals of Thought: The Intelligence of Emotions*. Cambridge: Cambridge University Press, 2001.

Ottinger, Didier. "The Circus of Cruelty." In *La Grande Parade: Portrait of the Artist as Clown*, edited by J. Clair, 35–46. New Haven, CT: Yale University Press, 2004.

Otto, Beatrice K. *Fools Are Everywhere: The Court Jester Around the World*. Chicago and London: University of Chicago Press, 2001.

The Oxford English Dictionary Online. Oxford University Press, 2009. http://oed.com/

Palmer, D. J., ed. *Shakespeare's Later Comedies: An Anthology of Modern Criticism*. New York: Penguin, 1971.

Park, Clara Claiborne. "As We Like It: How a Girl Can Be Smart and Still Popular." In *The Woman's Part: Feminist Criticism of Shakespeare*, edited by Carolyn Ruth Swift Lenz, Gayle Greene, and Carol Thomas Neely, 100–116. Urbana: University of Illinois, 1980.

Partridge, Eric. *Shakespeare's Bawdy*. London and New York: Routledge Classics, 2001.

Paster, Gail Kern. "*Much Ado About Nothing*: A Modern Perspective." In *Much Ado About Nothing*. New York: Simon and Schuster, 1995: 213–230.

Patterson, Annabel. *Shakespeare and the Popular Voice*. London: Blackwell, 1989.

Payne, Robert. *Charlie Chaplin (Orig. Title: The Great God Pan)*. New York: Ace Books, 1952.

Pepys, Samuel. *The Diary of Samuel Pepys*. Edited by Robert Latham and William Matthews. London: Bell, 1976.

Perl, Jed. "Clown as Hero." *The New Republic*, September 27, 2004: 25–30.

Poirier, Richard. *The Performing Self: Compositions and Decompositions in the Language of Contemporary Life*. New York: Oxford University Press, 1971.

Pope, Alexander. *The Poems of Alexander Pope*, edited by John Butt. New Haven, CT: Yale University Press, 1963.

Porter, Joseph A. *Shakespeare's Mercutio: His History and Drama*. Chapel Hill and London: University of North Carolina Press, 1988.

Presson, Robert K. *Shakespeare's Troilus and Cressida and the Legends of Troy*. Madison: University of Wisconsin Press, 1953.

Price, Joseph G. *The Unfortunate Comedy: A Study of All's Well That Ends Well and Its Critics*. Toronto: University of Toronto Press, 1968.

Purdie, Susan. *Comedy: The Mastery of Discourse*. New York: Harvester Wheatsheaf, 1993.

Putt, S. Gorly, ed. *Essays and Studies 1963*. London: John Murray, 1963.

Puttenham, George. *The Arte of English Poesie*. Kent, OH: Kent State University Press, 1970.

Pye, Christopher. *The Regal Phantasm: Shakespeare and the Politics of Spectacle.* London and New York: Routledge, 1990.

———. *The Vanishing: Shakespeare, the Subject, and Early Modern Culture.* Durham, NC: Duke University Press, 2003.

Pyle, Sandra J. *Mirth and Morality of Shakespeare's Holy Fools.* Lewiston, NY: Edwin Mellen Press, 1998.

Rabkin, Norman. "*Troilus and Cressida*: The Uses of the Double Plot." In *Essays in Shakespearean Criticism*, edited by James L. Calderwood and Harold E. Toliver, 304–22. Englewood Cliffs, NJ: Prentice Hall, 1970.

Rabelais, Francois. *Gargantua and Pantagruel.* In *The Complete Works of Francois Rabelais*, III. Translated by Donald M. Frame. Berkeley: University of California Press, 1991.

Rayner, Alice. *Comic Persuasion: Moral Structure in British Comedy from Shakespeare to Stoppard.* Berkeley: University of California Press, 1987.

Redfern, Walter. *Puns.* Oxford and New York: Blackwell, 1984.

Richards, I. A. "*Troilus and Cressida* and Plato." In *Troilus and Cressida*, edited by Daniel Seltzer, 229–37. New York: Signet, 1963.

Richmond, Hugh M. *Shakespeare's Sexual Comedy: A Mirror for Lovers.* Indianapolis: Bobbs-Merrill Company, 1991.

Ricoeur, Paul. "Metaphor and the Main Problem of Hermeneutics." *New Literary History* 6 (1974): 95–110.

Righter, Anne. *Shakespeare and the Idea of the Play.* London: Chatto & Windus, 1964.

Ringler, William A. "An Epilogue Possibly by Shakespeare." *Modern Philology* 70 (1972): 138–39.

Rolls, Albert. *The Theory of the King's Two Bodies in the Age of Shakespeare.* Lewiston, NY: Edwin Mellen Press, 2000.

Rose, Mary Beth, ed. *Renaissance Drama.* Chicago: Northwestern University Press, 1991.

Rose, Steve. "Love and Self-Love in *Much Ado About Nothing.*" *Essays in Criticism* 20 (1970): 143–50.

Rossiter, A. P. *Angel with Horns and Other Shakespeare Lectures.* Edited by Graham Storey. New York: Theatre Arts Books, 1961.

Rothman, Jules. "A Vindication of Parolles." *Shakespeare Quarterly* 23 (1972): 183–96.

Rymer, Thomas. *Short View of Tragedy.* Reprinted in *A Casebook on Othello.* Edited by Leonard F. Dean. New York: Crowell, 1961.

Salingar, Leo. *Shakespeare and the Traditions of Comedy.* London and New York: Cambridge University Press, 1974.

Santayana, George. *The Works of George Santayana.* New York: Scribner's, 1937.

Schaeffer, Neil. *The Art of Laughter.* New York: Columbia University Press, 1981.

Scot, Reginald. *The Discoverie of Witchcraft.* London: William Brome, 1584.

Sedinger, Tracey. "'If Sight and Shape Be True': The Epistemology of Cross-dressing on the London Stage." *Shakespeare Quarterly* 48 (1997): 63–79.

Segal, Eric. *The Death of Comedy.* Cambridge, MA: Harvard University Press, 2001.

Seidel, Michael and Edward Mendelson, editors. *Homer to Brecht: The European Epic and Dramatic Traditions*. New Haven, CT: Yale University Press, 1977.

Seiden, Melvin. "The Fool and Edmund: Kin and Kind." *Studies in English Literature* 19, no. 2 (1979): 197–214.

Selleck, Nancy. *The Interpersonal Idiom in Shakespeare, Donne, and Early Modern Culture*. New York: Palgrave Macmillan, 2008.

Seltzer, Daniel, ed. *Troilus and Cressida*. New York: Signet, 1963.

Shakespeare, William. *The plays of William Shakespeare in eight volumes: With the corrections and illustrations of various commentators; to which are added notes by Sam Johnson*. Edited by Samuel Johnson. London: J. and R. Tonson, 1765.

———. *The Riverside Shakespeare*. Edited by G. Blakemore Evans, Harry Levin, Herschel Baker, Anne Barton, Frank Kermode, Hallett Smith, and Marie Edel. Boston: Houghton Mifflin, 1997.

Shapiro, James. *A Year in the Life of William Shakespeare: 1599*. New York: HarperCollins, 2005.

Shenk, Linda. *Learned Queen: The Image of Elizabeth I in Politics and Poetry*. New York: Palgrave Macmillan, 2010.

Sher, Anton. "The Fool in *King Lear*." In *Players of Shakespeare 2: Further Essays in Shakespearean Performance*, edited by Russell Jackson and Robert Smallwood, 151–65. Cambridge: Cambridge University Press, 1988.

Shickman, Allan R. "The Fool's Mirror in *King Lear*." *English Literary Renaissance* 21 (1991): 75–86.

Sidney, Sir Philip. *Sir Philip Sidney's Defense of Poesy*. Edited by Dorothy M. Macardle. London: Macmillan, 1964.

Siegel, Paul N., ed. *His Infinite Variety: Major Shakespearean Criticism since Johnson*. Philadelphia and New York: J. B. Lippincott, 1964.

Skura, Meredith Anne. "Shakespeare's Clowns and Fools." In *Shakespeare Set Free*, edited by Peggy O'Brien, 19–24. New York: Washington Square Press, 1993.

Smith, Bruce R., ed. *Twelfth Night, or What You Will: Texts and Contexts*. Boston: Bedford/St. Martin's, 2001.

Smith, Emma, ed. *Shakespeare's Comedies*. Malden, MA: Blackwell, 2004.

Smith, Gordon Ross, ed. *Essays on Shakespeare*. University Park and London: Pennsylvania State University Press, 1965.

Smith, James. "*Much Ado About Nothing*." *Scrutiny* 13 (1946): 242–57.

Smith, Molly. *Breaking Boundaries: Politics and Play in the Drama of Shakespeare and His Contemporaries*. Aldershot, UK: Ashgate, 1998.

Snyder, Susan. "*All's Well That Ends Well* and Shakespeare's Helens: Text and Subtext, Subject and Other." *English Literary Renaissance* 18 (1988): 66–77.

———. *The Comic Matrix of Shakespeare's Tragedies: Romeo and Juliet, Hamlet, Othello, and King Lear*. Princeton, NJ: Princeton University Press, 1979.

———. *Shakespeare: A Wayward Journey*. Cranbury, London, and Ontario: Associated University Presses, 2002.

Southworth, John. *Fools and Jesters at the English Court*. Phoenix Mill, UK: Sutton, 1998.

Starobinski, Jean. *Portrait de l'Artist en Saltimbanque*. Paris: Gallimard, 2004.

Stevens, Martin, and James Paxson. "The Fool in the Wakefield Plays." *Studies in Iconography* 13 (1989–90): 48–79.

Stevens, Wallace. *The Collected Poems of Wallace Stevens*. New York: Knopf, 1965.

Stoll, Elmer Edgar. *From Shakespeare to Joyce: Authors and Critics, Literature and Life*. Garden City, NJ: Doubleday, Doran, 1944.

Stott, Andrew. *Comedy*. London: Routledge, 2005.

Styan, J. L. *Shakespeare in Performance: All's Well That Ends Well*. Manchester: Manchester University Press, 1984.

Swain, Barbara. *Fools and Folly During the Middle Ages and the Renaissance*. New York: Columbia University Press, 1932.

Tave, Stuart M. *Lovers, Clowns, and Fairies: An Essay on Comedies*. Chicago: University of Chicago Press, 1993.

Taylor, Charles. *Sources of the Self: The Making of Modern Identity*. Cambridge, MA: Harvard University Press, 1989.

Taylor, Gary, and Michael Warren, eds. *The Division of the Kingdoms; Shakespeare's Two Versions of King Lear*. Oxford: Clarendon Press, and New York: Oxford University Press, 1983.

Thomas, Keith. "The Place of Laughter in Tudor and Stuart England." *Times Literary Supplement*, January 21, 1977: 77–78.

Thompson, Ewa Majewsk. *Understanding Russia: The Holy Fool in Russian Culture*. Lanham, MD: University Press of America, 1987.

Thomson, Peter. "Clowns, Fools, and Knaves: Stages in the Evolution of Acting." In *The Cambridge History of British Theatre, I, Origins to 1660*, edited by Jane Milling and Peter Thomson, 407–23. Cambridge: Cambridge University Press, 2004.

Thorne, Christian. *The Dialectic of Enlightenment*. Cambridge, MA: Harvard University Press, 2009.

Tillyard, E. M. W. *The Nature of Comedy and Shakespeare*. London: Oxford University Press, 1958.

———. *Shakespeare's Early Comedies*. London: Longmans, Green, 1960.

———. *Shakespeare's Problem Plays*. Toronto: University of Toronto Press, 1949.

Towsen, John H. *Clowns*. New York: Hawthorn Books, 1976.

Traub, Valerie. *Desire and Anxiety: Circulations of Sexuality in Shakespearean Drama*. London and New York: Routledge, 1992.

Traugott, John. "Creating a Rational Rinaldo: A Study in the Mixture of the Genres of Comedy and Romance in *Much Ado About Nothing*." *Genre* 15 (1982): 157–81.

Tromly, Frederic B. "Macbeth and His Porter." *Shakespeare Quarterly* 26 (1975): 151–56.

Turner, Victor. *The Forest of Symbols: Aspects of Ndembu Ritual*. Ithaca, NY, and London: Cornell University Press, 1967.

———. *From Ritual to Theatre: The Human Seriousness of Play*. New York: Performing Arts Journal Publications, 1982.

———. "Variations on a Theme of Liminality." In *Secular Ritual*, edited by Sally Falk Moore and Barbara G. Myerhoff, 36–52. Assen, Netherlands: Van Gorcum, 1977.

Vaughan, Virginia Mason. *Othello: A Contextual History*. Cambridge: Cambridge University Press, 1994.

Vaughan, Virginia Mason, and Margaret Lael Mikesell, eds. *Othello: An Annotated Bibliography*. New York: Garland, 1990.

Videbaek, Bente A. *The Stage Clowns in Shakespeare's Theatre*. Westport, CT: Greenwood Press, 1996.

Waith, Eugene M. "The Appeal of the Comic Deceiver." *Yearbook of English Studies* 12 (1982): 13–23.

Walcott, Derek. *Collected Poems 1948–1984*. New York: Farrar Straus and Giroux, 1986.

Waller, Gary, ed. *Shakespeare's Comedies*. London and New York: Longman, 1991.

Warde, Frederick. *The Fools of Shakespeare: An Interpretation of Their Wit, Wisdom and Personalities*. Los Angeles: Times-Mirror Press, 1923.

Webster, Noah, ed. *The Holy Bible, Containing the Old and New Testaments, in the Common Version. With Amendments of the Language*. New Haven, CT: Durrie and Peck, 1833.

Weimann, Robert. *Shakespeare and the Popular Tradition in the Theater: Studies in the Social Dimension of Dramatic Form and Function*. Edited by Robert Schwartz. Baltimore and London: Johns Hopkins University Press, 1978.

Wells, Stanley. *Looking for Sex in Shakespeare*. Cambridge: Cambridge University Press, 2004.

Welsford, Enid. *The Fool: His Social and Literary History*. London: Faber & Faber, 1935.

Weschler, Lawrence. *Boggs: A Comedy of Values*. Chicago: University of Chicago Press, 2000.

———. *Mr. Wilson's Cabinet of Wonder*. New York: Vintage, 1996.

———. *Shapinski's Karma, Boggs's Bills, and Other True-Life Tales*. New York: Penguin, 1990.

Wheeler, Richard P. *Shakespeare's Development and the Problem Comedies: Turn and Counter-Turn*. Berkeley: University of California Press, 1981.

White, R. S., ed. *New Casebooks: Twelfth Night*. London: Macmillan, 1996.

Willeford, William. *The Fool and His Scepter*. Chicago: Northwestern University Press, 1969.

Wiles, David. *Shakespeare's Clown: Actor and Text in the Elizabethan Playhouse*. Cambridge: Cambridge University Press, 1987.

Williams, Paul V. A., ed. *The Fool and the Trickster: Studies in Honour of Enid Welsford*. Cambridge: D. S. Brewer; Rowman and Littlefield 1979.

Wilson, John Dover. *The Fortunes of Falstaff*. Cambridge: Cambridge University Press, 1943.

Wilson, Thomas. *The Art of Rhetoric*. Edited by Peter E. Medine. University Park: Pennsylvania State University Press, 1994.

Woodbridge, Linda. *The Scythe of Saturn: Shakespeare and Magical Thinking*. Urbana: University of Illinois Press, 1994.

Wofford, Susanne L., ed. *Case Studies in Contemporary Criticism: Hamlet*. Boston: Bedford/St. Martin's Press, 1994.

Wright, George T. "Hendiadys and *Hamlet*." *Publication of the Modern Language Association* 96, 1981: 168–93.

Wynne-Davies, Marion. *Much Ado About Nothing and The Taming of the Shrew.* Houndmills, Basingstoke, Hampshire; New York: Palgrave Macmillan, 2001.

Young, David. *The Heart's Forest: A Study of Shakespeare's Pastoral Plays.* New Haven, CT: Yale University Press, 1972.

———. *Something of Great Constancy: The Art of A Midsummer Night's Dream.* New Haven, CT: Yale University Press, 1966.

Young, David. *Bats in the Belfry: A Joyous Evocation of Architectural Eccentricity.* London: David & Charles, 1987.

Zacha, Richard B. "Iago and the *Commedia dell'Arte*." *Arlington Quarterly* 2, no. 2 (1969): 98–116.

Zamir, Zachi. *Double Vision: Moral Philosophy and Shakespearean Drama.* Princeton, NJ: Princeton University Press, 2007.

Zijderveld, Anton C. *Reality in a Looking Glass: Rationality Through an Analysis of Traditional Folly.* London: Routledge, 1982.

Zitner, Sheldon P. "The Worlds of *A Midsummer Night's Dream*." *South Atlantic Quarterly* 59 (1960): 397–403.

Index